The Art of Robert Burns

THE ART OF
ROBERT BURNS

edited, with an introduction, by
R. D. S. Jack and
Andrew Noble

VISION
and
BARNES & NOBLE

Vision Press Limited
11–14 Stanhope Mews West
London SW7 5RD

and

Barnes & Noble Books
81 Adams Drive
Totowa, NJ 07512

ISBN (UK) 0 85478 274 5
ISBN (US) 0 389 20203 7

Printed and bound in Great Britain by
Unwin Brothers Ltd.,
Old Woking, Surrey.
Phototypeset by Galleon Photosetting,
Ipswich, Suffolk.
MCMLXXXII

Contents

Introduction

by R. D. S. JACK and ANDREW NOBLE

Our primary desire in editing this new volume of essays on Robert Burns was that the distinct literary modes and poetic forms employed by him should receive equally distinct and fresh treatment. Along with this we wished, in so far as it is possible within the form of the essay, to place Burns in a wider literary, social and political context than, especially in Scotland, he is normally accorded. Having beyond this point prescribed neither content nor critical method, we found it a pleasurable bonus to discover that the essays, as they came before us, displayed a frequent and discernible pattern of pre-occupation with several key themes and problems regarding Burns. The existence of such mutual concern came in part from the fact that not a few of our essayists are relatively young. Inevitably a new generation brings with it a new perspective. By inviting Iain Crichton Smith and Alan Bold to contribute to the volume, we sought not only the kind of talent the creative writer can bring to literary criticism, but also to set a tone for the whole collection which, if achieved, would give the lie to the inevitable separation of academic writing from the relevance and vitality to be found in imaginative prose. What we sought in all our contributors, in short, was critical intelligence, the function of which is always to question the facile assumptions and dull, received opinions which can accrue round even the greatest of writers. Burns's genius, more than most, has been overlaid by such banal accretions. Indeed, with the admirable exceptions of David Daiches and Tom Crawford, augmented by some fine American scholarship, the situation in Burns studies is not significantly changed from that denounced by Hugh MacDiarmid in 1926:

> All this spate of essentially meaningless verbosity—the product of a stupid conventionalism reinforced by no first-hand

7

authoritative re-study of the poet and his work, still less by any consciousness of the history, functions and problems of Scottish literature—would not matter, or would not matter so much at any rate, if there was a single strain of a different kind of activity maintaining a real criticism or seeking to relate the poetry of Burns effectively to the changing needs and tastes of the world or endeavouring to carry on his work for Scottish literature or to preserve his spirit and work for his ideals in contemporary life. But of genuine Burns criticism in this sense there is scarcely a vestige. Burns, as a poet, has long ceased to be taken seriously by anyone really interested in literature. Exhaustive studies of the technique and output of other poets pour annually from the presses. But not of Burns's work. Even the personality, the man himself, has never been maturely studied. There is not a single book upon him—scarcely a single comprehensive essay—that is passably well written. Most of the biographical matter concerning him has been strung together in a very mediocre fashion, vitiated by a provincial morality and a lack of *savoir faire*. It is high time the Burns legend was destroyed and the man himself, 'in the round', a credible human figure, rescued from the eponymous proliferation of moralitarian excrescences under which he is buried—a human palimpsest in which all that is significant and immortal has been overwritten with tawdry and trivial scribblings of all kinds. From the strictly literary as against the broadly human point of view the things that principally want doing to-day, amongst all the things which should have been the first concern of the Burns cult, are to resume Burns in his proper historical setting—to see him as he really is in relation to world poetry as a whole—to consider what effect he has had upon Scottish literature in particular—and to consider his handling of the vernacular.[1]

In Tom Crawford's book most of MacDiarmid's highly demanding tests are met. We hope that these essays also meet his challenge and that, accordingly, much of the present work is an extension of Crawford's seminal criticism. Crawford's essential virtue is his anti-parochial attitude. He has a broad understanding of Burns's historical background, so that he can perceive him as a key poetic witness to the severe agrarian crisis that gripped Ayrshire and, indeed, all Britain in the late eighteenth century. He gives weight to the intellectual complexities inherent in Burns as a figure of the latter days of the Enlightenment bearing painful witness to all the humanistic and social aspirations of that age in the process of being either checked or wholly destroyed. Perhaps Crawford's most significant proximity to several of our essayists in this book is his awareness of the quite extraordinarily elusive nature of both Burns's personality and his rhetorical and poetical modes. Capable of a stark, simple lyricism, he was the least simple of men. Thus the complexity of Burns's language in relation to the convoluted manoeuvrings, spontaneous or imposed, of that seemingly almost fissiparous personality is subject to extended analysis in several of these essays. Burns's use and arguable abuse of a poetic *persona*; the distinction discernible between the creativity present in his best, mainly early, poetry and songs and the much more questionable 'self-creativity' displayed in his letters is, for several essayists, a theme of considerable interest. Indeed, one of the principal preoccupations of this volume and part of its claim to originality is the degree to which we have been drawn into analysing the letters. (We do regret having to go to press before the appearance of the new Oxford edition under the editorship of Professor Ross Roy.)

The virtues of Burns's letters are manifold. They cast a great deal of documentary light on society and politics. The broad social spectrum of Burns's social connections not only illuminates his age, but demonstrates the plasticity Burns felt he had to adopt in order either to fashion a tone suitable to his correspondent or to achieve the social role or position he desired. The letters, too, were often composed not only ironically but as deliberate parodies, so that it becomes extraordinarily difficult to deduce the degree to which highly conscious artifice or genuine naïveté is the motivating factor in specific letters. The hardest problem is, then, to decide not only the degree of sincerity present towards the person addressed, but also the degree of sincerity in the writer towards himself at the moment of composition. Our essayists present no final solution to this enigma, but our intention is rather that they should increase our awareness of its complexity. We agree with Edwin Muir's proposition that:

> One feels that it is from this self-dramatisation that the Burns legend originally arose. When a man is a natural actor he becomes more easy to understand in one way and more difficult in another, but we are left to guess what is behind the acting.[2]

9

Several intelligent guesses are made in this volume. We have attempted to 'read' Burns in the light of the kind of criticism of his age so well exemplified by Professor Lionel Trilling. To deal with Burns is not to deal with a provincial rustic. He demands of us as close attention as the fictional Rameau's nephew with his disconcerting remark that 'I am myself, and I remain myself, but I act and speak as occasion requires.'[3] With Burns, however, we are not always certain of even this. Nor is it specious to compare him to a fictive, foreign character, for the whole difficulty about the late eighteenth century is that the lachrymose mists that shroud it stem from an inherent confusion of life and art throughout literary Europe.

As well as stressing the complexity of Burns, we also seek to destroy the stereotype of Burns as a simple man and cosy representative of Scottish virtues. Scotland treated Burns harshly in his lifetime and, after his death, repressed much of what was most original and valuable in him and made him the *locus* for its sentimental, compensatory national fantasies. Lured by the promise of agricultural improvement, he only experienced the brutalizing blows of farm labour on marginal land. After being made a kind of nine-day wonder in Edinburgh, he was later treated with condescension by the mediocrities of the *literati* and never received proper remuneration for his genius. He ended a rootless man: the later letters show him as a tragically isolated figure living bitterly with the ghosts of his lost hopes, connected neither to rural nor to urban Scotland. As Hazlitt wrote:

> When a man is dead, they put money in his coffin, erect monuments to his memory, and celebrate the memory of his birthday in set speeches. Would they take any notice of him if he were living? No!—I was complaining of this to a Scotchman who had been attending a dinner and a subscription to raise a monument to Burns. He replied, he would sooner subscribe twenty pounds to his monument than have it given him while living; so that if the poet were to come to life again, he would treat him just as he was treated in fact. This was an honest Scotchman. What *he* said, the rest would do.[4]

Arguably the most incisive and certainly the wittiest of all English commentators on Scotland in the early nineteenth century, Hazlitt discerned in Scottish self-admiration a deep need for the nation to assuage its sense of guilt over the Union and its subsequent inferiority complex towards England by investing its cultural achievements with considerably more importance than they could bear. Thus he wrote in 'On the Scotch Character':

> You would think there was no other place in the world but Scotland, but that they strive to convince you at every turn of its superiority to all other places. Nothing goes down but Scotch Magazines and Reviews, Scotch airs, Scotch bravery, Scotch hospitality, Scotch novels, and Scotch logic. Someone the other day at a literary dinner in Scotland apologised for alluding to the name of Shakespeare so often, because he was not a Scotchman. What a blessing that the Duke of Wellington was not a Scotchman, or we should never have heard the last of him! Even Sir Walter Scott, I understand, talks of the Scotch novels in all companies; and by waiving the title of author, is at liberty to repeat the subject *ad infinitum*.[5]

Unfortunately Burns died before he could profit from such patriotic zest; though, no doubt, there were strong elements in his own composition which would have led him into the middle of such nonsense. Before the second decade of the nineteenth century was out, however, sumptuous memorial suppers replete with garrulous self-congratulation were being held in Edinburgh.[6] Intent on replacing an authentic nationalism with a sentimental one, Scotland created for itself a perfect populist totem in the image of a suitably censored Burns. Stemming from Jeffrey's initial critique, middle- and upper-class Scotland were able to fashion a figure almost as unlike the real Burns as possible.[7] Like the false nationalism, the reason for this was essentially political. Both Burns's sexual frankness and his personal and political discontents endangered the torpor which they believed was the guarantee of Scottish stability and their own continued supremacy. We will not understand that age unless we comprehend the degree to which the spectre of revolution haunted the consciousness of the Scottish establishment. The randy, insurrectionary figure was replaced as quickly as possible by one of sentimental rural piety. Burns, however, is partly to blame for this. His not infrequent rustic posturing, perhaps most manifest in 'The Cotter's Saturday

11

Night' (to become a kind of ark of the political covenant for bourgeois Scotland), was all too easily converted to such purposes. Like other unsettling eighteenth-century voices such as Swift and Smollett, Burns was expurgated. The long, claustrophobic night of Scottish Victorian gentility, prudery and social and political stagnation hid him from view.

Burns's partial resurrection came with a new generation of Scottish writers working in the very changed atmosphere which existed in Scotland after the First World War. The verities of bourgeois Scotland with their basis on the longevity of British imperialism were, if not wholly destroyed, deeply fractured. As in Burns's own age, economic depression, social discontent, heightened individual aspirations and rumours of foreign revolution were abundant. Inspired by the innovations, aesthetic and psychological, of European modernism, writers like MacDiarmid, Muir and Catherine Carswell—whose personal friend and literary hero, D. H. Lawrence, also shared a predilection for Burns as being, like himself, a man of the people and sexual revolutionary—looked to a radical reshaping of Scottish life. They identified strongly with Burns's radicalism, with his struggles with Scottish repression and with the harsh economic business of being an artist in Presbyterian Scotland. They wished, as we have already observed MacDiarmid asserting, 'to preserve his spirit and work for his ideals in contemporary life'. While their radical aspirations, especially MacDiarmid's rampant Anglophobia, somewhat distorted the actual literary and historical conditions prevailing in Burns's own lifetime, there is no doubt that in feeling and spirit they were much closer to the Ayrshire poet than were their sentimental, 'conservative' predecessors. The fruits of these labours were Mrs. Carswell's fine biography, MacDiarmid's brilliant poetry on the theme of Burns (his prose is much less convincing) and Muir's admirable essays.[8] In an essay published in the *Left Review* at the depths of the Depression, Muir presented a minor critical and comic masterpiece which encapsulates so much of the falsity surrounding Burns, which these essays seek to dispel, and also defines the social and literary problem which does so much to hinder such a clearing away of the layers of sentimental political sediment which cover Burns over. The occasion of Muir's essay was a description of Ramsay MacDonald unveiling a new

12

monument to Burns in a churchyard, with the odd cry of execration from the excluded unemployed ringing in his ears but not disturbing the deadly flow of his grandiloquence. Muir also noted that:

> The symbolism implicit in the scene is quite casual and involuntary. The churchyard could only hold a certain number of people; the 'platform party' (in Scotland one is always hitting against platform parties) was naturally chosen from the more well-to-do admirers of the poet: landlords, baronets and officers in the British Army. Objectively one can see that Scotland being what it is, a ceremony in honour of its greatest poet should take this form and no other. But at the same time one is driven to ask what can have happened to Burns since his death to make him now the implicit property of the middle and upper classes, when he was the property of the poor man at the beginning. The change may be briefly described by saying that Holy Willie, after being the poet's butt, has now become the keeper of his memory.
>
> . . . Something has happened to him since his death, and it is what happens to all writers after their death, no matter what they have written. It may not be true that all writers reflect the economic ideology of the society in which they live—I do not think it is—but it does seem to be true that their writings are finally and in the long run made to reflect that ideology, by a process of elimination and transformation, until the most influential classes in society can finally put their seal on the result.[9]

Sensing the oncoming war, feeling profoundly isolated in his native land, Muir's mood when he wrote this was peculiarly bleak. The wit, in fact, is an ironic reflection of this. His writing is characterized much more by a sense that the imagination can, despite all, free us. In our limited fashion the following essays are about Burns and freedom because, even if spasmodically, he and it went together.

Probably no modern Scottish poet can respond to Burns without a fair degree of ambiguity. The main reason for this, as MacDiarmid noted, was that the populist manner of his assimilation into Scottish society made both the production and reception of subsequent genuine poetry less rather than more likely. In his essay on Burns's lyric poetry, Iain Crichton Smith perceives Burns's partial culpability for this situation, but he also sees in his lyricism not simply a transparent and peculiar purity—'which allows us to look through the poet to the universal things that he is writing about'—but a capacity, arguably stemming from his Scottishness, to create a medium which is both popular and profound. It is a kind of profundity which is not analysable by modern critical techniques. Smith seems close to Catherine Carswell's belief that, discarding the merely couthy elements in Burns, there remains an exceptional kind of magic:

> Because a poem of the sort Burns had in mind must combine magic with homeliness in a manner so natural-seeming that the art with which it is done shall defy detection as absolutely as it woos the ear and wins the heart. If homeliness were enough, Scotland could show a galaxy of great singers: if magic were enough, a recitation from Keats or Shelley would hold a Bank Holiday tavern spell-bound. But in this rare accomplishment Shakespeare is the English master, and he and Burns are un-approachable except by a few scattered, often anonymous, authors of folk song.[10]

Smith looks back to this reconciliation of the homely with the magical with a certain nostalgia. Poetry's shrinking provenance and the more tortuous sensibility of the contemporary poet make a repetition of Burns's achievement seem impossible. Or, in MacDiarmid's prescient stanza:

> The trouble is that words
> Are a' but useless noo
> To span the gulf atween
> The human and the 'highbrow' view.

As befits a rightly celebrated MacDiarmid scholar, Professor John C. Weston stresses the bitter anger that, although often formally and ironically disguised, is present in Burns's satire. While he does not detect quite the degree of misanthropy in some of Burns's work that MacDiarmid did, Weston shows the justified nature of his anger based as it was on his experience of deprivation, toil and continually thwarted ambitions. It is salutary that the actual details of the harsh farm life Burns experienced (especially at Mt. Oliphant) should come from an American scholar, because Scotland still lacks an adequate social history of that period. If Professor Weston's views should prove controversial to Scottish historians, it is hoped that the controversy will act as a spur to bridging the unhappy gap between Scottish historians and literary critics which still mutually debilitates both groups. Satire, for Burns, is not regarded as a very high or even reputable mode, but when he does adopt it, his motives tend to be more personal and less benevolent than has generally been realized—self-therapy, revenge and protection. Analyses of eleven of his most important satires follow, aimed at substantiating this thesis. And if Burns is not finally ranged beside Juvenal, his aims and practice are clearly differentiated from those of gentle practitioners in the Horatian line. Weston, however, is also keen to demonstrate the linguistic skill of a poet who employs the very rural language which his opponents held to be a deficiency in order effectively to attack their entrenched positions. The variation of mood and *persona* which is so characteristic of Burns's satiric writings is also discussed and a reassessment of his contribution to European satire presented.

Burns is first and foremost a lyrical poet, a fact admitted by Robert Wells in his essay. He argues, however, that earlier studies of his narrative verse have been limited by the failure, first of all, to define exactly what is meant by 'narrative'. Distinguishing between a true 'story' and what he terms 'Mimetic Transcripts' (works containing a large number of narrative features but lacking *peripeteia*) he places only 'Tam o' Shanter' in the first class, while such varied works as 'Death and Doctor Hornbook', 'Holy Willie's Prayer', 'The Cotter's Saturday Night' and 'The Jolly Beggars' are in the second. This initial distinction provides the necessary theoretical base for a series of analyses, leading to the conclusion that, in this area of his work, Burns was more concerned with didacticism than earlier critics have supposed.

Catarina Ericson-Roos's contribution, 'The Young Lassies, Love, Music and Poetry', serves to remind us that the eighteenth-century vernacular revival in Scotland, of which Burns represents the zenith, was very largely a 'singing' revival. Focusing on the poet's love lyrics and dealing in turn with courting songs, more reflective expressions of longing, and the trials of motherhood, she shows how, in different ways, the full effect depends on a fusion of poetry and music. Thus, in 'Tam Glen', while Burns uses various rhetorical devices to transmit the girl's eager, nervous chattering, the quick tempo of the tune

15

with its syllabic setting, monotonous melody and even rhythm underlines these characteristics even more powerfully. Moreover, her increasing desperation is mirrored in the last bar of each stanza where the melody (in minor mode) rises suddenly, then slowly descends to the tonic again. Dr. Ericson-Roos's dual qualifications as literary and musical scholar guarantee that she can discuss these songs as complete units, over-emphasizing neither words nor tune. It is a matter of some sadness that few earlier Burns scholars have been able to achieve a similar balance.

What these first four essays all demonstrate is an essential feature of Burns's creative genius which is his quite remarkable power of empathy and dramatization. Hazlitt immediately recognized his ability, and it was his lectures which inspired Keats also to see in him that creative quality which he placed above all others—the capacity in the poet for 'negative capability'. Hence Burns's uncanny capacity to adopt the *persona* of the person he hated or feel himself into the identity of the beloved. As Edwin Muir has cogently remarked:

> His vision of the world was unusually complete. Generally praised as a lyric poet, he was more truly a kind of dramatist. He expressed very seldom in his songs the emotions of Robert Burns, and when he expressed them, he often did it badly. 'To Mary in Heaven' and 'Man was made to Mourn', poems obviously composed under the stress of deep personal emotion, were among the worst he wrote, and had none of the absolute sureness of dramatic lyrics like 'Tam Glen' or 'Whistle and I'll come tae ye, my lad'. In his songs he put himself in a certain attitude, or rather, a certain number of attitudes, and the voices which spoke through them were those of the entire Scots peasantry of his time. All his songs written for women were especially exquisite; in throwing the emotion of a woman into a song he did not once fail.[11]

Several of the following essays, especially those of Wilson and Simpson, are centrally concerned with the troubling discrepancy between Burns's dramatic genius and his highly suspect talent for self-dramatization. It is perhaps an intractable problem. Increasingly Burns felt himself as living in a kind of vacuum or, even worse, a vortex, and it is impossible to say to what degree this was imposed on him by Scottish society or the inevitable result of his impulsive search for a condition which was not so much one of personal freedom as of amorphous licence. The Edinburgh *literati* had not the slightest doubt that it was the latter, dark insurrectionary force that Burns represented. Sexual freedom being an inevitable plank of any revolutionary platform, Burns's love poetry came in for particular disfavour. As Jeffrey wrote in 1808:

> He has expressed admirably the feelings of an enamoured peasant, who, however refined or eloquent he may be, always approaches his mistress on a footing of equality; but has never caught that tone of chivalrous gallantry which uniformly abases itself in the presence of the object of its devotion. Accordingly, instead of suing for a smile, or melting in a tear, his muse deals in nothing but locked embraces and midnight rencontres; and even in his complimentary effusions to ladies of highest rank, is for straining them to the bosom of her impetuous votary.[12]

If Jeffrey was anxious about such amorous aspirations to transgress the strict boundaries of social class, he would have been not only disgusted but politically terrified had he known of Burns's appetite and aptitude for more exotic erotica. In 'Burns and Bawdy' Ronald Jack examines an area of the poet's verse, seldom given due critical attention either because of censorious prudery such as Jeffrey's, an erroneous belief that these works contain little of poetic merit, or, more usually, because of the grave editorial problems facing those who wish to establish the exact extent of Burns's own contribution to older songs and ballads. Dealing first with the poet's adaptations, Jack demonstrates the great care taken by Burns when handling older material. Also, although in some instances (e.g. 'John Anderson') he purified the originals, in others (e.g. 'The Reel o' Stumpie') he increased the bawdy content for the benefit of the Crochallan Fencibles and their like. Two groups of his original bawdy verses are then discussed in turn. A study of the religious bawdry underlines both the poet's thematic range and his satiric skills—different from but just as varied as those practised in the more respectable Kirk Satires. His scurrilous parodies of pastoral ('Ode to Spring') and ballad ('Grim Grizzle') also reveal poetic talents of a sort not encountered elsewhere in his verse. These analyses lead to the conclusion

17

that, while Burns is heavily influenced by eighteenth-century folk bawdry, his contribution is at the same time unique and impressive. In particular he shows much greater imagistic ingenuity in this area of his verse than elsewhere. By shyly casting a veil over such material, critics give an incomplete picture of the poet's skill and omit some of his finest work.

It has usually been accepted that the Scots for whatever reasons have found it convenient, necessary or expedient to create myths around their 'national bard'. Scott Wilson, by examining the poet's letters and (especially) his verse-epistles, shows how Burns actively created roles for himself. The famous letter to Moore, for example, presents his biography not in a factual, chronological way but re-arranges the life story in a manner which would make the poet more readily acceptable to his new literary audience. The image of the Scottish 'Tom Jones' is enthusiastically pursued when he writes to Ainslie and the Fencibles; that of the posturing man of sentiment dominates his correspondence with Clarinda. But if such examples show to a greater or lesser degree the corrupting power of image-making, the verse-epistles written at Mauchline between 1784 and 1786 provide a refreshing contrast. Wilson not only demonstrates the high literary artistry of these works but argues that, in this instance, poetry itself becomes the major means of projecting a more vital and honest image. 'We see a man discovering a talent, revelling in it, and elevating the practice of it to a style of living—combative, cocky, independent, fiercely alive. As an extension of this, society's treatment of the poet becomes, in a sense, the touchstone for that society's moral, political and religious health. Such a study reveals not only a nation keen to mythologize a poet but a poet anxious to mythologize himself.'

In his essay Kenneth Simpson also pursues the devious (wounded?) hare of Burns's epistolary style and multiple personality. This essay argues that Burns's letters, in many cases works of conscious literary artistry, exemplify the linguistic energy of the Scottish tradition (best epitomized in the flyting) and the Scottish capacity for ironic voice. The letters offer an outlet for the expression of Burns's considerable dramatic talent, and they permit him to follow, like Sterne, the impulse of wit. Detailed similarities show that the legacy of Sterne was

18

considerable, with Burns adopting from Sterne the *persona* of sentimentalist. Burns's self-dramatization was ultimately limiting in that he in effect *became* the *personae* and came to write almost automatically in the appropriate modes. The compulsive use of voices reflects the fragmentation of the self; and this helps to account for both Burns's Scottish and his twentieth-century appeal.

In his essay Andrew Noble argues for a recognition of the creative affinity and revolutionary aspirations of Burns and Blake. While Sterne's manifest Irishness makes him a fairly easily acceptable associate for Burns, most Scottish critics have anglophobically dismissed the possibility of his having a profound connection with the English Romantic poetry of his age. A close examination of Burns and Blake disproves this. Both men suffered from being geniuses with a working-class background. Both men sought not only to overthrow the rigid neo-classic aesthetic forms of their age but to overthrow the decorous, moderate psychological type who was their social superior. Both men looked to revolution abroad and at home as a form of necessary change. Both sought a resurrection of their respective national art forms; though in Burns's case this was to prove particularly difficult. Both were also attracted to Milton's Satan, though in Burns it was mainly in a comic manner and not in terms of the transvaluation of orthodox Christian values to which Blake aspired. Given Blake's advantage of living considerably longer and being nourished by a much deeper spiritual and intellectual tradition, the essay displays Burns's very considerable power of deep, penetrating thought. His sheer intelligence is still perhaps undervalued.

Like Scott Wilson and Kenneth Simpson, Alan Bold underlines the way in which Burns was anxious to create roles for himself. Even more ominously, however, Bold points to the fact that Scotland has not only been too ready to applaud some of Burns's more suspect performances, but has put on stage a figure which has much more to do with its own compulsive devising than it has to do with Burns. This is Robert Burns—'Superscot'. Or, as Edwin Muir brilliantly described this exemplary national hero in 1935:

> To every Scotsman Burns is a familiar figure, a sort of house-

hold god, and most Scotsmen, I suppose, could reel off a few proverbial tags of his poetry, and one or two of his songs set to music. But that is all. This public effigy, in which the lover, the boon-companion and the democrat are the main ingredients, with a hard-working farmer in the background all but subdued to respectability by time, is the real object of worship of the Burns cult. It is not a literary cult but a social one. It has very little to do with Burns, and is concerned chiefly with the perpetuation of a myth. In that myth Burns becomes an ordinary man like his devotees which he was not. He also becomes a successful lover and a free and glorious companion which everybody would like to be. His myth is thus based on a firm foundation of sanctified illusion and romantic wish-fulfilment. This legendary figure is a Scotsman who took upon him all the sins of the people, not to redeem them, but to commit them as ideally as they should be committed, that is freely and guiltlessly, in an imaginary world beyond good and evil, a Paradisal Kailyard with a harmless domesticated serpent; for even to the most respectable of Burns's worshippers, to elders and ministers of the Kirk, Burns's sins are in a special category, and his fornications have the prescriptive right of King David's. He was a scapegoat driven out to sweet pastures while the people elected to stay in the wilderness; a god who sanctified the meagre indulgences of the many by unlimited loving and drinking.[13]

Like Muir, Bold sees the Scottish need for Burns as an absurd, compensatory fantasy. Historical evidence is adduced to prove that a nation, suffering under the successive hammer-blows of Flodden, the two Unions, and the two Jacobite rebellions, desperately needed such a figure at such a time. His contemporaries like Maria Riddell and our contemporaries like John Cairney continue the presentation of Burns as an almost superhuman figure. The myth thus becomes further exaggerated and jealously protected by people who have only the slightest knowledge of his verse. Most insidiously (and ironically) a poet who had himself a very keen appreciation of his position within a continuing tradition of Scots writing, has been equated with our entire National Literature, casting into obscurity both the great names of the past and the present. His vast band of admirers may turn to their pints and to a few half-remembered lines from 'To a Mountain-Daisy'. They are much less likely to turn to Henryson or MacDiarmid, Fergusson or Muir.

NOTES

1. 'The Burns Cult (1)', *Contemporary Scottish Studies* (Edinburgh, 1976), p. 113; David Daiches, *Robert Burns* (London, 1950; Revised Edition, 1966); Tom Crawford, *Burns: A Study of the Poems and Songs* (Edinburgh, 1960); Hoxie Fairchild's 'Robert Burns' in his *Religious Trends in English Poetry*, Vol. III (New York, 1949) is a minor masterpiece in the genre of intellectual biography. With regard to the complex problems of Burns's language David Murison's 'The Language of Burns' in *Critical Essays on Robert Burns*, ed. Low (London, 1975), pp. 54–69, is first-rate.
2. Review of Hilton Brown's *There Was a Lad* in *Edwin Muir: Uncollected Scottish Criticism*, ed. Noble (London: Vision Press; Totowa, N.J.: Barnes & Noble, 1981), pp. 202–3.
3. *Rameau's Nephew* and *D'Alembert's Dream*, trans. Tancock (London, 1966), p. 82.
4. Cited in *Burns—The Critical Heritage*, ed. Low (London, 1974), p. 327.
5. *Collected Works*, Vol. XII, ed. Waller and Glover (London, 1904), p. 253.
6. John Gibson Lockhart, *Peter's Letters to his Kinsfolk*, ed. Ruddick (Edinburgh, 1977).
7. Review of *Cromek's Reliques* in *Burns—The Critical Heritage*, pp. 178–95.
8. Carswell, *The Life of Robert Burns* (London, 1930). All Muir essays in *Edwin Muir: Uncollected Scottish Criticism*; cf. footnote 2.
9. 'Burns and Holy Willie', *Edwin Muir: Uncollected Scottish Criticism*, pp. 189–92.
10. 'Robert Burns', in *From Anne to Victoria*, ed. Bonamy Dobrée (London, 1937), p. 413.
11. 'Robert Burns', in *Edwin Muir: Uncollected Scottish Criticism*, p. 185.
12. *Burns—The Critical Heritage*, p. 182.
13. *Scottish Journey* (Edinburgh: Mainstream, 1979), p. 90.

1

The Lyrics of Robert Burns

by IAIN CRICHTON SMITH

I must say that I have never considered Burns a great poet in the same sense as I think of Dante as a great poet. I believe that Burns wrote one indisputably great poem, that is, 'Holy Willie's Prayer', and I consider this a great poem because it is artistically articulated, and because it expresses perfectly the hypocrite immersed in his own accepted way of life. As for the rest of Burns's work I do not think that it reached the pitch of artistic perfection that this particular poem reaches. 'A Cotter's Saturday Night' seems to me to be responsible for much of the very bad sentimental poetry that we had in Scotland up until the time that MacDiarmid opened his little country out to the universe, and set it by implication in its true perspective. His parody of a Burns Supper as delivered by a Chinaman says much of what I myself think of that extraordinary ceremony. There is also in Burns an unhealthy Scottish chauvinism which I find disquieting.

Thus it seems to me that Burns has been responsible for much of the inferior poetry that depends on the idea of the 'heart'. The kailyard for example is implicit in 'A Cotter's Saturday Night', and I often think it odd that Burns himself could see no discrepancy between his own mode of life and that which he praised in 'A Cotter's Saturday Night'. His attack on the villain who might remove the daughter's virginity might very well have been an attack on himself if he could have seen more clearly than he did. 'A Cotter's Saturday

Night' is a perfect example of much that is wrong with a certain kind of Scottish poetry.

Nevertheless the cult of Burns has to be explained, and I do not simply mean by that the admiration which the Russians and the Chinese have for him, an admiration which is probably political. There is in Burns a quality which makes an appeal to ordinary people and which obviously has little to do with 'artistic articulation'. They read him, for example, when they do not read Ezra Pound or Eliot or, for that matter, Mac-Diarmid. MacDiarmid is a poet's poet in a way that Burns is not. We go to MacDiarmid for interesting ideas, for a larger vision than we can find in Burns. Where we find in Mac-Diarmid a continual interest in life itself and man as merely one manifestation of that life, we obviously do not find this in Burns, for Burns is not interested in ideas, and in comparison with MacDiarmid—and for that matter Wordsworth and Coleridge—he is almost naïve. He is not in fact a self-conscious poet in the way that we expect of our moderns and even in the way that Pope was self-conscious.

There is not in Burns's work any artistic obsession, and it seems to me that the corpus of his work looks disturbingly occasional. In a sense Burns was more like Clare than he was like a Wordsworth or Coleridge, except that he is more universal than Clare. For his philosophy is not a complicated one, and amounts to little more than an adage, 'A man's a man for a' that'.

And yet and yet . . . Burns cannot be as easily dismissed as this. In spite of saying that he is not philosophical, that he does not use language in a specifically artistic way, that he is often sentimental and that he is naïve, there is a quality in Burns that cannot easily be turned aside. It is a quality that one finds in his lyrics and that haunts and lingers. It is not the case that any weight of modern learning can be brought to bear on these lyrics, for they are not, for instance, ironical, and irony is perhaps the most common weapon in modern consciousness. Irony implies that a writer is not only concerned with his writing but is also concerned with himself being concerned. What I find in Burns is an unusual simplicity and transparency. It seems to me that Burns was a poet as a 'rose is a rose'; that is to say, we hardly ever find any sense of strain

23

in his work, and especially in the lyrics. We never feel that he is looking for a variant to what he is writing down, and in this sense the lyrics look as if they have been made almost without intervention. There is a speed and rightness in these lyrics which make them almost become part of our poetic corpus, without our wishing to attribute them to anyone. It is useless to say, 'This is a Burns lyric' in the same way as one can say, 'This is a Stevens poem' precisely because the poetry is so naïve. It is as if we were looking through the poet to the universal things that he is writing about.

When I say that we can talk of a 'Stevens poem', what we are concerned with is not only the poem that we are reading but all the other poems that are leading up to this poem and of which this poem forms a part. It is also a question of language and of a specific tone which can be seen as belonging to Stevens alone. But all the time we are aware of a particular mind and consciousness behind these poems in a way that we are not when we read a Burns lyric. In a sense nothing much can be said of a Burns lyric except that it is there. No resources of modern scholarship can be brought to bear on it. And yet it speaks of intense emotion, it is powerful, and it resonates.

For instance, suppose we have a look at the lyric 'The Silver Tassie', which runs as follows:

> Go fetch to me a pint o' wine,
> And fill it in a silver tassie;
> That I may drink before I go,
> A service to my bonie lassie:
> The boat rocks at the Pier o' Lieth
> Fu' loud the wind blaws frae the Ferry,
> The ship rides by the Berwick-law,
> And I maun leave my bony Mary.
>
> The trumpets sound, the banners fly,
> The glittering spears are ranked ready,
> The shouts o' war are heard afar,
> The battle closes deep and bloody.
> It's not the roar o' sea or shore,
> Wad make me langer wish to tarry;
> Nor shouts o' war that's heard afar—
> It's leaving thee, my bony Mary!

$\qquad\qquad\qquad\qquad\qquad\qquad\qquad\qquad\qquad$ (I, 445)[1]

I can imagine a scholar trying to find something to say about this poem. For instance he might point to the internal rhymes, or he might remark that the colours in the poem are silver and red, that for instance the silver tassie is linked up with the silver spears and trumpets, or that the wine in the cup links up with the blood mentioned in the second stanza. He might say all these things but they would be irrelevant. In a Stevens poem they might not be irrelevant for he might have used silver and red in other poems for a specific reason. But in Burns they would be irrelevant for Burns does not use these colours significantly as part of an artistic consciousness. All we can say about this poem is found in the cadence, 'It's leaving thee, my bony Mary' or 'And I maun leave my bony Mary'. The poem is there on the page. It is easy to forget about Burns and simply look at what he has created as if it were a stone. There is no sense of strain, no sense of alternative possibilities.

If we look at Blake's lyrics we can imagine other possibilities, other ironies. But Burns's lyrics are presented to us, whole and fresh, and they are open to any reader in a way that Blake's lyrics are not. Of course behind those words are the cadences of the songs based on them, and it is very difficult for one to see and read them without being haunted by these cadences. Nevertheless, what astonishes is their extreme self-confidence and simplicity.

One of his very great lyrics is 'Ae Fond Kiss', and again there is this naïve self-confidence as in

> I'll ne'er blame my partial fancy,
> Naething could resist my Nancy: (II, 592)

where the girl is so specifically and easily named.

The fact that the greatest verse perhaps in Burns's lyrics could flow so effortlessly shows not merely the self-confidence of the poet but also the strength of a tradition:

> Had we never lov'd sae kindly,
> Had we never lov'd say blindly!
> Never met—or never parted,
> We had ne'er been broken-hearted.   (II, 592)

25

There is no sense in which this verse makes the rest of the poem seem inferior, because the poet does not in any way strain after the greatness of the verse. As on a piece of land a flower might grow beside an old tin can, so this verse lies with the others and does not appear out of place. For the following lines are not so fine, especially the ones:

> Thine be ilka joy and treasure,
> Peace, Enjoyment, Love and Pleasure! (II, 592)

However, if we compare this with a love lyric by MacDiarmid we are immediately in a different country. The lyric is called 'In the Hedge-Back':

> It was a wild black nicht,
> But i' the hert o't we
> Drave back the darkness wi' a bleeze o' licht,
> Ferrer than men could see.
>
> It was a wild black nicht,
> But o' the snell air we
> Kept juist eneuch to hinder the heat
> Meltin' us utterly.
>
> It was a wild black nicht,
> But o' the win's roar we
> Kept juist eneuch to hear oor herts beat
> Owre it triumphantly.
>
> It was a wild black nicht,
> But o' the Earth we
> Kept juist eneuch underneath us to ken
> That a warl' used to be.[2]

Now it seems to me that this is a great lyric, but it is different from Burns's lyrics in many ways. For one thing the last two lines are beyond Burns. He didn't have that kind of imagination, and perhaps it was not possible to have written like that in the eighteenth century in any case. But there is a drive towards these last two lines which is not typical of Burns, though it is typical of MacDiarmid. But the real difference is this, that this poem does not have the lucid universality that Burns's lyrics have.

A poet who I think derives more from Burns than Mac-Diarmid does is Sidney Goodsir Smith, as for instance in 'Loch Leven':

> Tell me was a glorie ever seen
> As the morn I left my lass
> Fore licht in the toun o snaw,
> And saw the dawn
> O' burnan cramasie
> Turn the grey ice
> O' Mary's Loch Leven
> Til sheenan brass—
> And kent the glorie and the gleen
> Was but the waukenin o her een . . .[3]

It seems to me that there is a Burnsian quality haunting that poem, and yet it is not as great a lyric for us as MacDiarmid's lyric is. There is a thinness here precisely because the poet relies so much on the cadences. The simplicity that is to be found in this poem looks too simple for the twentieth century. Yet, in their own context, though Burns's poems are simple, they are not irritatingly so.

It is possible that the reason why Wordsworth admired Burns so much was not just because of his creed of independence and humanity, but rather because he envied the tradition that could allow a poet to speak so clearly and so confidently and so unself-consciously. It is rather as if Eliot were envying MacDiarmid for the way in which he can move up and down the ladder of a Scottish democratic language, while, for instance, Eliot's pub scene in *The Waste Land* sounds artificial and strained. There are, for instance, in 'Auld Lang Syne' two verses which are powerful because Burns could almost take for granted that his readers would have done exactly what is being described in these verses, and indeed we have.

> We twa hae run about the braes,
> And pou'd the gowans fine;
> But we've wander'd mony a weary fitt,
> Sin auld lang syne.

We twa hae paidl'd in the burn,
Frae morning sun till dine;
But seas between us braid hae roar'd
Sin auld lang syne.   (I, 444)

I think that these lines are very close to great poetry because
they are so universal. Again they are written with supernatural
ease and self-confidence and are things which neither Wordsworth nor for that matter Coleridge could have written. And I
think that this has a great deal to do with a Scottish tradition.
It is true that Wordsworth wrote about childhood, but I am
sure he did not write as simply and with such naturalness and
resonance as this. This union of the familiar and the large was
one of Burns's outstanding gifts. There is a directness about
these lines which Wordsworth never attained (though he did
great things in another mode) and perhaps by the nature of
things never could have attained, unless, perhaps, he had
written in the Cumberland dialect.

Burns can even do it in 'John Anderson my Jo' which seems
to me to be sentimental and gooey in the verse:

But now your brow is beld, John,
Your locks are like the snaw;
But blessings on your frosty pow,
John Anderson my Jo.   (II, 529)

Nevertheless, in spite of these lines, which seem to me to be
analogous with 'My Granny's Hieland Hame' for sentiment,
he can be pure and clear as in:

John Anderson my jo, John,
We clamb the hill the gither;
And mony a canty day, John,
We've had wi' ane anither.   (II, 529)

Better and very fine indeed is the verse:

The soger frae the war returns,
The sailor frae the main,
But I hae parted frae my Love,
Never to meet again, my dear,
Never to meet again . . .   (II, 876)

where the pause at 'my dear' is like a catch at the heart.

28

It is possible that much of the simplicity and emotional strength of these lyrics comes from the language and from a tradition, and yet this may not wholly be true, for a poem on childhood which I myself have much admired is 'A Boy's Song' by James Hogg:

Where the pools are bright and deep,
Where the gray trout lies asleep,
Up the river and o'er the lea,
That's the way for Billy and me.

Where the blackbird sings the latest,
Where the hawthorn blooms the sweetest,
Where the nestlings chirp and flee,
That's the way for Billy and me.

Where the mowers mow the cleanest,
Where the hay lies thick and greenest;
There to trace the homeward bee,
That's the way for Billy and me.

Where the hazel bank is steepest,
Where the shadow falls the deepest,
Where the clustering nuts fall free,
That's the way for Billy and me.

Why the boys should drive away
Little sweet maidens from the play,
Or love to banter and fight so well,
That's the thing I never could tell.

But this I know, I love to play,
Through the meadow, among the hay;
Up the water and o'er the lea,
That's the way for Billy and me.[4]

This poem seems to me to have the purity of the verses I have quoted from 'Auld Lang Syne', and it occurs to me that the reason for this purity is perhaps not so much to do with language as with the nature of Scotland. It may be that these poems have their power because of the fact that the poet could assume that most of the people of Scotland could have done something like this in their childhood: in other words, that the power has to do with the relative democratic nature of a country, for in a sense these poems seem to me to get closer to the pathos of childhood than Wordsworth's poems do, precisely because they are unweighted by a philosophy. As I have said already, Clare would have got closer to this than either Wordsworth or Coleridge, and as far as Blake is concerned it is possible that the cadences he created are more personal and idiosyncratic than those which Burns employed.

Now it is quite impossible for a poet to write like this in the twentieth century, and indeed, if he were directly influenced by these lyrics, he would, I think, appear out-of-date, for we cannot look on women and children as Burns did. A poem like 'A Red Red Rose' begs too many questions, is too set in one inflated mood for us to write like it, because we would be far more concerned with the shadows. How could we possibly, in our world, speak of such permanency?

> Till a' the seas gang dry, my Dear,
> And the rocks melt wi' the sun:
> I will love thee still, my Dear,
> While the sands o' life shall run. (II, 735)

That is why I think Goodsir Smith's lyrics, some of them I think deriving from Burns, seem so thin in this century simply because of what they have left out. A largeness such as this is beyond us. We could not speak with such eloquence.

In fact, though nothing can diminish my admiration for Burns's lyrics, I feel that they are less individual poems than emanations from a people. And however much we may regret the fact that poetry can no longer be the voice of the people, it is nevertheless the case. When Burns wrote these lyrics he was not speaking out of his own dark life, he was articulating moods. It is interesting in this connection how Goodsir Smith, who began with lyrics, ended as a self-parodist and ironist, and was in fact the greater poet because of it, for the lyric is not the typical poem of the age.

An early poem of Goodsir Smith's like 'Kinnoul Hill' reads rather like a Burns lyric:

Kinnoul Hill lies white wi snaw,
The lyft is pale as stane,
My burd's dark een 're far awa—
It's dreich tae bide alane.

It's cauld an gurl on Kinnoul Hill
As Janiveer gaes oot,
But neer a blast sae shairp an fell
As whorls my saul aboot.

O black's the ice on Kinnoul Brae,
Dark scaurs like wa's o doom—
But nane sae mirk 's this dumb wae
That maks aa Perth a tomb.

My loo, I lang yir airms the nicht,
My lane's sae fremt an drear—
An Kinnoul Hill stans bleak an white
I' the goulin wunds o Janiveer.[5]

The Burnsian cadence can be heard in this lyric, but at the same time it is to be noticed that Smith feels it necessary to break it in the last line as if he felt that the lyric was moving too smoothly.

MacDiarmid once remarked that the most beautiful line in Scottish poetry was that one, 'Ye are na Mary Morison'. But I do not think that 'Mary Morison' is a typical Burns lyric. It seems to me to be too vitiated by a foreign poetic diction, such as in the second verse:

Yestreen when to the trembling string
The dance gaed through the lighted ha',
To thee my fancy took its wing,
I sat, but neither heard nor saw . . .   (I, 42)

The directness and speed which are the true characteristics of the Burns lyric seem to me to be missing.

I come back again to a lyric like 'It Was a' for our Rightfu' King', which has these qualities:

It was a' for our rightfu' king
    We left fair Scotland's strand;
It was a' for our rightfu' king,
    We e'er saw Irish land, my dear,
        We e'er saw Irish land.—

31

> Now a' is done that men can do,
>   And a' is done in vain:
> My Love and Native Land fareweel,
>   For I maun cross the main, my dear,
>   For I maun cross the main.
>
> He turned him right and round about,
>   Upon the Irish shore,
> And gae his bridle-reins a shake,
>   With, Adieu for evermore, my dear,
>   And adieu for evermore.
>
> The soger frae the wars returns,
>   The sailor frae the main,
> But I hae parted frae my Love,
>   Never to meet again, my dear,
>   Never to meet again.
>
> When day is gane, and night is come,
>   And a' folk bound to sleep;
> I think on him that's far awa',
>   The lee-lang night and weep, my dear,
>   The lee-lang night and weep.   (II, 876)

This lyric seems to me perfect of its kind. There is an energy which is never dissipated by hesitation on the part of the poet. Burns shows complete confidence in the way he moves from description to generalization, as in the fourth verse. It is as if he wrote his best verses as absentmindedly as he wrote the other verses, so that we never feel with him that he is building up to something special. In other words, we are in the presence of an unself-conscious poetry which is, because of its purity and simplicity, universal. What is even more interesting is that this directness and simplicity can be found in his comic poems as well as in his 'romantic ones', and this is the sign of an unusual talent. We find these qualities for instance in 'Duncan Gray':

> Duncan Gray cam here to woo,
>   Ha, ha, the wooing o't,
> On blythe Yule night when we were fu',
>   Ha, ha, the wooing o't.

> Maggie coost her head fu' high,
> Look'd asklent and unco skiegh,
> Gart poor Duncan stand abiegh;
>> Ha, ha, the wooing o't. (II, 667)

It seems to me that Burns in these lyrics has an unusual speed of thought which allows the poem to move very fast and with great energy. It is not, however, the kind of thought that will issue in ideas. It is rather the speed of thought of a poetically gifted mind, sure of itself at all times.

I know no other writer in Scottish literature able to write this sort of universal lyric, dealing so intimately and with such great power with the concerns of ordinary humanity. Mac-Diarmid's lyrics are something else again: they are new and almost idiosyncratic in a way that Burns's lyrics are not. They are the product of a highly conscious artistic mind. They show genius of a different kind from Burns's. It was possible for Burns to write at a particular moment in history with a freedom and assurance and ease that allowed him to articulate the passions of ordinary people as if they were his own.

There is of course much that these lyrics do not touch on, but they do touch on many important aspects of our emotional lives. They tell us about forsaken love, happy love, about love in old age, about domestic comedy. Time and time again their cadences have a piercing quality as in for instance:

> There's wild-woods grow, and rivers row,
> And mony a hill between;
> But day and night my fancy's flight
> Is ever wi' my Jean. (I, 422)

There seems to me nothing that he cannot handle in the territory that he has chosen for himself. What we do not have, in all this perfection, is the idiosyncrasy of Burns himself, of the darknesses that he must at times have felt. What we do not have is the slant oddness of a Blake, or the strangeness of some of Wordsworth's lyrics. What we do have is the pure universality of the moods and thoughts of the ordinary person.

I do not think that any twentieth-century writer could learn anything from these lyrics, for Burns exhausted all new possibilities in their perfection. It is true that certain nineteenth-century writers followed him in concentrating on the 'heart' rather than on the mind, and that this was for a long time a bad thing in Scottish poetry. But to write as Burns wrote one would have to have lived at that time and to have been a Burns. There is nothing left that one can draw on, for it is only on imperfection that one can draw. The time was to come when poetry was to move away from these universals and to become self-conscious and idiosyncratic, so that we do not think much now of any poet who does not have a style of his own and one that is easily recognizable. The time was to come when a MacDiarmid was to look for something more intellectual than he was to find in earlier Scottish poets. There is much in sentimental Scottish songs that derives from the lyrics of Burns, for the appeal to the 'heart' has allowed an entry to the kailyard. Only Burns himself had the ability to maintain the miraculous poise which his lyrics at their best have. Others would assume that the 'heart' alone could create poetry, which of course is not true. Burns had the technical power to make constructions which were not simply effusions of the 'heart'. He also had the power to make the selection of detail necessary and poetic. It is true that there is sentiment in 'Auld Lang Syne', and certainly the linking of hands of drunken guests has not helped the poem much. But beyond and behind all that there are lines like

> We twa hae paidl'd in the burn,
> Frae morning sun till dine;
> But seas between us braid hae roar'd,
> Sin auld lang syne,   (I, 444)

which seem to me to be close to great poetry. There are hundreds of Scottish songs which derive from the sentimental side of Burns, but the lyrics of Burns are far better than these, though by their nature they have allowed territory to the sentimental.

It is true that 'A Red Red Rose' is almost destroyed by sentimental singers, but nevertheless it does express the feelings that lovers have when they are young. No poet could write like this now, for the statements are far too large: but this is not to say that certain people do not feel like this. It seems to me that there is a central humanity in Burns's lyrics and songs which one does not, for instance, find in those of Moore.

The lyrics of Burns are perfect of their kind, and their perfection, poised precariously between sentiment and universal truth, tells us that nothing more can be added. We do not have the confidence to write like this now. We do not have the extraordinary control over the cadence that Burns had. And in any case, after Freud and the rest, we do not have the lack of self-consciouness to write like this. We are no longer able as poets to speak so universally and with such authority and rightness. All we can do is write from within ourselves alone.

NOTES

1. All quotations come from *The Poems and Songs of Robert Burns*, ed. James Kinsley, 3 vols. (Oxford, 1968).
2. *Collected Poems of Hugh MacDiarmid*, ed. C. M. Grieve (Edinburgh and London, 1962), p. 15.
3. Sydney Goodsir Smith, *Collected Poems 1941–1975* (London, 1975), p. 63.
4. *James Hogg: Selected Poems*, ed. Douglas S. Mack (Oxford, 1970), p.152.
5. Goodsir Smith, op. cit., p. 4.

2

Robert Burns's Satire

by JOHN C. WESTON

> And aye his harns wi' smeddum birl'd aroun
> And spied the maist fause-herted in his toun,
> And heez'd them up on laughter's gallow tree.
> —William Jeffrey on Burns from
> *On Glaister's Hill*

There has long been a belief that Burns's satire is essentially comic, that there is really no bite to it, that it proceeds from a person of gentle good humour, whose veins flow with the milk of human kindness. Answering Francis Jeffrey's indignation over a letter by Burns published in 1808 which expresses the most extreme and violent hatred of the Evangelicals, Josiah Walker in his memoir of Burns (1811) said that the poet's 'tumidity' was 'merely a playful effusion of mock-heroic, to divert a friend'.[1] Such attempts to reduce Burns's fierce anger to gentle proportions have continued. Auguste Angellier makes no distinction between the humour in 'Death and Dr. Hornbook' and in 'Holy Willie's Prayer', characterizing the 'raillery' found in all Burns's comic and satirical poems, except a few political pieces and lampoons motivated by personal anger, as without gall, full of friendly good nature, written from no moral viewpoint and intended to inflict no reprimand.[2] More recently Robert Dewar, as part of his attempt to de-emphasize the importance of Burns's criticism of life and powers of analysis in favour of his 'passionate love and enjoyment of life', has claimed that even those poems

36

which have a note of criticism or satire are 'altogether without venom and . . . reformative aim'.[3] Robert T. Fitzhugh asserts that Burns is pre-eminent among English and Scottish satirists in 'overwhelming good humor and almost sympathy with the victim'.[4] Finally, Christina Keith asserts that Burns's satires are all Horatian and show a sympathetic understanding of their victim, a quality which failed him after Edinburgh.[5] It is easy to take the edge from Burns's poems because of his obvious charm, *joie de vivre*, and sentimental benevolence. And one is tempted to do so in order to make Burns a cheery companion generally pleased with his world. But one must not do so, because his edges were formed by the harsh world in which he struggled and to which his satire responds.

Burns certainly does not have a misanthropic view like Swift's, nor does he effect his satiric purpose, as Juvenal does, by disgusting us with loathsome descriptions of physical detail reflecting moral depravity. If we were to divide all satire into Horatian (comic) and Juvenalian (tragic), Burns's satires, with the single exception of 'Address of Beelzebub', would be on the Horatian side of the line, although unlike Robert Fergusson, whose satires are all strikingly like Horace's, only 'To a Louse', if indeed it is a satire at all, and perhaps 'Address to the Deil', are strictly Horatian. But that Burns's satires are not tragic, black, visceral does not mean that they are merely gently bantering and wittily amusing. Their power derives from the fierceness of Burns's hatreds and his intention to wound his adversary. The splenetic and the friendly temperament can exist together, as Burns wrote of his friend William Smellie: 'Yet, tho' his caustic wit was biting rude,/ His heart was warm, benevolent, and good' (335) (II, 588).[6]

Burns was a great hater, as Maria Riddell made clear a few weeks after his death:

> Much allowance will be made by a candid mind for the splenetic warmth of a spirit whom 'distress had spited with the world', and which, unbounded in its intellectual sallies and pursuits, continually experienced the curbs imposed by the waywardness of his fortune. . . . His passions rendered him, according as they disclosed themselves in affection or antipathy, an object of enthusiastic attachment, or of decided enmity . . . he acknowledged in the universe but two classes of objects, those of adora-

tion the most fervent, or of aversion the most uncontrollable. . . . It is said, that the celebrated Dr. Johnson professed to love a good hater, a temperament that would have singularly adapted him to cherish a prepossession in favour of our bard, who perhaps fell but little short even of the surly Doctor in this qualification.[7]

Since Maria Riddell described Burns during the last five years of his life when she was acquainted with him, some might explain that he was more given to decided animosity during these later dark and troubled years than when he wrote all his greatest satires before going to Edinburgh. But although his capacity to hate and his tendency to anger undoubtedly increased after he left Ayrshire, he always reacted to social injustice with anger, never with sweetness and compliance. It was not just his sexual freedom, general wildness, and non-conformity which created such a degree of hostility around Mauchline as to make him an outcast, 'skulking from covert to covert',[8] bent on escaping to Jamaica. His brilliant ridicule of local kirkmen in the poems eagerly passed about in manuscript, first with 'The Twa Herds' and then with 'Holy Willie's Prayer', and his practice of questioning kirk doctrine in conversation, or 'puzzling Calvinism', as he put it,[9] equally contributed to his virtual outlawry by the community. His social conversation in the early 1780s was so laced with 'satirical seasoning' as to cause, besides glee, 'suspicious fear'; and he was for his heterodox religious beliefs, even at that early date, considered by his neighbours 'an heretical and dangerous companion'.[10] He was always a dangerous man, always a radical, powerful, extremist force, although near the end established power compelled him to modulate his voice. He was never the comfortable bourgeois many of his admirers have mismade him.

He maintained, until his judgement was formed, a manner, as a witness reports of a meeting in 1783, 'distant, suspicious, and without any wish to interest or please'.[11] Dugald Stewart was impressed with Burns's social manner in late 1785 and 1787, but found him lacking in 'gentleness and accommodation', somewhat 'decided and hard', perhaps from over-compensation to any appearance of servility, and in pursuing his favourite topic in conversation of the characters of individuals 'frequently inclining too much to sarcasm'.[12] This habit of speaking ironically and wittily about people continued to the last years, for Maria Riddell also wrote of his 'keenness of satire' in conversation as his most 'dangerous talent' and as often 'the vehicle of personal . . . animosity'.[13] The following description of himself in January 1783, suggests the opposite of the man of unrestricted benevolence:

> one of the principal parts in my composition is a kind of pride of stomach; and I scorn to fear the face of any man living: above every thing, I abhor as hell, the idea of sneaking in a corner to avoid a dun—possibly some pitiful, sordid wretch, who in my heart I despise and detest.[14]

Burns's pride of stomach rose in response to the owning class, its minions and dupes, and its institutions. It came from his own personal outrage and pain from social and economic injustice experienced by him and his family during the starvation years from six to eighteen at Mt. Oliphant farm. The memory of the owner's agent's threats to evict the family and seize their cattle, tools, and stores for non-payment of rent when he was about sixteen continued a dozen years later: 'my indignation yet boils at the recollection of the scoundrel tyrant's insolent, threatening epistles, which used to set us all in tears.'[15] In a fragment of a poem written at the time of the threatened eviction, he first protested the injustice: 'With tears indignant I behold th' Oppressor,/ Rejoicing in the honest man's destruction,/ Whose unsubmitting heart was all his crime.'[16] In 'The Twa Dogs' (1785), in the famous passage recalling the threats ten years before, he protests that 'Poor tenant-bodies, scant o' cash,/ How they maun thole a factor's snash/ . . . [and] stand, wi' aspect humble,/ An' hear it a', an' fear an' tremble' (71). In the same poem, he singled out 'want of maisters', on the same level as illness, as a 'sair disaster' of the cotter class (sub-tenants who give a small cash rent supplemented by labour for a cottage, garden, and pasturage). He thus recognized the rural unemployment caused by the agricultural revolution, which by 'improvements' like engrossing and enclosing put not only cotters out of land, house, and employment but also tenant farmers, like Burns's father, if they could not meet the growing competition to pay increasingly higher rents. The poignant horror of a person begging to be allowed to work for his family's own survival, but for the owner's benefit, Burns expresses in 'Man Was Made to Mourn' (1785) where he attacks Cassilis,[17] a rich aristocrat whose castle was a few miles to the south of Mt. Oliphant:

> See, yonder poor, o'erlabour'd wight,
>   So abject, mean and vile,
> Who begs a brother of the earth
>   To give him leave to toil.   (64) (I, 118)

Thomas De Quincey is the only person of the next generation to have recognized the poignancy and importance of these words: 'I had for ever ringing in my ears . . . those groans which ascended to heaven from his over-burthened heart—those harrowing words, *"To give him leave to toil"*, which record almost a reproach to the ordinances of God—and I felt that upon him, amongst all the children of labour, the primal curse had fallen heaviest and sunk deepest.'[18] Gilbert Burns, who laboured as a boy with Robert as the only field-helpers to their father at Mt. Oliphant, said that his brother 'could not conceive a more mortifying picture of human life, than a man seeking work' and that he wrote this poem to express it.[19] Most of Burns's very early poetry, even his love lyrics, is full of protests of class inequality and assertions of his own worth in spite of his poverty. As a result of his suffering at Mt. Oliphant, class injustice early becomes central to Burns's consciousness.

But most of the biographers who comment on this period forget the everyday cold, dirt, solitude, hunger and crippling work on the farm and tell us only about schooldays in Ayr and Dalrymple and summers in Maybole. We avert our eyes with shame from such horrors suffered by the national poet in his formative years. But they made their mark on him, nonetheless, which was in part an irascible reaction to affronts by the owning class to himself and his class and a tendency to lash back with the only weapon he had, his wit and his satire. Burns himself is not reticent about these hard times: 'We lived very poorly. . . . This kind of life, the chearless gloom of a hermit with the unceasing moil of a galley-slave, brought me to my sixteenth year.'[20] Brother Gilbert confirms the picture of life on their first farm: 'the very poorest soil in a state of cultivation . . . To the buffettings of misfortune we could only oppose hard labour, and the most rigid economy. We lived very sparingly.'[21] It is tempting to translate these abstractions and generalizations into images, facts. A book of inferential detail could (and should) be written about Burns's daily farm work in his teens, but for the present purpose of showing an important source for his class anger and satire, this summary will be enough.

For twelve crucial years Burns helped his ageing father farm seventy-five acres of mossy, rocky uplands, perhaps less than half tillable and of that only half productive because of the sparse friable soil on the top of high, broad ridges with large unproductive balks between. Younger brother Gilbert was the only additional help because the family did not have money to hire a ploughman. The land was unimproved, that is un-drained, unenclosed by stone fences or ditches with hedge-rows, ridges not straightened and flattened, unproductive soil not brought into use. The steading was isolated, not even on the main pony path from Ayr to Dalrymple. They lived in a stone, thatched house, along with their stock, no bigger than the mud cottage with a turf roof Burns was born in. It was heated by peat, dug by themselves from the muirs. They were forced by lack of cash, not by ignorance, to use the old style farming, that is, dunged infield and an unmanured outfield, both used without rest until exhausted. Their old 'Scotch plough' was a heavy wooden monster thirteen feet long for cultivating rocky ground, with only a bit of iron in the sock and coulter. It was drawn by four horses and made a v-shaped rut. For their harrow, they probably could not afford iron teeth and instead used wood pegs hardened in fire. Their £40 rent had to be paid by selling oats, and maybe a little barley, peas, beans, and butter (from one or two cows). Oats were cut with a sickle, thrashed with a flail, winnowed by wind, and ground by hand daily on a knocking stone. They tethered (not having fences) a sufficient number of sheep and grew enough flax to make their own clothes. They grew no hay for winter forage, using straw and wild bog hay cut with a sickle. They ate nothing but skim-milk, oats, cabbage and maybe potatoes; and when there was none of that they starved. The little lime they used to make the soil less sour, they bought because they had no kiln to burn it

41

themselves. They hauled it on sledges or in creels on horse-back, because they had no cart with wheels.[22]

If the Burns family knew no other life than this life, which we now find almost incomprehensible, it could have been endured as natural and inevitable. But the Burnses knew they did not have to live and farm this way by the examples of lots of modern farms in Ayrshire for richer farmers than they were. Most of these farms were improved and leased by the two main landowning aristocrats, Eglinton and Loudon, from money acquired from the state as compensation for losing their feudal jurisdictions in 1747,[23] an example of pampered privilege which would not have been lost upon Burns. William Burness had no such money to pay rent for an improved farm or to improve the one he leased, nor had his landlord, a working professional. Burns knew he was trapped in a life which did not have to be: 'Our lands . . . are mountainous and barren . . . our landholders, full of ideas of farming gathered from the English and the Lothians, . . . make no allowance for the odds of the quality of land, and consequently stretch us much beyond what . . . we will be found able to pay. We are also much at a loss for want of proper methods in our improve-ments of farming: necessity compels us to leave our old schemes; and few of us have opportunities of being well informed in new ones.'[24] Burns suffered from the agricultural and industrial revolution not by labouring in a new cotton mill or iron factory or in the fields as a hired hand—but by being raised to the traditional life of family farming and clinging to it during years when, if you had little cash, it became increasingly impossible to do so, without starvation and insecurity and constant dunning and legal harrassment.

Born, he wrote, 'a very poor man's son',[25] Burns found himself in that dwindling class of farmers because his father, born a farmer, went with the times and turned labourer, and then when his first child was six, for old-fashioned values of family and class, went against the times and turned farmer again. According to the old popular values, a farmer belonged to a respectable class. In the famous chapbook, Jockey's mother's remarks about her future stepchild show the popular feeling about the three rural classes above servants and labourers: the pregnant servant's father 'was but a poor cotter carle', while *her* son is 'a good fu' fat farmer's son, but ae laigher nor a laird'.[26] Burns's father struggled to regain the old respectability of the farmer class into which he was born, but did not realize that he was living in a new world in which the class was now too small and rich for him to re-enter. Burns learned not to accept his father's class goal, to loathe and fear the diminished life entailed by the struggle to achieve it, to hate the owning class and the system which insured that class its riches from the drudgery and starvation of farmers and other workers. By genius and his early suffering, he in effect became declassed. On the one hand, avoiding like the pains of hell the miserable life of the poor farmer, he cultivated, for the influence and culture he needed, first professionals and lairds and then aristocratic acquaintances—his means: Freemason brotherhood, elegant letters in fashionable English, romantic primitivist poses as in 'Cotter's Saturday Night', and Popean couplets. On the other hand, he learned he could never become bourgeois either by acquiring wealth or changing his consciousness; he resented, mistrusted and hated the rich, especially when he was soliciting favours; and sought the company and the culture of the labouring poor—the result: sarcasm and caustic wit in conversation among the bourgeoisie; working-class companions at home and in the tavern; folk song collecting and writing; poems in Scots about farmers, like 'Tam o' Shanter'; and Jacobin Jacobitism.

These class conflicts and economic insecurities make his satire complex and full of felt emotions. His kirk satires attack the Evangelical faction on the parish level and thus social control and by implied extension the state church, Whigs, and Hanoverianism; but they nevertheless attack a popular tradition and side by implication with the Moderates and Deists, the upper hierarchy of the kirk and the controlling class supporting it through patronage. However, in several kirk satires the warmth, fun, and colourful humanity of the popular religion shows through the ridicule of Calvinism and in at least one ('Holy Fair') the Moderates get their lumps for being boring, English, and sycophantic. The political satires consistently attack the possessing class and the state: landlords, reactionary politicians, monarchy. But with the exception of one poem, 'Address of Beelzebub', the attack is softened, modulated by indirection (dialogue, dramatic voice, humour). When he attacks one hated anti-Jacobin, the corrupt and powerful Robert Dundas, in a rollicking and sarcastic song,[27] he did not send it off to be printed although as an editor of song books he easily could have. Burns could not afford to alienate the class without whose influence he would find himself back on the farm. That is why he hid and even publicly recanted his Jacobinism. The one exception, 'Beelzebub', he never printed. It is his most savage and direct formal verse satire and very significantly about his most painful memory—eviction of farmers by landlords. The unfettered expression of his hate he saved for his letters, conversation, and unpublished epigrams and lampoons. The printed satire of a poor family man who knows and fears poverty is limited in its targets and its force.

A comparison to the only later Scottish poet ranking with Burns, Hugh MacDiarmid, is useful. It is no accident that the two supreme poets of capitalist Scotland came from the working class because that class inherited the native culture, language, and mental and emotional vigour required of great poetry. But MacDiarmid never softened his satire as Burns did, because no memory of crushing poverty in his youth made him fear offending powerful people in print. The later poverty in the Shetlands and Glasgow only seems to have increased his public bellicosity. He was circumspect, formally polite, even ingratiating, in society, savage in print—reversing Burns's compromise in dealing with the possessing class. Burns also could have declared with MacDiarmid, 'it had never been my aim to rise above the class into which I was born',[28] but fear of poverty kept politic what Burns printed. By contrast, MacDiarmid kept up in print 'perpetually a sort of Berserker rage'.[29] Much of MacDiarmid's prose and poetry, early and late, seethes with hate emerging in the most scurrilous, vicious flytings. The tendency culminates in the attack on the fascist Roy Campbell in *The Battle Continues* (1957), 'an operation . . ./ To remove the haemorrhoids you call your poems/ With a white-hot poker for cautery,/ Shoved right up through to your tonsils!' In this poetry of hate, MacDiarmid works quite consciously and proudly with the Scottish flyting tradition, as the occasional alliterative spitting scorn of some lines indicates: Campbell has no bays nor laurels, 'But this sanguine and fecal halo in their place/ That truly better fits your forcible-feeble face.'[30]

Burns in personal insult had no taste for this quite traditional scatological aspect of Scots flyting that MacDiarmid relished, nor was he, for that matter, much inclined to the genre at all, although his occasional practice shows he knew it and he doubtless had read at least one of the late medieval flytings.[31] 'Address to the Tooth-Ache' (500) and 'The Brigs of Ayr' (120), Burns's two imitations of Fergusson's use of parts of Scottish flyting, have no personal venom. Neither do his prose flytings.[32] He expressed his personal hatred in the epigrams, epitaphs, and other extemporaneous thrusts and squibs that he scattered about him on his way through life to give ease to his wrath. He copied them into letters or enclosed them on scraps of paper, scratched them on window panes, wrote them on fly-leafs or in his Commonplace Book or journals.[33] Sometimes he felt aggrieved enough to lengthen a vengeful lampoon, polish it, and send it off to a newspaper. For instance, on the occasion of his convivial pleasures at an inn being interrupted by a rich person's funeral, 'the iron pride of unfeeling greatness', he wrote a vicious 'ode' against a local monied family.[34] His two most laboured and deliberate personal attacks, one on William Creech, a petit bourgeois, and two on Maria Riddell, a middle-class intellectual with ties to local gentry, he never printed. They are full of hate but feeble because they are in Burns's second language and in foreign modes.[35] After Edinburgh, his tendency to write in English, except in folk song or the folk tale, limited his effectiveness in personal satire. To sum up: sharing with MacDiarmid a class rage against the rich and their insti-tutions, Burns did not, like MacDiarmid, express his rage openly in his poetry; but, fearing reprisals, he either softened or disguised it in his published pieces or expressed it in private to give himself relief.

Satire for Burns is simply an instrument of self-therapy, revenge, and protection. Only very seldom does he take the customary high (and to my mind disingenuous) ground of all satirists from Horace to Pope, that the satirist intentionally employs his sacred weapon in the service of morality and public order; the only instance that I can find is when he justifies attack on evil men as 'surely not merely innocent, but laudable', but he probably felt guilty in this instance for writing election ballads for Patrick Heron, a candidate for member of parliament.[36] It is significant that the only time, or at least one of the few times, he wrote satire to curry favour, he justified himself for doing so by the plea of public service. Usually he writes to please himself: 'For me, an aim I never fash;/ I rhyme for fun.'[37] On another occasion when some complained that another ballad burlesquing an election was not partisan enough ('the butter not thick enough spread'), he defended his indiscriminate ridicule of all concerned by stating that he would belong to neither side 'unless devilishly well paid'.[38] In other words, when his own interest or antipathies were not involved, he would not attack in satire.

He usually explains the motive for his satire as a relief for feelings and as a means of hurting those who have hurt or offended him or his friends, either by actions or by merely being the way they are. The former motive we see illustrated in the amusing story John Syme tells of Burns's behaviour during a tour of 1793. In a towering and seemingly inconsolable rage at having ripped his wet boots to shreds one morning, Burns, at Syme's instigation, transferred the rage to the Earl of Galloway, 'with whom he was offended', and against whom, 'he expectorated his spleen, and regained a most agreeable temper'. Burns's purge presumably was accomplished by the four famous epigrams on Galloway (415). Burns recognized this characteristic of himself, for he wrote after a lengthy flyting against Poverty: 'Well, Divines may say what they please, but I maintain that a hearty blast of execration is to the mind, what breathing a vein is to the body: the overloaded sluices of both are wonderfully relieved by their respective evacuations.'[39] He seems always to have composed satire under the immediate emotion of resentment, just as he invariably, as he several times reported, composed love lyrics only when he experienced the emotions of love. To Mrs. Dunlop in 1789, he wrote that he intended 'serving up ... again in a different dish' his old High-flyer foes, and even if he failed to make them ridiculous, 'I shall at least gratify my resentment'.[40] Sometimes a light-hearted squib would result from a minor affront to his pride, as Burns reported that the beginning of 'The Mauchline Wedding' (74) was composed after a girl 'huffed [his] Bardship' and he 'in the heat of [his] resentment resolved to burlesque the whole

46

business'.[41] In this instance he did not want to publish the result widely, because he did not want to hurt the people involved, but more often gratifying his resentment through satirical composition went beyond mere relief of hostility to the pleasure derived from causing injury to enemies, quite frankly the pleasure of revenge. He speaks not only of his lampoons as 'instruments of vengeance', a 'conspirator's dagger', 'satiric aquafortis, to gnaw the iron pride of unfeeling greatness',[42] but he also writes in late 1787 of his satirical plans for the Evangelical faction, who were at that time charging the Moderate clergyman William M'Gill with Socinianism:

> I ever could ill endure those surly cubs of 'chaos and old night'—those ghostly beasts of prey who foul the hallowed ground of Religion with their nocturnal prowlings; but if the prosecution which I hear the Erebean fanatics are projecting against my learned and truly worthy friend, Dr. M'Gill, goes on, I shall keep no measure with the savages, but fly at them with the faucons of Ridicule, or run them down with the bloodhounds of Satire, as lawful game wherever I start them.[43]

His motive for attacking his enemies is that

> . . . I gae mad at their grimaces,
> Their sighan, cantan, grace-prood faces,
> Their three-mile prayers an' hauf-mile graces,
>   Their raxan conscience,
> Whase greed, revenge, and pride disgraces
>   Waur nor their nonsense.

Burns wants to hurt his proud and powerful enemies by exposure.

> O Pope, had I thy satire's darts
> To gie the rascals their deserts,
> I'd rip their rotten, hollow hearts
>   An' tell aloud
> Their jugglin' hocus-pocus arts
>   To cheat the crowd.   (68) (I, 124–25)

His motive is anger over personal affront, his purpose injury. In other words, satire for Burns is an instrument of revenge. Dundas injured enemies—many more and much more deeply

47

than Burns was ever able—by the political-economic control
his wealth and rank gave him. Cut off by class inequality from
such material power, the poor farmer's son took joy in his only
weapon and defence, the satiric power his carefully cultivated
genius gave him. He hugged his satire to him as a poor poet's
sole defence of pride and outlet for resentment.

I suspect that all satirists operate thus, especially those from
the labouring poor, but Burns is more truthful in parading no
pretence that his weapon is heaven-sent nor parallel in its civic
function to the power of the pulpit and the bench. He knew he
was not going to change his society. His muse has an obli-
gation to 'erect her head/ To cowe the blellums', not in pursuit
of a plan of national moral regeneration but to injure the great
who have hurt him and his class. He seems, in fact, to have
had rather a low view of satire. In 'The Vision' (62), where he
sets out his patriotic view of a Scottish national revival in all
departments of life, he gives satire no place at all, although he
provides for James Beattie's *Minstrel*, for love songs, and for
descriptive poems. We are tempted to conclude that, however
much joy his satire gave him as a personal weapon, he did not
consider satire a social instrument, at least one worthy the
dignity of the serious literary kinds.

Critics have conceived of Burns as a friendly, comic satirist
not only because of the obvious warm humanity of his character and their desire to mystify his radicalism but because of his
almost invariable satiric practice of using an ironic voice, what
he called 'ironic satire, sidelins sklented'.[44] The speaker of the
poem represents the group attacked, the ostensible view of the
poem is the very view attacked in it. In the kirk satires, the
speaker is sympathetic to the Evangelicals; in the political
satires, to the Whigs, the Hanoverians, and repressive landlords, and anti-Jacobins. We take direct expressions of hostility
as more sincerely felt. Artfulness and cunning indirections seem
to soften the force of the enmity. Further, the imaginative
projection of self necessary to speak from the position of one's
enemy, indicates a humane understanding, and even at times
produces a somewhat sympathetic villain, like Holy Willie,
whose very high spirit of pretence and gall we are awed by.

To show how important the ironic voice is to Burns's satires,
I present a list of what most would accept as his important

satires.[45] I also put those nearest the top which I think most would agree are superior.

'Holy Willie's Prayer'	Scots-English	(1785)	(53)
'The Holy Fair'	Scots	(1785)	(70)
'Address to the Deil'	Scots	(1785–86)	(76)
'The Twa Dogs'	Scots	(1785–86)	(71)
'The Twa Herds'	Scots	(1784)	(52)
'The Ordination'	Scots	(1785–86)	(85)
'Address of Beelzebub'	Scots	(1786)	(108)
'The Kirk's Alarm'	Scots-English	(1789)	(264)
'A New Psalm'	Scots-English	(1789)	(260)
'The Dean of the Faculty'	Scots-English	(1796)	(515)
'A Dream'	Scots	(1786)	(113)

We note that Burns composed all the best satires in the two years before going to Edinburgh (because afterwards he was concentrating on songs and new non-lyric modes and perhaps having committed himself to Scotland, he feared by giving offence to be forced back to the farm). And we note that most of those written before Edinburgh are in Scots, because satire and humour require concrete particulars which Burns could only express in his native language and because characteristically in satire Burns spoke in the colloquial language of his opponent. In fact, this trick of adopting the voice of his enemy determines, as we shall see, all the other aspects of his satiric act. Nine of the eleven satires use, in various degrees of emphasis, the voice of the opponent. The other two ('The Twa Dogs' and 'A Dream') employ an irony which results from the poet's speaking in some degree other than what he means, but not, as in the more typical, speaking, more or less, the opposite of what he means.

Where did Burns learn a manner so central to his satires? Swift, of course, is the satirist whose name springs to mind as the master of the ironic *persona*, but, unlike Sterne, this Irishman had no deep influence on him. And besides, in his Scots poems he invariably follows Scots models. Robert Fergusson, his favourite Scots poet,[46] failed in this instance to provide him with one. Much more Horatian and mild than the fiery radical Burns, Fergusson wrote many burlesques but only a very few Scots satires which clearly attack or ridicule sets of values, like 'Braid Claith', 'The Ghaists', 'Hame Content', and none of these employ the ironic point of view of the enemy, the voice of the party ridiculed. Fergusson utters his satire in pretty much his own voice, Burns characteristically in an assumed one. My guess is that Burns knew about this kind of poem before he discovered Fergusson in 1784. He developed in his mind and put together what was suggested from two sources. The first was the ironic voice in one of Ramsay's poems, all the more attractive to Burns because it was an anti-kirk satire, 'Elegy on John Cowper, Kirk-Treasurer's Man' (1718), a lament in Standard-Habbie measure by a pious Calvinist for the death of the kirk's official in charge of suppressing fornication.[47] The Scots comic elegy seems more designed to present biographical and professional detail than to ridicule by ironic statement, but the satirical purpose is there in a secondary way and Burns was to make it primary in similar poems. The second source was the dramatic voice of the important non-satiric genre of the revival, which at times nevertheless had satiric elements, the last-dying-words poem, like the anonymous 'The Mare of Colintoun' and Hamilton of Gilbertfield's 'Last Words of Bonny Heck, a Famous Greyhound in the Shire of Fife',[48] and most important Ramsay's 'Lucky Spence's Last Advice' (1721), in which an old bawd tells all the tricks of the trade to the young whores in her establishment. Burns had used the dramatic voice of the last-dying-words genre masterfully in his first non-lyric Scots poem 'The Death and Dying Words of Poor Mailie' (1782 or 1783), where he had included, as did Ramsay in 'Lucky Spence', a satirical element, in this case, a ridicule of middle-class complacency and Anglo-Scottish snobbery. And his first Scots satire without musical setting and the first poem he circulated in manuscript locally, according to his own testimony,[49] 'The Twa Herds' (probably late 1784), used the opponent's voice to full advantage, a method to become the distinctive feature of Burns's satire. All Burns had to do was put the dying-words-type utterance in the mouth of an enemy on a dramatic occasion other than death and 'Holy Willie's Prayer' would result. Do the same thing for an enemy observer, rather than a principal, of other dramatic occasions (an ordination, a dispute between two neighbouring auld-licht ministers, an annual communion day, George III's recovery from insanity, news of suppression of emigration in the Highlands, the election of a right-wing head of the Scottish bar association, and so on) and almost all his other satires would result. This would appear a simple enough formula, but only Burns did it. That Burns derived this important method mainly from Ramsay rather than from Fergusson, although the latter's 'Elegy on John Hogg' (1773) must also have been running in his head a bit when he wrote 'The Twa Herds', supports in a new way DeLancey Ferguson's claim, made in connection with Burns's epistles, that 'Ramsay rather than Fergusson showed the way to the sort of poetry without musical setting in which Burns found his genuine freedom and inspiration.'[50] Ramsay showed him a beginning of the possibilities of the dramatic voice, central to Burns's epistles[51] and, ironically used, at the heart of his satire.

If the satirist uses the voice of his enemy, he can degrade him by putting low words and figures in his mouth. Thus the satiric device of what David Craig calls 'subjugation'[52] is with Burns a product and ancillary of his characteristic method of the opponent's voice. Of the nine satires in the list which employ the voice of the opposing faction, all but two ('Holy Fair' and 'Address to the Deil') cause the speaker to degrade himself and impugn his motives by his speech. Two are prayers of sorts, 'Holy Willie's Prayer' and 'A New Psalm'; they expose the speaker's religion by the crudeness of his terminology and his provincialism by giving his Deity a completely local orientation. Holy Willie uses the pulpit diction of a country High-flyer to portray his primitive God, who seeks pleasure and glory by whimsically choosing a few and letting the rest of His creation suffer in Hell-fire and brimstone, and who is called upon to blast the basket, store, kail and potatoes of Willie's village enemies and to reward Willie himself with 'temporal mercies'. He exposes his moral insensibility by the gutter-talk of his confession and his craven excuses.

The psalmist in his hymn treats British politics in the same terms as the members of a kirk session would speak of parish affairs. A provincial Calvinist dialectic is imposed upon matters of high state. This is a kind of satirical levelling: by calling down the same anathema upon both the enemies of George III and a local Moderate minister, the Scots-Whig kirkman exposes his own provincial inability to discriminate. He is shown to see the whole world through the small lenses of his local vision.

Both 'Twa Herds' and 'The Ordination' employ the traditional figure of the minister as a shepherd protecting his congregation as a flock of sheep against such heretical dangers as weasels, badgers, foxes, and poisoned water. The first of this pair uses the metaphor centrally, as the title suggests, to determine the whole poem. The expanded metaphor creates an allegorical beast fable. Both degrade the affairs of the Evangelical party by the speaker's expressing those affairs in their own barnyard images and figures. In both, the speakers show their unfeeling enthusiasms by the bloody terms of their appeal for floggings, hangings, and transporting of personified qualities of the Moderate faction.

'The Dean of the Faculty' uses subjugation less extensively than those we have been considering, but it is clearly there. Burns has his speaker degrade himself by his ludicrous Biblical allusions, his partisan assumption that God is on his side, his vulgarity ('Which shews that Heaven can boil the pot/ Though the devil piss in the fire'), and in general his tendency, like the New Psalmist, to interpret politics from a Calvinistic viewpoint: like the Calvinist God, the Faculty chose Dundas not for merit (parallel to works) but to demonstrate their own 'gratis grace and goodness'.

One need not explain the more straightforward choice of 'Address of Beelzebub': the devil speaks in character and thus condemns his own position, which is equated with that of the rackrenting peers. Burns is saying, in effect, that the rapacious Highland landlords are of the devil's party. The devil speaks to them in language they can understand, their own. There is no trace here, of course, of Burns's more common treatment of the devil (from *Paradise Lost*) as hero (as in 'Address to the Deil') and (from Scots folklore and sermons) as comedian (in 'Tam o' Shanter' and in 'The Deil's awa wi' th' Exciseman', [386]).

The speaker of 'The Holy Fair' is an Evangelical only ambiguously, unlike the unfaltering zealous spokesmen of 'Twa Herds' and 'Ordination'; and only by understanding the difference can one understand 'The Holy Fair'. If Burns had merely wanted in 'The Holy Fair' to attack Calvinism generally for petty puritanism and tyranny, as in the other two poems, his speaker in this would have upheld those values. He would have accompanied to the fair those allegorical personages introduced at the beginning of the poem, Hypocrisy and Superstition, and he would have attacked Fun. But Burns wanted to attack Calvinism for something more particular, its blind inability to cope with the human spirit, its incapacity to relate meaningfully to human desire, in other words, its unreality, its inappropriateness to people. Thus Burns chose a speaker who is generally on the side of life and enjoyment without thinking about it much, so that he reports on pleasures with innocent, wide-eyed admiration, but who admires the pulpit oratory of Evangelical preachers and condemns the cold sermon of one Moderate and the favour-seeking sermon of the other (stanzas 14–15, 17). He implies his rejection of Hypocrisy and Superstition as companions to the fair, but applauds both in the auld-licht sermons. The auld-licht bias of the speaker is not only historically accurate, because the Evangelicals were the popular party, but emphasizes the ironic anomaly of the parishioners' views. The speaker does not much like the 'greedy glowr' of the elder who takes the admission fee, nor the 'screw'd-up, grace-proud faces' of a group of saints, but he admires the frenzied preaching of Moodie and condemns the 'cauld harangues,/ On practice and on morals' of the new-licht Smith. He defends alcoholic drink at length but is very affected by Black Russell's rant. The whole poem is determined by ironic contrasts between social pleasure and religious fear, between the body and the soul, between erotic and divine love; and the division in the speaker between his allegiance to the High-flyer preachers and to social pleasures is just another one of these ironic contrasts that serve to indict Calvinism for unreality, for being, in spite of its pride in a rigorously logical theology, a religion full of the wildest contradictions because its message, if not its manner, is not adjusted to warm humanity.

The speaker of 'The Kirk's Alarm' has the same general views as those in the other kirk satires, but they do not function strongly. He calls for support for orthodoxy in united opposition to M'Gill's dangerous book, but he insults the auld-licht ministers at the same time he calls them forward to do their duty. There is consistent subjugation, by the use of low diction and imagery. There is obvious amusement in having one enemy, unconscious of the effect he is producing, insulting more enemies, but, unlike all the others, there is no exploitation of the ironic voice to achieve consistent effects, Burns being in a too rousingly disrespectful mood in this boisterous song to be very fastidious about singleness of viewpoint.

In 'Address to the Deil', Burns uses an interesting variation of his favourite satiric technique. Instead of causing the dramatic voice to express the sentiments of his opponent unalloyed, he makes a mixture. He wanted to ridicule certain Scots attitudes towards the devil: the superstition, love of folk lore, the intimacy, the scapegoating. Therefore he causes the person who makes the address to demonstrate these attitudes. But Burns also wanted to contrast a warm humanity to the kirk's hostility to the devil. Therefore he caused the speaker to have, besides those traditional Scots attitudes to the devil just mentioned, a sentimental heart, one appropriate to a man of feeling, capable of pitying the devil (stanza 21) and incapable of understanding how even a devil could take pleasure in the pain of others (stanza 2). Thus for a complicated satire, he created a comic, mixed voice, part ridiculed, part exemplary.

The two remaining satires on the list are departures from Burns's usual technique in satire. His gentle ridicule of the royal family in 'A Dream' is done by assuming the pose of a naïve, downright, frank country person, a moderately loyal Hanoverian, who innocently runs on, with occasional sarcasms, in the royal presence. Burns in his ordinary manner would allow us to hear how a wild Whig, a rabid royalist, anti-Jacobite celebrates the king's birthday. 'The Twa Dogs' is of course a dialogue poem, and the voices, therefore, after the opening narrative, are those of a working-class dog and an aristocratic dog. The attack on the cruelty, moral indifference, triviality, and psychosis of the aristocracy is not accomplished by a single ironic voice, as in his other satires, but by both voices, more particularly by the two naïve misunderstandings made by Luath: (1) that the aristocrats have to be absent from their estates to serve Britain; (2) that they are happy. Both of these errors provide Caesar with an occasion for damning descriptions. Luath is a kind of straight man in a comic routine. And his simplicity calls into question his idealized description of the generally happy life of the poor, in spite of the injustices they suffer, which heightens by ironic contrast the self-inflicted miseries of the gentry.

Because Burns spoke his satires in the dramatic voice of his

Scots adversaries, most are in vernacular Scots, a few in Scots-English. Thus he avoided in his satires the genteel pose of Henry Mackenzie's Anglicized man of feeling, which is a dreadful poison in much of his poetry, one of his serious deficiencies. Tied to colloquial expression by his chosen satiric manner, he wrote a body of serious poetry in Scots, contrary to his usual practice of writing in English when he felt very solemnly serious about something: see the disastrous English of 'Elegy on the Late Miss Burnet of Monboddo' (324), which he worked doggedly at for months without satisfaction. He was able to express his most serious class resentments in Scots vernacular satire, turning to his advantage, by the device of the enemy's voice, the severely truncated native language and literary tradition he inherited, which has been said, with too little discrimination, to be too exclusively rural to communicate serious, contemporary ideas.[53] Burns's adversaries had deficiencies Burns wanted to expose. Part of those deficiencies was a rural language of relatively narrow reference and restricted purview. Burns used that very language to attack them and in so doing he wrote some satires which rank very high in eighteenth-century European literature.

NOTES

1. *Works of Robert Burns*, ed. William Scott Douglas (Edinburgh, 1879), V, p. 252n.
2. *Robert Burns: La Vie et les Oeuvres* (Paris, 1893), II, pp. 118–19.
3. 'Burns and the Burns Tradition', *Scottish Poetry*, ed. James Kinsley (London, 1955), pp. 198–99, 206.
4. *Robert Burns: His Associates and Contemporaries* (Chapel Hill, 1943), p. 13.
5. *The Russet Coat* (London, 1956), pp. 24–5.
6. Here and henceforth an arabic number in parentheses in the text or notes gives the poem number in *The Poems and Songs of Robert Burns*, ed. James Kinsley, 3 vols. (Oxford, 1968)—hereafter cited as Kinsley, *Poems*.
7. *Works of Robert Burns*, ed. James Currie, 2nd ed., 4 vols. (Edinburgh and London, 1801), I, pp. 250–52.
8. *Letters of Robert Burns*, ed. J. DeLancey Ferguson, 2 vols. (Oxford, 1931), I, p. 115. Henceforth, *Letters*.
9. *Letters*, I, pp. 107–14.
10. Letter of David Sillar to Robert Aiken published in James Morison's edition of Burns, 1811, as reprinted in *Life and Works of Robert Burns*, ed.

Robert Chambers, rev. William Wallace, 4 vols. (Edinburgh and London, 1896), I, pp. 68–9.

11. From Dr. John Mackenzie's reminiscence of his first meeting with Burns published in Josiah Walker's memoir (1811) and reprinted in *Works*, ed. Douglas, IV, p. 365.

12. From Stewart's memoir of Burns provided for Currie's edition (1800) and reprinted in *Works*, ed. Douglas, IV, pp. 375–77.

13. Currie, *Works*, 2nd ed. (1801), I, p. 250.

14. *Letters*, I, p. 14.

15. *Letters*, I, pp. 107–8.

16. Kinsley, *Poems*, No. 5; compare No. 106, ll. 7–10: 'I've seen th' Oppressor's cruel smile/ Amid his hapless victim's spoil;/ And for thy [money's] potence vainly wish'd/ To crush the Villain in the dust.'

17. . . . 'hundreds labour to support/ A haughty lordling's pride', 'lordly Cassilis' in First Commonplace Book, Kinsley, *Poems*, No. 64, ll. 19–20.

18. From 'Autobiography of an English Opium-Eater', *Tait's Magazine* (February 1837), reprinted in *Robert Burns: The Critical Heritage*, ed. Donald Low (London and Boston, 1974), p. 431.

19. Kinsley, *Poems*, III, p. 1087.

20. *Letters*, I, pp. 107–8.

21. Currie, *Works*, 2nd ed. (1801), reprinted in Chambers-Wallace, *Works*, I, p. 35.

22. William Fullarton, *General View of the Agriculture of the Country of Ayr* (1793), pp. 13–53; *The Statistical Account of Scotland*, ed. John Sinclair, *passim*, but particularly, for reconstructing life at Mt. Oliphant, accounts from the parishes of Ayr (I), Kilmarnock (II), Dailly (X), Kilwinning (XI), Dalry (XII), Sorn (XX); J. E. Handley, *Scottish Farming in the Eighteenth Century* (London, 1953), pp. 53ff; John Strawhorn, 'Farming in 18th-Century Ayrshire', *Collections of the Ayrshire Archaeological and Natural History Society*, 2nd series, III (1955), 136–73 (this is the first part of the series, 'The Background of Burns', and is especially valuable; the second part, 'Industry and Commerce in 18th-Century Ayrshire', also uniquely useful for students of Burns, appeared in Vol. 4 [1957, pp. 182–215] but a third part promised and much needed, on Burns's social background, was cancelled in favour of *Ayrshire at the Time of Burns*, cited just below, which, however, presents only the data, not the analysis); *Ayrshire at the Time of Burns*, Vol. 5 of *Ayrshire Collections* (Kilmarnock, 1959), particularly Strawhorn's 'Burns's Ayrshire as Portrayed by his Contemporaries', pp. 34–94; James Barke, *The Wind That Shakes the Barley* (1946), pp. 43ff, has some useful hints; William Aiton's second part (1811) of Fullarton's *General View* is important but could not be obtained to use for this study.

23. Strawhorn, *Ayrshire Collections*, III, 164.

24. *Letters*, I, pp. 15–16 (21 June 1783).

25. *Letters*, I, p. 105.

26. 'Jockey and Maggy's Courtship', *Collected Writings of Dougal Graham*, ed. George MacGregor (Glasgow, 1883), II, p. 33.

27. 'Dean of the Faculty', Kinsley, *Poems*, No. 515.

28. *Lucky Poet* (London, 1943), p. 231.
29. *Lucky Poet*, p. 79.
30. Pp. 1, 27.
31. Alexander Montgomerie's flyting with Polwart was reprinted in Watson's *Choice Collection*, II (1711), which Burns must have read.
32. *Letters*, II, pp. 7, 51–2, 77.
33. A few typical and good ones: 'Lines on Stirling' (166), 'On James Grieve, Laird of Boghead' (28), 'Pinned to Mrs R's Carriage' (448), 'On a dog of Lord Eglintons' (622), on a rich Galloway laird (411A, 411B), on a club of super patriots in Dumfries (450), 'To Symon Gray' (155).
34. 'Ode, Sacred to the Memory of Mrs. Oswald of Auchencruive' (243); *Letters*, I, p. 296.
35. Kinsley, *Poems*, No. 335, additional 12-line fragment after l. 55; 'Monody on Maria' (443), 'Epistle from Esopus to Maria' (486). Burns's commentators show their class snobbery and sexism by taking Maria Riddell's side in this estrangement and condemning Burns's lampoons as vulgar and tasteless. Why should not Burns, rubbed raw by a life of class affronts, attack a 'lady' who made a choice to stick to her family and class against a son of a farmer?
36. *Letters*, II, p. 292.
37. 'Epistle to James Smith', stanza 5 (79).
38. *Letters*, I, p. 376, commenting on 'The Five Carlins' (269).
39. *Letters*, II, p. 52.
40. Ibid., I, p. 345.
41. Ibid., I, p. 248.
42. Ibid., I, pp. 268, 296.
43. Ibid., I, pp. 135–36.
44. I.e., 'sideways squinted', from 'To William Simpson' (59).
45. These are, in fact, all or almost all the satires if we exclude foreign modes and doubtful cases: pure burlesque (literary parody, like 'Grim Grizzle' [530] and 'Ode to Spring' [481]); brief satiric songs, epigrams, epitaphs, and fragments; imitations of Pope; election ballads; poems with only passages of satire or with only a subsidiary satiric intent (e.g., 'Epistle to John Goldie' [63]); comic poems whose object of attack is diffuse and generic (e.g., 'Address to the Unco Guid' [39] and 'To a Louse' [83]); poems which clearly fail in their satiric intent ('Adam Armour's Prayer' [88]) or are clearly unfinished ('The Mauchline Wedding' [74]).
46. 'I am pleased with the works of our Scotch Poets, particularly the excellent Ramsay, and the still more excellent Ferguson [sic]', Commonplace Book (August 1785, Douglas, ed. *Works*, IV, p. 91).
47. *The Works of Allan Ramsay*, eds. Burns Martin and John W. Oliver (*S. T. S.*, 1945), I, pp. 14–17. Alexander Pennecuik (d. 1730) wrote a good satire in Scots, which Burns probably knew, about the subject, *The Presbyterian Pope* (see *Collection of Scots Poems* (Edinburgh: James Reid, 1756), pp. 106–13), a long conversation in the Habbie stanza between an Edinburgh kirk-treasurer's man and a whore about their plans and methods.

48. Both published in Watson's *Choice Collection*, Vol. I (1706).
49. *Letters*, I, p. 114.
50. *Pride and Passion* (New York, 1939), p. 248.
51. John C. Weston, 'Robert Burns' Use of the Scots Verse-Epistle Form', *Philological Quarterly*, XLIX (1970), 180–210.
52. *Scottish Literature and the Scottish People, 1680–1830* (London, 1961), p. 77.
53. Craig, *Scottish Literature*, pp. 78ff. The belief continues strong: e.g., consider the astounding belief of Matthew P. McDiarmid that the Scots language of Hugh MacDiarmid's early lyrics and long poem *A Drunk Man* caused him to avoid 'ideas' (*Agenda*, V, No. 4 (1967), 76–7).

3

Burns and Narrative

by ROBERT P. WELLS

Almost everyone, if asked to categorize Burns's work, would describe him as a lyric poet; indeed, the popular image is that of incomparable master of love-songs. Burns, in keeping with his lyrical inclinations, is very much an occasional poet; his canon, in fact, contains well over one hundred poems of a more expository or dramatic nature: verse epistles, addresses, laments and elegies, a cantata, dramatic prologues and fragments, descriptions, epigrams, dialogues, and dramatic monologues.

No one, I believe, would place Burns among the narrative poets. Including 'Tam o' Shanter', there are barely a handful of poems Burns himself thought of as 'a true story' or 'a tale'. My present purpose is not to challenge the established view. Yet Burns's 'occasional' poems do make use of a variety of narrative techniques; and in this essay I intend to examine some of these poems in terms of narrative kind and structure.

The first task in such an undertaking is to establish a definition of narrative,[1] momentarily omitting from the general description considerations of genre and tone. I am concerned here only with fictitious narratives. Fictitious narratives may be divided into two basic kinds: stories, and story-like narratives which I shall call mimetic transcripts.

Story (or *Tale*): in prose or verse, a narrative which is a sequence of connected mimetic events or episodes, the sum of which comprises a complete whole (i.e. represents an action)

59

with a definite beginning, middle, and end; further, it has unity in that the transposition or removal of any of its connected incidents will disjoin and dislocate the whole. A story must be concerned with human or anthropomorphic agents. A story must have the element of *peripeteia*, depicting a change of some kind in the agent or agents (e.g. misery to happiness, or vice versa), an unexpected change which, though unforeseen, is a necessary or probable outcome of the agents' actions. This *peripeteia* frequently but not invariably involves *anagnorisis*, recognition in the agents of this change and their own part in effecting it. Most often recognition means movement from illusion or opinion to fact or reality, a shift from ignorance to knowledge. A story must also have a sense of being addressed directly to a real or imagined audience (as opposed to lyric forms, which do not necessarily presuppose an external audience). A story may be brief, a single complete episode, such as an anecdote; or developed, a story of several or many episodes. Stories may be simple or interwoven. By simple, I mean a single unified tale usually but not necessarily unfolding sequentially (events may be removed from chronological sequence, as in a flashback); by interwoven, two or more tales joined together to form a whole. Stories may be told from the point of view of the first or third person, or in combination. These qualities are equally applicable to tragic or to comic tales.

There are many varieties of stories, often based on non-fictional narrative modes: mimetic autobiographies, biographies, epistles, journals, reports of experience, allegories, and fantasies (e.g. faerie tales, 'science fiction'). In these latter two unrealistic modes especially sequential events are often impossible or highly improbable in nature and so neither necessary nor probable outcomes of antecedent episodes, although such stories usually follow an internal logic. These separate categories may also appear in combination with one another; thus we may find allegory joined with fantasy (e.g. Aesop's *Fables*), and so on.

Mimetic Transcript: in prose or verse, a fictional narrative which may have many or all save one of the essential qualities of a proper story, that one element being the lack of a distinct *peripeteia*. Without *peripeteia*, the 'story' must be considered a mimetic transcript. A mimetic transcript may have many or all of the recognizable appurtenances of a story, such as fictional characters or real characters in fictional situations, dialogue, a sequence of connected mimetic incidents, or even contain a tale or tales within the whole work, yet not of itself comprise a story as previously defined. Mimetic transcripts sometimes lack unity as well as *peripeteia* in that episodes may not relate the chronicle of an agent or agents but that of a distinct group of people; or in that episodes may be transposed or deleted without seriously disrupting the whole work.

There are several varieties of mimetic transcripts, corresponding largely with the different varieties of story: biography, allegory, diary, fantasy, and so forth. This is to be expected of story-like narratives. One major kind of mimetic transcript, equivalent to the anecdote among stories, is the situational mimetic transcript. A situational mimetic transcript is one in which meaning is not dependent upon 'story' but upon a particular context; it involves narrative elements at only a rudimentary level. It tends to be brief, a whole but usually single episode; and it does not in itself comprise an action, although it may involve descriptions of activity. In verse it is often cast in a lyric form, and may take the shape of a mimetic complaint, lament, argument, dialogue or dramatic monologue reported by or tacitly assumed to be reported by another witnessing it. 'Situational' does not mean static—i.e. purely descriptive—but a single scene that raises the impression of mimetic action by providing details of an agent's life and thought even though no action takes place and so no change occurs in the characters' circumstances and emotional states.

The basic difference between stories and mimetic transcripts, reflected in their structures, is one of purpose. It is a division that arises from different patterns of emphasis. Stories can often appear to have no ulterior aim other than self-fulfilment; mimetic transcripts almost invariably appear to have been written as a means of conveying a particular idea or set of ideas. A story concerns itself with, and closely directs itself toward, the expression of plot. A story may have an underlying theme, but theme is usually subordinate to the plot, made manifest through plot. A mimetic transcript conversely tends to place much greater emphasis on theme. The expression of theme takes precedence over the vehicle conveying it. That is, dominated by thematic considerations, mimetic transcripts often appear as 'dramatic' expressions of observation (e.g. fictional travel books, addresses, catalogues), discourse (e.g. philosophy, monologue, debate, dream-vision, parable), and satire, a mode necessarily governed by theme. Divided by differences of design rather than subject matter, both forms have an equal potential for aesthetic excellence.

What may seem complex in the abstract will become clearer as this theory is applied in practical terms. To that end, I shall begin with a comparison of 'Tam o' Shanter' and 'Death and Doctor Hornbook' as narratives,[2] and then proceed to discussions of various other narrative poems. I do not intend to examine more than a few examples representative of Burns's narrative art—for instance, 'Holy Willie's Prayer' (a dramatic monologue), 'The Cotter's Saturday Night' (observation of scene), and 'The Holy Fair' (a peasant festival), among others. But I believe the exploration of only a few of the available kinds of stories and mimetic transcripts will enable us to draw some general conclusions about Burns and narrative verse.

I begin with 'Tam o' Shanter' and 'Death and Doctor Hornbook' because, according to their subtitles, both poems are tales in Burns's own estimation. 'Tam o' Shanter' (No. 321) is a comic tale of the supernatural, the account of Tam o' Shanter's drunken confrontation with the Devil and several of his devotees; it is told by an ironical 'I'-narrator outside the action described. Tam's adventure is simple and, if fantastic, straightforward. Despite the poem's elaborate introduction, the narrator's frequent digressive intrusions, and the mocking *moralitas* which summarizes the import of the night's events, it may be demonstrated that the poem fits the criteria of a story as defined above. It has unity, in that a complete action is portrayed in a sequence of episodes that lead logically but not inevitably from one to the next: Tam, drunk on market-day, leaves a tavern for home at midnight in a terrible storm; on the way he spies the haunted kirk of Alloway ablaze with light, and, riding up to investigate, he is amazed to see a witches' dance at which the Devil himself provides the music; struck by the charms of the scantily clad young witch Nanny, Tam forgets himself and cries 'Weel done, Cutty-sark!' (189); instantly the

witches give chase, and Tam narrowly escapes over the Brig o'
Doon and home, his gray mare Meg sacrificing her tail to
Nanny during her frantic dash for safety. The loss of any
component episodes or the disruption of their sequence would
seriously affect the story as a whole.

The story has a probable but unforeseen outcome. The
reversal of fortune is an unexpected movement from joy ('O'er
a' the ills o' life victorious', 58) to terror at the threat of
destruction ('In hell they'll roast thee like a herrin'', 202). This
peripeteia occurs when Tam unwittingly calls attention to himself by shouting his encouragement to Nanny. We may say that
his drink-induced mistake is accompanied by *anagnorisis*, for he
immediately recognizes his error and its consequences. The
dénouement and resolution of the action swiftly follow, a comic
anticlimax in which the threat of death is absurdly reduced to
the loss of a horse's tail.

Even the lengthy introduction and deliberately inappropriate concluding 'lesson', although strictly speaking not part of
the action, are essential components in the narrative's comic
structure. The opening stanzas establish the scene (1–16), set
the comic tone in discussing wifely wisdom (17–28), and
provide a foreshadowing of events (29–36). This foreshadowing
turns out to be ironical, in that what almost happens to Tam
coincides with the far-fetched, nagging warnings of his wife
Kate:

> She prophesied that late or soon,
> [Tam] would be found deep drown'd in Doon;
> Or catched wi' warlocks in the mirk
> By Alloway's auld haunted kirk. (I, 558)

Except that this is an outsider's account (and apart from the
comic eroticism of Nanny's dance), Tam's adventures sound
suspiciously like an excuse concocted by a drink-fuddled
husband to turn aside his wife's wrath. We can almost visualize
her grudging acceptance of it, as the tale obligingly confirms
her dire predictions. This quality of private joke further
increases the ridiculousness of the tale.

The narrator, however, calls the story's veracity into question
himself by referring ironically to 'this tale o' truth' (219). The
tongue-in-cheek *moralitas* that follows is an example of comic

misdirection, humorously confounding the reader's expectations by providing absurdly inappropriate commentary. The sabotaged 'lesson' rounds off the ironic strategy of the poem: by drawing our attention to the sufferings of Meg (an innocent creature) and away from Tam (a sinner who escapes physically unscathed), the narrator completely deflates the seriousness of the final admonition. In effect he winks at Tam's follies, and mocks those who give the story credence.

The narrator is omnipresent although he does not seem to be fully omniscient; he could be considered a secondary character. He hovers close to the action, shaping our perceptions of and guiding our responses to events. Seventy lines, a third of the poem in fact, are taken up with the narrator's commentary. 'Atmospheric' catalogues comprise a further twenty lines, lists of the horrible places that Tam passes on the road and of the grisly sights displayed as a kind of macabre stage-dressing to the witches' sabbath. The narrator, placing himself among the neighbourly tavern-frequenters, introduces the scene in his own *persona* (1–36). A little later, when the tale is barely begun, he steps back from the immediate scene to offer philosophical reflections on the transitory nature of pleasure (59–68), and—with mock-heroic delight—on the follies of courage induced by drink (105–8). He further interrupts with a comic apostrophe on the appearance of the witches (151–58); with a brief use of the traditional humility *topos* (179–80); and with a warning addressed directly to Tam in full flight (201–4). Still in character, he finally offers his ironical *moralitas* (219–24).

The narrator seems to adopt different 'voices' for his various discursive intrusions. For example, he briefly elevates his diction to a rather Latinate, formal English in order to achieve a philosophical tone (59–66); or he mimics the shrewish quality of Kate's 'advice' to Tam, scolding advice that sounds like a medieval flyting: 'thou was a skellum,/ A blethering, blustering, drunken blellum' (19–20), et cetera. These dramatically effective postures represent basic shifts in perspective, in tone, but equally different levels of the narrator's involvement in the action—now a drinking companion, now musing aloud outside and above the scene, now at Tam's side advising him. The teller and the tale are inextricably linked, and our appreciation of the story depends as much on our knowledge of the narrator's personality and sympathies as on our awareness of the slowly unfolding action.

'Death and Doctor Hornbook' (No. 55) bears a certain broad similarity to 'Tam o'Shanter'. Both deal humorously with supernatural encounters, and both are told by genial 'I'-narrators who purport to be inebriated. 'Death and Doctor Hornbook', however, is a fantastic mimetic transcript of a dialogue between a narrator-character and the personification of Death; the poem is intended to satirize a pretentious but otherwise unqualified local apothecary, John Wilson. The poem, constructed with some of the constituent components of narrative, projects a story-like appearance. It has an ironical introduction; it animates two fictional agents in a particular locale who meet one night and carry on a dialogue; and it is a single, unified episode (although incomplete in that their dialogue is interrupted before Death makes a final revelation of his planned vengeance against the usurper Hornbook, 181–84). But the narrative lacks a necessary *peripeteia*. There is no action other than discussion. While engaged in conversation neither Death nor the narrator takes actions or makes choices that result in any kind of reversal for themselves or others. They do not even alter in condition, physical or emotional: when they take their separate roads the narrator is no less drunk and Death no less ineffective than before their meeting. Nothing is different; nothing has *happened*, apart from an exchange of information. Without *peripeteia*, it follows that there is no *anagnorisis*, no recognition of a self-wrought reversal. The narrative could be considered the account of a situation, their meeting; but it could not be described as a story.

We learn a great deal about Hornbook, who is exaggerated into a larger-than-life figure in order to sharpen the comic contrast with his lowly reality. But his malignant activities are reported to us, not presented dramatically. The reason for this is simple: the focus of the poem, as is common among mimetic transcripts, is on theme rather than on plot. The impossible dialogue becomes a convenient and memorable vehicle for ridiculing Burns's victim, Wilson; it provides a solid foundation upon which to build his ideas, offering a maximum of satirical effectiveness and a minimum of personal risk.

The poem's basic premise rests on the incongruity of Death being made redundant due to the ministrations of Hornbook, who deals out life and death in the form of absurdly named medicines. Through the device of Death's self-pitying complaints, the poem is structured in such a way as to turn Hornbook into an inhuman object. Rather than a self-animated character with complex wants, needs, abilities, and choices, Hornbook is depicted as the mechanical, impersonal, ubiquitous force that death is traditionally thought to be. Death, in contrast, has a variety of human personality traits, and decided limitations. Because Hornbook is transformed into an object, sympathy for him is put out of reach, enhancing his ridiculousness. Ironically, we are instead invited to sympathize with Death, unable to earn his bread for the first time 'Sin [he] was to the butching bred' (71–8), and piqued at the inequity of Hornbook slaying a score with malpractice for every one Death used to take off naturally (145–50). The use of this theme, which has its roots in Classical literature, is a potent, and well-executed, satiric strategy. Further, the narrator saves himself from the accusation of slander by carefully establishing his context: first, he claims his account 'Is just as true as the Deil's in h–ll,/ Or Dublin city' (9–10), superstitious nonsense; and second, he claims to be drunk, predicating unreliability. He is able to make wild, insulting, and damaging charges against 'Hornbook' while at the same time ironically disclaiming them as lies.

Initially, this may seem a dry method of approaching two vibrant, joyously comic poems; but an understanding of narrative structure is an essential first step toward appreciating the poet's purposes, his thematic emphases. The eighteenth century, known foremost as an age of satire, continued to value the ancient justification for imaginative literature, to teach and delight (*utile et dulce*). In narrative art, mimetic transcripts are particularly well suited to didactic productions of all kinds—to debate, satire, discourse, propaganda, parable. Stories may be didactic as well. But where an imbalance exists between the two functions, stories tend to be weighted more heavily toward delight; mimetic transcripts tend to be orientated toward education. Mimetic transcripts seem to be driven primarily by thematic considerations: that is, we can imagine Burns first deciding he wanted to ridicule Wilson, then casting about for the best method of achieving his purpose; we cannot imagine the reverse of that process. However, with 'Tam o' Shanter', we can envisage Burns holding the initial desire to tell a good story. For this reason mimetic transcripts often appear to be set pieces, stationary single episodes raising and resolving a limited theme. While this is by no means an inflexible rule, the majority of Burns's mimetic transcripts follow this pattern. Burns is not generally considered a didactic poet. Yet given the predilections of the age, no one should be surprised to find that a high percentage of Burns's narrative poems—not to mention various addresses and epistles—are fundamentally exemplary in nature, even if only mockingly so as in 'Tam o' Shanter'.

Satire is particularly favoured as an educational device, able to expose the ridiculous and discourage the emulation of folly in a delightful way, bringing credit to the satirist. And nowhere is satire more effectively employed than in Burns's dramatic monologue, 'Holy Willie's Prayer' (No. 53), the situational mimetic transcript of a hypocrite's confession and supplication to the Lord. As a satire it achieves the desirable state of serving both topical and universal interests.

'Holy Willie's Prayer', brilliantly conceived, compact and energetic, is not a story. Through the device of overhearing his devotions we learn everything essential about Willie's nature; but although he reveals the secrets of his heart Willie does not experience any kind of reversal while confiding in his image of God. He does not change one jot from first to last; in fact, the poem would be destroyed if he did, if he realized even for a moment what he was truly saying. He is, and must be, fixed in his ways, comically inflexible and thus, by implication, past redemption. Dispensing with a wry or mocking narrator, Burns gets inside Willie's mind, causing him to damn himself, unconsciously and so ironically. Willie remains serenely unaware of his many transgressions and of his uncharitable—not to say unchristian—attitudes. Or, if he does acknowledge a fault—for instance, confessing to several forays into the gratification of 'fleshly lust' (37–54)—he displaces the blame (55–

60), compounding the sin through a failure to recognize his responsibilities.

Out of Willie's mouth drop blind admissions of all of the traditional Seven Deadly Sins. He confesses to *lust*, which he sees as visited on him to try his spirit (lest he 'O'er proud and high should turn', 57); and he uses *gluttony* in the guise of drunkenness to excuse himself ('that Friday I was fou/ When I cam near her', 51–2). He is *envious* of his foe Gavin Hamilton, not of Hamilton's venial slips ('He drinks, and swears, and plays at cartes', 68), which are tame compared to Willie's own malefactions, but of the 'mony taking arts' that enable him to steal 'frae God's ain priest the people's hearts' (69–72). Proof of Hamilton's success lies in his ability to raise the congregation's laughter at the accusations of the auld-licht faction against him. Willie has been publicly humiliated by Hamilton and the lawyer Aitken, and his revenge takes the shape of self-righteous *wrath*. He maliciously—and, of course, impotently—calls down the Lord's terrible 'curse' and 'vengeance' upon them and upon all those of 'that Presbytry of Ayr' (76–96), unwitting comic blasphemy. Then, having distributed the Lord's punishments to suit himself, his *avarice* manifests itself as a request for enlarged

> mercies *temporal* and divine!
> That I for grace *and gear* may shine,
> Excell'd by nane!   (I, 78; my italics)

He had earlier described his salvation in terms of 'gifts and grace' (10), seeming to equate showy, material prosperity with the singular blessings of Providence, temporal bounty with spiritual grace. With this request his prayer has returned to its place of beginning, having explored the idea of sin and salvation. This gives the poem a circular structure.

From the phrase 'excell'd by nane' it is apparent that *pride* is Willie's chief sin. He conceives of himself as 'a chosen sample . . . a pillar . . . a guide, a ruler and example/ To a' thy flock' (25–30), like so much of his prayer absurd presumption. He is indeed an example, but not, ironically, in the way he thinks: he is a ridiculous, negative model to be eschewed by all true Christians. Spiritual *sloth* is born out of this pride in that, though he admits he is mere 'dust/Defil'd wi' sin' (41–2), he regards himself as one of the elect, predestined for salvation, and so has no fear of damnation, whatever he does. His belief that he is a righteous man is of course comical to any outside observer. But worse, even if it were true, moral behaviour is quite pointless. It does no good to serve the people as an example if salvation is denied them in any event, if damnation exclusively depends on God's whims and 'no for ony gude or ill' committed in this life. 'Holy Willie's Prayer', masterfully exposing a creed in a sharply defined dramatic setting, does not merely condemn an odious and adept practitioner of religious double-think but the whole system of extreme Calvinist belief which necessarily produces such creatures.

Almost all of Burns's satires and burlesques—for example, 'The Holy Tulzie' (No. 52), 'The Mauchline Wedding' (No. 74), the 'Address to the Deil' (No. 76), or the mock-heroic testament 'Death and Dying of Poor Mailie' (No. 24)—are mimetic transcripts. Most are intended to edify as well as poke fun at persons, ideas, or literary genres. But Burns's efforts to be movingly informative are not invariably satiric or comic. 'The Cotter's Saturday Night' (No. 72), to cite a well-known instance, employs the structure of a mimetic transcript in order to depict the life of the average farm family and to discourse seriously on the felicities of such an existence.

The poem's narrative elements are arranged to explore a series of scenes, not to relate the tale of an individual's actions and their results. Narrated by an omniscient 'Patriot-bard', the poem traces the activities and especially the attitudes of one cottage family from dusk through the reading of the Bible before retiring to bed one Saturday in November. The time-scale is narrow, but the implications of the scene are universal. The account is purely descriptive, interspersed with commentary by the narrator. We follow in detail the family's home-gathering after toil, supper, the arrival of Jenny's young man, and their homely worship services. There is no dialogue. Only a few moral imperatives or prayers are quoted (50–4, 108; 158–62); and, in the same unrealistically elevated diction, the poet is once moved to declare his emotional experience of love (77–81). The few characters who are distinguished as individuals, the Father, Mother, Jenny and her beau, are representative stereotypes. Real personalities are better fitted for stories, where circumstance, motive and choice precipitate the plot. These characters are not real personalities but highly idealized figures. Indeed, the entire portrait is intended to represent the ideal, despite the realistic touches by the way. Each scene, each character, becomes a subject for extended philosophical discussion by the poet, who weaves together the several related themes of the good life, order, obedience, simplicity of heart, patriotism, and the manifestations of love, which descend as grace and bounty from the Creator and encompass even the smallest child. The scenes, insignificant in themselves, build into a pattern of moral consequence. In fact, the narrative's structure and materials (the scene, the characters, the narrator's rhapsodic or reverent tone) are wholly governed by didactic demands. Like 'The Auld Farmer's New-Year-morning Salutation' (No. 75), it is a narrative of distilled emotion. The list of soberly didactic mimetic transcripts, including 'The Vision' (No. 62), 'Man Was Made to Mourn' (No. 64), 'To a Mouse' (No. 69), and even the allegorical 'John Barleycorn' (No. 23), is somewhat shorter than the list of humorous didactic narratives, but it is nonetheless substantial.

Though I have pointed out that didacticism is a neglected aspect of Burns's art, I do not mean to imply that his narratives are solely or necessarily intended to offer serious moral instruction or even to be comically edifying. Most do have a moral point to make, and are designed to satisfy powerful thematic motives as well as aesthetic pleasure. Some, however, seem to be born primarily out of a spirit of fun: for example, 'The Holy Fair' (No. 70) and 'Love and Liberty' (No. 84), more popularly known as 'The Jolly Beggars'. Both poems, to be sure, are comical mimetic transcripts; but both are more celebratory than informative. They are lively, exuberant, and roguishly attractive.

The personification of Fun, in fact, is the narrator's guide in 'The Holy Fair'. Superstition and Hypocrisy are also in attendance, assuring a satirical flavour as well. This poem is identical in prosody, and similar in episodic development, tone and intention, to 'The Ordination' (No. 85) and 'Halloween' (No. 73). It may therefore serve as a representative of the group.

70

'The Holy Fair' chronicles the activities of a gathering of Christians during a typical summer religious festival in Mauchline; it is a portrait of social *mores* and not a tale. Narrative components—episodic development, a heterogeneous congregation of characters pursuing a variety of activities and interests, dialogue, the visible spectrum of emotions—are set in motion for the purpose of painting a comedy of manners. The narrator, aloof from the scenes he describes, roves among the throng like a good-humoured camera, focusing, as it were, at random. Stanzas regularly begin or change direction with 'Here' or 'Now', signals pointing to each fresh set of observations, observations which act as implicit social criticisms. The foibles of both sexes and of all professions are much in evidence, but no one is scrutinized for very long, nor earnestly ridiculed. Few characters are even named; most are character types, representative figures, or indistinguishable in their various groups. They have recognizable traits, but are not full-blooded personalities.

A tableau effect is built up piecemeal. The events follow a rough chronology, growing ever more boisterous, but no other pattern; scenes seem to be haphazardly arranged, to appear less well-knit than in the sequential unfolding of a story. Unity is not fully apparent, a feature of some mimetic transcripts: scenes could be rearranged or even deleted without seriously damaging the structure of the whole poem. But the narrator's quick leap from one small, deftly sketched cameo to the next helps to ensure the rollicking pace and lively tone of humane delight. It is a narrative of comic behaviour, concerned with atmosphere, motive and faithful observation rather than action. Its air of jollity sharpens the incongruity of juxtaposing carnal and divine love throughout, the secular and spiritual aspects of charity, both generously lubricated with strong drink. The narrative's quick metre, indulgent comic tone, and episodic structure act in concert to preclude any suggestion of seriousness or indecorous disapproval. Because his levity is not diminished, the narrator's implicit superior judgements of his neighbours' ethics and beliefs do not give offence by striking a holier-than-thou attitude. Involvement in the revels, personal remarks, would destroy his neutral vantage. As it is, he can poke fun in all directions without behaving as a spoilsport or

71

colouring his observations by partaking in the action.

'Love and Liberty' is concerned wholly with secular matters; however, the same riotous, bacchanalian spirit of 'The Holy Fair' still prevails. As the title suggests, freedom and love—of the most basic kind—are the twin themes that bind the various songs together. The poem is a celebration of freedom from social responsibilities and moral obligations, expressed by a varied cast of vivacious low-life characters, outcasts who harbour no higher desires than enjoying the fleeting pleasures of warmth, sex, and alcohol in an atmosphere of convivial fellowship. They have nothing to lose, and consequently nothing to fear, scorning the values and flouting the conventions that pertain to social stations above their own.

The poem, a cantata, is a collection of 'character'-songs linked by the bridging recitative passages of an omniscient narrator. Burns no doubt identified himself with the Bard who closes the poem. But the Bard is distinct from the narrator, who simply observes, and does not comment on, the festive scene. The narrative contains at least one story, the rivalry of the Fiddler and the Tinker for the 'raucle Carlin's' affections. The Fiddler attempts to charm her with a carefree song; the bullying Tinker threatens the Fiddler, and sings to the doxie an aggressive song of self-advertisement; 'o'ercome' with passion—and liquor—'th'unblushing fair' surrenders to the Tinker's blandishments (181–84), resulting in felicity for him and short-lived grief for the Fiddler, who soon finds comfort elsewhere. However, the presence of one or more stories in a text is not enough to transform a narrative into a story: 'Love and Liberty' is the mimetic transcript of a beggars' revel, an interweaving of separate character-revealing songs and tales into a complex, thematically unified new whole.

The songs, as exemplified by the Fiddler–Tinker rivalry, are appropriate to their assigned speakers. The crippled Soldier sings a swaggering, patriotic air; his trull, with an agreeable comic self-awareness, expresses her preferences for the camp follower's life; the pickpocketing Highland widow laments the political forces that turned her into an outlaw; and, after the Tinker's quarrel, the Bard rounds off the foregoing with a toast to love and women. Asked for an encore, the Bard provides a general climax to the libertines' feast which tightly knits together the different thematic threads: his song rejoices in sensual pleasure, freedom from care, love in its many forms, and scorn for the laws of society as represented by the church and court. Although the previous songs are more amoral than openly rebellious in nature, we are to understand that he functions as spokesman, his attitudes epitomizing the spirit of the group at large. It is a vibrant song conducted with the characteristic *brio* of Burns at his rakish best. The patriotism of the Soldier aside, the various views expressed throughout are anti-Establishment in the extreme, and the poem can hardly be described as exemplary or edifying.

Certain songs could be reordered, but there is a general pattern discernible in their presentation. The Soldier loves his country, the doxie loves the soldiers; the Tinker and Fiddler campaign for the attentions of the unattached widow, the strong prevailing but without violence or genuine loss of amicability; and the Bard voices an all-embracing salutation to earthy, unsentimental love. The structure is that of theme-and-variations, the unity of idea, rising to a crescendo climax in the final song. In fact, most of the mimetic transcripts that I have examined or mentioned are organized on the principle of theme-and-variations.

It should be evident by now that Burns rarely attempts to animate or explore complex personalities in his narratives. The characters in his mimetic transcripts are usually personifications (Death, Fun) or stereotypes. They are figures of convenience, presented entire and not developed. Occasionally, as with Holy Willie, we see deep into the core of an individual. Yet even Willie symbolizes a code of belief (extreme Calvinism) as well as the Seven Deadly Sins. Most often, as in 'Love and Liberty', with its characters drawn from low-ranked occupations, the agents are limited to fixed qualities associated with a trade, a trait, a belief, a narrow aspect of behaviour. They function in a proscribed way; and they are usually used to illustrate a point or promote an idea, as do the rich and poor dogs or the new and old bridges in the slightly comic but essentially philosophical dialogues of 'The Twa Dogs' (No. 71) or 'The Brigs of Ayr' (No. 120). Burns's use of character types and spokesmen reflects the fundamental aim of mimetic transcripts aptly to express ideas.

Burns wrote only a few verse stories,[3] and those rather late in his career. Most of his efforts in narrative modes come in the form of mimetic transcripts—monologues, dialogues and dramatic scene-paintings harnessed in the service of satire, comical and sentimental observation, and philosophical discourse. The majority of these mimetic transcripts were written prior to his first trip to Edinburgh, near the beginning of his professional career. Many of his verse addresses and epistles also appeared at this time, so he was then obviously interested in philosophical issues, questioning behaviour in individuals and in society at large, and exploring concepts. He had always written lyrics. But later, as the work of song-collecting and song-writing increasingly demanded his attention, Burns virtually abandoned theme-orientated verse in favour of more purely emotive expressions. Despite his numerous efforts in narrative genres and the lasting popularity of 'Holy Willie's Prayer' and 'Tam o' Shanter', Burns is remembered as a lyric poet. This bias has nothing to do with the quantity of lyric as opposed to narrative verse produced over his lifetime. The reason for this lies instead in the natures of lyrical and occasional verse. A number of his songs have a timeless, universal quality which has helped to assure them a lasting place in people's hearts. Lyrical emotions have not changed, whereas interest in the topical issues and social concepts of his philosophical verse has largely faded from the world.

Limited by considerations of space, I have had to slight significant features of Burns's narrative art: for example, his use of traditional genres, rooted in Classical and especially medieval and folk literature; or matters of craft—prosody, patterns of imagery, techniques of creating tone, all of which contribute to the final experience of the poem in the reader's mind. I have instead concentrated on aspects of kind and structure—narrative perspective, the use of character types, the arrangement of scenes—especially as they relate to thematic purpose. First it has been necessary to establish the existence of a body of verse which may be properly described as narrative. In considering narrative function and effect, I think it should be evident by now that, early on, Burns was strongly concerned with didacticism, and that most of his narratives are of a kind designed to express ideas in an agreeable form.

NOTES

1. The following principles represent the summation of a more extensive argument for a model of narrative literature. See R. P. Wells, *Middle Scots Humorous Narrative Verse* (Unpublished Ph.D. Thesis, University of Edinburgh, 1981), pp. 22–38.
2. Quotations from Burns's poetry follow *Robert Burns: Poems and Songs*, ed. James Kinsley, 3 vols. (Oxford, 1968).
3. Apart from 'Tam o' Shanter' there are only a few ballads that tell stories: e.g. 'Grim Grizzle' (No. 520), 'Kellyburnbraes' (No. 376) etc. These songs, however, are usually reworkings by Burns of traditional tales and not entirely original compositions.

4

The Young Lassies: Love, Music and Poetry

by CATARINA ERICSON-ROOS

> There is certainly some connection between Love, Music, and
> Poetry. . . . For my own part I never had the least thought or
> inclination of turning Poet till I got once heartily in Love, and
> then Rhyme and Song were, in a manner, the spontaneous
> language of my heart.[1]

The majority of Burns's songs[2] deal with love, love seen from
the poet's point of view or love seen through the eyes of one of
the lovers. There are conventional pieces, droll and humorous
scenes, young love, mature love, and erotic love. There are
love-songs where the emphasis lies on sentiment, others where
it lies on character or on action. Among all these songs we find
Burns's most interesting and exciting characters. These are his
young girls in love and particularly those who speak for themselves in the songs. Here Burns shows an extraordinary
psychological insight into the feminine mind and as Christina
Keith points out, at the time he wrote them he had 'had great
experience of girls, at any rate of the particular girl he had
chosen as his type'.[3] These girls display a considerable amount
of independence, of self-confidence, of self-knowledge, and of
knowledge of the world. Their world is love, and love exclusively, but into this world they grow and through love they
grow, from the first stage of girlhood and innocence into

womanhood and experience. They come into conflict with convention and the code of female behaviour and with their parents' opinions, but in all situations they show strength of mind and individuality. A passive woman who lets herself be subdued cannot be found among these young women. Furthermore, as Christina Keith has shown,[4] Burns carried on the tradition of the Scottish folk-songs and ballads in which free love had managed to survive in spite of the Reformation. In the ballads of the Borders and the Highlands we find the women of the old Scotland, women who 'were captivating, free and elegant, without the remotest shadow of subjection'.[5]

The youngest and most innocent of these girls is to be found in 'Tam Glen' (236),[6] a song which portrays a highly infatuated girl who is totally engrossed in the thoughts of her lover. Excitedly, she chatters away without stop about her dear Tam Glen, naïvely she believes in superstitious omens, and with growing self-confidence she reacts against her parents' opinions. The situation is common enough: the mother warns her against flattering men and the father wants her to marry for money. She listens to neither for the only advice she wants to hear is to marry Tam Glen. With the impatience of a very young girl in love, she begs and bribes her sister:

> Come counsel, dear Tittie, don't tarry;
>   I'll gie you my bonie black hen,
> Gif ye will advise me to Marry
>   The lad I lo'e dearly, Tam Glen.   (I, 436)

Her character, her girlishness and her state of mind with its agitation and restlessness is conveyed through words and music. The quick flight of her thoughts and the intensity of her chatter lie embodied in the quick tempo of the tune and in the syllabic setting (i.e. one syllable for each note) for the undotted notes, which makes one pronounce each word quickly and vigorously and with equal force. The girl speaks uninterruptedly, her heart seems to beat quickly, and she has hardly time to take a breath before she starts talking again. The shortness of the tune, the monotonous melody and the even rhythm captures this very well. Only at the end of the second and fourth bars does the tune come to a rest, and on these

cadences, or phrase-endings, the repeated name of Tam Glen
and its rhymes fall.

At one point in each stanza there is an intensification of the
girl's emotions. This happens in the last bar, where the
melody emphatically rises. There is a large and unexpected
upward skip to the highest note of the tune followed by a
gradual descent to the tonic.[7] This feature of the tune re-

"Tam Glen"
(236, SMM No. 296)

But what will I do wi' Tam Glen?

inforces the climax of the fourth line of each stanza and, as the
mode is minor, it lends them a sense of despair and exaspera-
tion. But there is also irritation and impatience in the expression and the high note brings out the important questioning
words 'what', 'when' and 'wha'. These lines are also the keys
to the girl's state of mind. Young as she seems and new as the
sensation is to her, she is full of wonder, questions and impatience: '*what* will I do', '*wha* can think sae' and '*wha* will I
get'.

Very free and independent for her eighteen years, mature
and full of opposition to her parents is the girl of 'O, for ane
and twenty Tam' (363). She will not be oppressed by them
any longer, nor will she marry a fool for his money. She knows
her worth, and as soon as she comes of age ('ane and twenty')
she will marry the boy she loves. Her maturity and strength
are expressed through both text and tune. The melancholy
high part with its stronger minor quality and intensifying
upward direction enhances the girl's bitter feelings against her
parents, expressed in the first stanza: 'They snool me sair, and
haud me down,/ And gar me look like bluntie, Tam.' It also
makes her opposition, expressed in the more relaxed chorus,
psychologically logical. This girl has none of the worries of the
girl in 'Tam Glen', she is not dependent on anybody, and in
the last stanza she gives her hand in pledge to the boy: 'But
hearst thou, laddie, there's my loof,/ I'm thine at ane and
twenty, Tam!' The girl in 'Tam Glen' is on her way to self-
confidence and independence, but she still feels that 'to anger

them a' is a pity' (meaning her parents) and she needs her sister's support. The tune of 'O for ane' is slow and much less excited than that of 'Tam Glen'. The emphatic high starts of the upbeats in the chorus ('*An* O', '*An* hey') give the girl's words a sense of conviction. She takes her time and rests on the cadences with the repeated 'twenty Tam', and there is also a refrain-line in each stanza and a chorus to give the song a more balanced expression. The younger girl in 'Tam Glen' is restlessly babbling on with no sense of pause anywhere: 'She keeps on at it too—as they do—dinning the name at you in verse after verse', as Christina Keith puts it.[8] Her conversation with her sister is intimate, worried, secret and whispering, whereas the girl in 'O for ane' is critical, extrovert, straight-forward and free.

Another young and inexperienced girl appears in 'I'm o'er young to Marry Yet' (195), an uncomplicated song with humorous implications. This girl is being courted by a man somewhat older than herself, but she rejects him, claiming that she is too young to marry. Yet she is intelligent—and witty—enough to see that it will not be long before she is ready to say yes. She measures time by the seasons, and half a year, from winter to summer, is what she believes she needs to be old enough to marry. The song is spun around the contrasts between winter and summer, young and old, mother's child and man's woman, innocence and experience, the present and the future. The girl is now her mother's 'ae bairn', she is 'o'er young', and 'o'er young' is repeated four times in the chorus. It is 'winter' and 'frosty' and both words are emphasized through the rise in the melody. But what will come is implied strongly enough in the last stanza of the song:

> Fu' loud and shill the frosty wind
>   Blaws thro' the leafless timmer, Sir;
> But if ye come this gate again,
>   I'll aulder be gin simmer, Sir.   (I, 384)

The light note of the song is struck already in the old chorus from which Burns took his start, and the skittish, cheerful and innocent character of the young girl is suggested in the light-tripping reel-tune, the even rhythm,[9] the quick tempo, the high register, the rising phrases, and the major mode. Thomas

Crawford acknowledges the importance of the tune and says that 'the words and music combine to give us a girl's mood shortly after puberty—shy, blushing, yet full of the knowledge of what she is and what she must become.'[10]

In the first line of the song ('I am my mammy's *ae* bairn') the significance and implications of the word 'ae' are emphasized in the musical context. It emphatically falls on a rising melodic line as well as on two notes in the otherwise syllabic setting of the song. The fact that the girl is her mother's only child is one of the reasons she gives to the man for not marrying him, and therefore ''twad be a sin/ To tak me frae my mammy yet'. The other reason for her denial of the man is that she shudders at the thought of creeping into bed with him: 'And lying in a *man's* bed,/ I'm fley'd it make me irie, Sir.' In this example (from stanza 1) 'man's' falls on two notes, emphasizing an implied antithesis—to lie in a man's bed and not in one's own—and in stanza 2 ('And you an' I in *ae* bed,/ In trowth, I dare na venture, Sir') the word 'ae' is accented. A man and one bed, that is a collocation which is quite beyond her field of experience.

Already married to an old man and trying to find her way out of the ill-mixed liaison is the girl in 'What can a young lassie do wi' an auld man' (347). Her situation seems rather hopeless at the beginning to judge from the way she repeats the opening, almost rhetorical questions: 'What can a young lassie, what shall a young lassie,/ What can a young lassie do wi' an auld man?' The repetitions are of course the conventional formula of the folk-song, but, coupled as they are to the minor tune, and in the context of the whole song, they become indicative of the girl's predicament and of her feelings.

The verbs fall heavy on the dotted first beats of the bars, 'shall' being more intense as it lies higher. This first part of the tune (A) has an energetic, but relaxed swing in the 6/8-time and a decisiveness in the melodic lines, which precludes an expression of passivity and perplexity on the girl's part. In

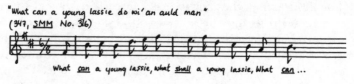

"What can a young lassie do wi' an auld man"
(347, SMM No. 36)

What *can* a young lassie, what *shall* a young lassie, What *can* ...

fact, she proves to be furious in her indignation, and with a terrific suppressed anger she swears at her match-making mother who was tempted to sell her daughter 'for siller and lan''. This happens in the second half of the tune (B), which has much more tension than the first. It lies low, but rises progressively on rhythmic snaps[11] and by small intervallic steps (see next example). Only in the last two bars is there relief from the tension when the tune resolves in the dotted swing of the first half. With the force needed to pronounce the consonants falling on the snaps, and with the very marked rhythm which they create, this part of the tune has an almost pictorial effect of the young girl, stamping her foot with impatience, indignation and irritation. But the rhythmic and melodic structure of the second half of the tune also has an emotive import: the sense of the accumulated but suppressed displeasure, the growing agitation and the relief of tension in the last two bars.

The two following stanzas give a vivid portrait of the horrible old man, and the girl's disgust with him is released. With full armoury she lets fly at him:

A He's always compleenin frae mornin to e'enin,
      He hosts and he hirples the weary day lang:
B He's doyl't and he's dozin, his blude it is frozen,
      O, dreary's the night wi' a crazy auld man!

A He hums and he hankers, he frets and he cankers,
      I never can please him, do a' that I can;
B He's peevish, and jealous of a' the young fallows.
      O, dool on the day I met wi' an auld man!   (II, 607)

As both stanzas have a similar structure with the repeated 'he', a read version of the song can hardly convey the range of emotion and temperament which lies behind the surface structure. It is particularly the girl's wavering between an outgoing expression of disgust in the first half-stanzas (on the dotted swing in the high register) and the inwardly directed, more forceful anger in the second half (for the low, 'snapped', section) that cannot be conveyed without the tune. Through the dotted rhythm the music reinforces the effective alliterations in lines 6 and 9, which are so expressive of the girl's

81

irritation and disgust ('hosts' and 'hirples', 'hums' and 'hankers'). Her impatience is also effectively brought forth through the plosive *d* in line 7, alliterations which are now accented by the snaps.

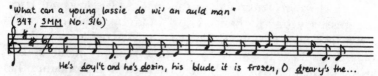

"What can a young lassie do wi' an auld man"
(347, SMM No. 316)

He's doyl't and he's dozin, his blude it is frozen, O dreary's the...

In the last stanza the girl proves to be cunning. Realizing that she never can please the old man whatever she does, she decides to follow her auntie's advice: 'I'll *c*ross him, and *w*rack him untill I hea*rtb*reak him.' Here the collected impact of the apt alliterations (*r* having a rough and forceful effect), the choice of verbs, and the low register of the tune are used to express anger and threat. However, the song has a humorous and happy ending. Relieved at the thought of getting rid of the spiteful man, the girl falls into the swinging lilt of the last two bars, and maybe she dances away while singing 'And then his auld brass will buy me a new pan.'

A young girl's wishes might not only conflict with the expectations of the parents but also with society's claims for virtue, innocence and honour. In 'Wha is that at my bower door?' (356) the girl makes strong attempts to resist the man, as it is expected of her, but the song shows her slowly yielding to him, only a little anxious that anybody will know. From an old broadside stanza and in the tradition of the night-visiting songs Burns develops the theme, creating, with a strong sense of humour, a 'carle' who is self-assured, masculine and straightforward in his attempts to be let in by the girl:

> Wha is that at my bower-door?
>   O wha is it but Findlay;
> Then gae your gate, ye'se nae be here!
>   Indeed maun I, quo' Findlay.   (II, 616)

Findlay's character remains constant throughout the song. His lines are only slightly varied with a touch of humour, as he teasingly takes up the preceding words of the girl: 'In my bower *if ye should stay,/ Let me stay*, quo' Findlay' or 'Here this night *if ye remain,/ I'll remain*, quo' Findlay.' He sets out with one intention—to make the girl let him in—and he makes no attempts to conceal this. He is certain that her hesitation is only a conventional attitude and that his honest, but slightly provoking manner will force her into a quicker decision. She, in turn, shows that she knows perfectly well what it is all about. She is on her guard and puts Findlay on trial by being seemingly resistant. 'Before the morn ye'll work mischief', she says and goes on:

> Gif I rise and let you in,
>   Let me in, quo' Findlay;
> Ye'll keep me waukin wi' your din;
>   Indeed will I, quo' Findlay.   (II, 616)

Crawford describes the situation this way: 'From the very start, despite all appearances to the contrary, she has wanted to let Findlay into the bower, and she ends as absolute mistress of the situation. Findlay has made a binding promise to her (to be secret)—that is, he has yielded to her femininity; and the joke is that he thinks that *he* has conquered her!'[12]

The tune suits the poem perfectly. It has a simplicity which allows the oppositions to be exposed, the oppositions between the questions and answers, between the apparent change in the girl's attitude and the constancy in Findlay's, and between her worries and his self-confidence. Significantly, the girl's words are matched to the descending phrases, whereas Findlay's lie on the more aggressive ascending ones. Especially the

"Wha is that at my bower door?"
(356, SMM No. 337)

Wha is that at my bower-door? O wha is it but Findlay;

second and sixth bars (corresponding to the second line of each stanza) are very emphatic in their assertive upward direction. This line is the climax of each stanza and the music helps to express the joy Findlay takes in challenging the girl's female code of coyness. It is also the point where he teases her by repeating her words (see above). A sense of strength and assurance is also embodied in the dotted four-beat rhythm[13] of the tune and in the lack of an upbeat.[14] The potency of the 'direct attack' on '*Wha* is that', '*What* mak ye', '*Gif* I rise' brings out a tone of irritation in the attitude of the girl. This points to a strong attempt to cover up the desire to let him in, but it is also a sign of her independence. The girl is, as has been pointed out, not completely in Findlay's power.

Even more illustrative of this double-standard of morality is the 'Scotish Ballad' (503). In this song it is very obvious how the girl tries to cover up her real feelings by keeping up a pretence of irritation and haughtiness. Yet she knows her feminine influence and when she risks the loss of her lover she is quick to act. Passivity is not a feature of Burns's heroines. Robert D. Thornton asserts that 'never was there a girl more confident of her charm or more able to turn her lover inside out by teasing'.[15] The song has a very human humour and touch of subtle irony, and it is set to a tune of splendid momentum and liveliness.

The irony in the handling of the characters and the pathetic overstatement in the love-effusions of the boy are to a great extent embodied in the way the words are set to the music. The middle-cadence in the fourth bar is an ascending line ending on a long dotted crotchet. The words falling on this note are subsequently prolonged, and dimensions and implications are brought out which cannot be heard in a read version. There is irritation in the girl's first lines: 'Last May a

"Scotish Ballad"
(503, SMM No. 522)

And sair wi' his love he did *deave* me; I said, there was *naething*...
My wooer he *caper'd*...

braw wooer cam down the lang glen,/ And sair wi' his love he did *deave me*', and mocking scorn in her rendering of the boy's pathetic words: 'He spak o' the darts in my bonie black een,/ And vow'd for my love he was *dying*.' In the first stanza she protests, 'I said, there was *naething* I hated like men', and her 'naething' is saucily spat out on an upward leap. However, already in the second stanza it is clear that she is desperately trying to keep up pretences ('I said, he might die when he liked for JEAN—/ The Lord forgie me for lying, for lying') and in the third one she reveals that she has some feelings for the boy ('I never loot on that I kend it, or car'd'). The irony lies in the opposition between what she says and what she actually feels, and the implications are obvious: she says one thing, but means and feels another.

As the story proceeds it is the lover's turn to pretend, and being close (as she believes) to losing him, the girl has to act. She gives him a wink and 'My wooer he caper'd as he'd been in drink,/ And vow'd I was his dear lassie, dear lassie.' Here the leap in the music makes the verb 'caper'd' illustrative of the physical demonstration of the lover's joy. Crawford speaks in terms of 'character, motive and mask' about this song,[16] and if the mask was indifference with the girl at the beginning, it has now developed into irony and humour. In the last stanza the boy is back to the passion of the first part of the song, but the girl's answer this time expresses compassionate understatement:

> He begged, for Gudesake! I wad be his wife,
> > Or else I wad kill him wi' sorrow:
> So e'en to preserve the poor body in life,
> > I think I maun wed him tomorrow, tomorrow,
> > I think I maun wed him tomorrow.   (II, 796)

The songs discussed so far have been songs of courtship. They have caught the young girls in the act of choosing (or refusing) a lover or a husband, and they have thrown light on the conflicts which might then arise. There has been a stress on personal strength, self-confidence and independence more than on the actual feelings of love. Some of the songs have been light-hearted, suggesting young girls, others have been humorous and most of them have been set to brisk, extrovert tunes. In another group of songs the themes are spun around longing and affectionate love, the relationships are more definitely established and the tunes are of a reflective character.

In an essay on different types of folk-songs Gavin Greig makes a distinction between 'apostrophic', introspective love-songs, and biographic, narrative ones,[17] a distinction which applies very well to the songs in the following. To the latter group belong 'My Harry was a Gallant gay' (164) and 'Young Jockey was the blythest lad' (310), in which the girls speak about their love and their longing rather than addressing themselves straight to the beloved. The apostrophic songs, on the other hand, represent 'the higher kind of lyric where the lover utters his own feelings in direct appeal to the object of his adoration'. Songs of this type are the musical and lyrical translation of a central feeling, and as Greig puts it, they give 'unlimited scope for intensity of feeling and expression'.[18]

Such a song is 'For the sake o' Somebody' (566) in which a most generous and tender love is expressed, a love which is not seeking its own ends but is directed to the beloved person. There is a continuous return to the word 'somebody' and preoccupation of thought around this person. The tune consists of two almost identical halves, one for the stanzas and one for the chorus. In the second bar there is an intensifying lift, and with his instinctive perception of the inherent expression of the tune, Burns makes the lyrical meaning in both stanzas correspond to it:

"For the sake o' Somebody"
(566, SMM No. 436)

My heart is sair, I dare na tell, My heart is sair for Somebody;

    My heart is sair, I dare na tell,
    My heart is sair for Somebody;
       . . . . . .

    Ye Powers that smile on virtuous love,
    O, sweetly smile on Somebody!
       . . . . . .
                              (II, 850)

Whereas the first line is tentative, the second is more definite and more passionate: 'My heart is sair' not for anybody, but for 'Somebody', and 'Ye Powers that smile' on all lovers, smile especially on 'Somebody'. In both stanzas one word is repeated in both lines to hold them more firmly together ('sair' and 'smile'). On the descent in the third bar the girl gives proof of her love: she could 'wake a winter-night' for her lover (stanza 1) and she bids the heavenly powers to keep him from danger (stanza 2).

For the second half of the tune there is a chorus. As the rhythmical swing in the music is stronger here, the first and

third beats being heavier and the upbeats lacking, these lines
seem more extrovert and more overflowing with the joy of love:
'Oh-hon! for Somebody!/ Oh-hey! for Somebody!' But the
four-beat lilt and the arched melodic contour are also very
expressive of sighing and yearning, and the intensity of the
long close *o* of '*O*hon' and '*O*hey' gives added emphasis to
these feelings. These lines lead up to the protestation in the
last couplet of each stanza, 'I could range the warld round'
and 'I wad do—what wad I not', and this 'For the sake o'
Somebody'. The fusion of the two arts, poetry and music, is
most perfect in this song. The generous love and the passionate
longing is embodied in both text and tune, and the simplicity
and sensitivity with which the one is coupled to the other
makes the song an organic whole, where each part is dependent
on and enhanced by the other.

Another apostrophic song is 'Ay waukin O' (287), the
lyrical and musical expression of a young girl lying awake at
night, unable to sleep for thoughts of her dearie. Her longing,
her unrest, her infatuation, and her sadness, all this lies
embodied in the short lyric and in its tune. The structure, the
diction and the tonal language are extremely simple and
nothing seems superfluous in this song. Through very small
means it captures the desolate situation like a Japanese lyric,
and the song itself is like a weary sigh.

The chorus expresses the girl's longing, her melancholy and
her sighing. On two long notes the 'Ay' and the 'Oh' fall, being
the utterance of her love-sick heart. The minor melody drops
here, enhancing that sadness, but it rises in the second bar
(line 2) as if to express her impatience and her unrest. In the
third bar it monotonously repeats the same note four times
before it falls again (line 3). It finally reaches its peak in the rise
of the last bar, reinforcing the intensity of the girl's feelings.

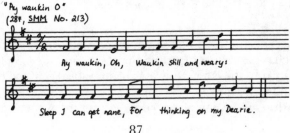

"Ay waukin O"
(287, SMM No. 213)

Ay waukin, Oh, Waukin still and weary:

Sleep I can get nane, For thinking on my Dearie.

The stanzas contain the thoughts occupying the girl's mind and keeping her awake. The second (see below) is only a variation of the chorus and the other two are impressionistic lines, capturing the tired thoughts passing through her mind:

> When I sleep I dream,
>> When I wauk I'm irie;
> Sleep I can get nane,
>> For thinking on my Dearie.—   (II, 510)

The music lies higher here, it has more dotted notes and seems to embody her unrest and excitement. But each poetical line is sung to a falling melodic phrase, each one starting anew as if it is an effort for the girl to express her thoughts, tired and sad as she is.

In the narrative 'My Harry was a Gallant gay' (164) the theme of longing and sadness is opposed to that of strength and vengeance. There are tensions within the girl of her tender feelings towards Highland Harry and of her bitter feelings towards those who saw to his banishment, and these tensions are embodied both in the tune and in the poetical interpretation of the tune. The predominant thought in the girl's mind is that of Highland Harry's return home, and in the refrain it is kept alive throughout the whole song. Burns has connected his own stanzas with the theme of the old chorus by letting each last line take up the refrain of the latter:

> My Harry was a gallant gay,
>> Fu' stately strade he on the plain;
> But now he's banish'd far awa,
>> I'll never see him *back again*.   (stanza 1)

> O for him back again,
>> O for him back again,
> I wad gie a' Knockhaspie's land
>> For Highland Harry *back again*.   (chorus)
>   (I, 347)

In the chorus the girl's emotions intensify. At this point the tune changes register (it rises an octave) and the long first beat for 'O' (n.b. the expressive lack of an upbeat) embodies all her unfulfilled longing.

With its interplay of dotted notes and snaps the tune is very powerful. In the first lines of the first and last stanzas the snaps are particularly effective, as they accent the alliterations and make the words sound forceful and fierce. There is pride

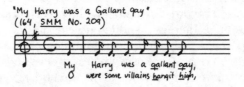

"My Harry was a Gallant gay"
(164, SMM No. 209)

My Harry was a gallant gay,
were some villains hangit high,

in the girl's voice when she sings, 'My Harry was a gallant gay,/ Fu' stately strade he on the plain', and for 'stately' the tune makes a large upward leap, emphasizing that word. But the girl's happy reverie comes to a sudden end in line 3, where she bursts out *But now* he's banish'd far awa.' Dramatically the tune now lifts and rises to the top note, before it descends into the refrain.

In the second stanza the girl's sadness is expressed. The descent of the tune in bar 2 here becomes finely expressive of the despondency in 'I wander dowie up the glen', as if she slowly drops her head. In the last stanza the girl gathers up strength, and its first half expresses suppressed anger and threat. On the melodic ascent in the third bar, however, she cheers up at the thought of seeing her lover again: 'Then I might see the joyfu' sight,/ My Highlan Harry back again.'

'Jamie come try me' (295) also expresses the longing of a girl, but is more purely a song of the senses and a song of passion. It is an interpretation of emotions only and says nothing about the circumstances around these emotions. It 'calls up a picture of someone "just waiting to be asked"—breathless with desire, and almost beseeching Jamie to take the first step', as Crawford puts it.[19] The contents, language and structure of the lyric in combination with the character of the tune also suggest a slightly older girl than the ones in the songs discussed above.

The chorus introduces the theme around which the two stanzas are spun:

> Jamie come try me,
> Jamie come try me,
> If thou would win my love
> Jamie come try me. (II, 519)

89

The first 'Jamie come try me' is sung on an assertively ascending melodic line going from the tonic to its octave. It lacks an upbeat, which makes the invitation more direct and straightforward. After this first attempt the girl becomes sensuous and alluring and her words are sung in a low register and with less directness. Then there is a sudden tone of despair in her tune. It leaps up one octave and on this high note the word 'if' falls. It jumps down again, but ascends from there and comes back to the last 'Jamie come try me.' This time it lies very high and therefore has a stronger intensity.

"Jamie come try me"
(295, SMM No. 229)

Jamie come try me, Jamie come try me,
If thou would win my love Jamie come try me.

The stanzas, set to the second half of the tune, are spun round the if-questions and the tune in this section remains in the high register, intensifying these questions. For 'Could I deny thee?' and 'Wha could espy thee?' the melody urgently rises, but with the return to the refrain of the song it passively descends: it is the last appeal, it is the least forceful, yet the snaps give it a certain urgency.

On the printed page this simple poem reveals very little of its emotional overtones. The sensuality, the urgent and alluring appeal, the intensity of the questions, the underlying despair, the wide emotional range of the song; all this lies embodied in the tune with its slow tempo, its great range, its melodic contour and the gentle lilt of the triple rhythm.

A love-song of a more uncomplicated and happy kind is 'Young Jockey was the blythest lad' (310). Through the frequent use of repetitions and words with pleasant associations Burns gives this lyric an extrovert character, which finely responds to the cheerful expression of the tune. He also takes advantage of the contrast between the two sections of the tune to convey the emotions behind the girl's words. The first four lines of stanza 1 describe the lad in an objective way: 'Fu' blythe' the lad whistles and 'Fu' lightly' he dances, and as if to imprint this on the listener the word 'blythe' is used twice. With the lift in the second half of the tune, its shift from minor to major and its less jerky rhythm, the lyric now speaks of the girl's feelings for the boy, and her face seems to light up at the thought of her own relationship with him:

> He roos'd my een sae bonie blue,
>   He roos'd my waist sae genty sma;
> An ay my heart came to my mou,
>   When ne'er a body heard or saw.   (II, 538)

In the second stanza the minor first part of the tune with its energetic, snapped rhythm becomes aptly descriptive of the scene—young Jockey 'toils' on the plain through 'wind and weet' and through 'frost and snaw'. In the last half-stanza the lad comes home, he takes the girl in his arms, and the gaiety of the situation is enhanced by the switch to the high register and the major quality of the tune, and the tension of the hard work is released through the smoother rhythm.

One group of Burns's females grow from girlhood to womanhood through the experience of motherhood. A common feature of Scottish life in the eighteenth century which is reflected in the folk-songs, is that of the young girl who has been seduced and deserted by her lover. Burns picked up this traditional theme and to tunes of both light-hearted and reflective character he wrote lyrics which mirror different aspects of such situations. He shows deep understanding and sympathy for these girls, and his fine psychological insight into the female mind reveals itself particularly in these songs.

A young and very inexperienced girl is depicted in 'To the Weaver's gin ye go' (194), in which the girl's encounter with the erotic side of love comes very abruptly. Her 'heart was ance as blythe and free/ As simmer days were lang', but innocence met with bitter experience and her singing changed to sighing. There is a foreshadowing of the disastrous event already at the beginning ('But a bonie, westlin weaver lad/ Has gart me change my sang'), and although there are elements of joy and excitement in the song, there is also a sense of doom hovering over it. The shame and fear of the girl is the underlying sentiment and it is expressed in the last stanza:

> But what was said, or what was done,
>   Shame fa' me gin I tell;
> But Oh! I fear the kintra soon
>   Will ken as weel's mysel! (I, 383)

Her words are sung to the low, monotonous part of the tune, which is centred round one note (F sharp) and has a descending melodic contour. Although it is lively, the tune also strikes

"To the weaver's gin ye go"
(194, SMM No. 103)

My heart was once as blythe and free As simmer days were lang,

a tone of regret and hopelessness through the incessant drumming character of the reiterated F sharp. This also calls to mind the regular thump of the loom, which accompanies the girl's sighing and sobbing (notice the monotonous effect of the repetition and alliteration in 'But the *w*eary, *w*eary *w*arpin o't').

But, as Kinsley points out, the 'blend of delight and regret' is also palpable in the chorus because of its 'melancholy final phrase'. This chorus, which is traditional, is a jocular, yet serious comment on the girl's words in the stanzas. What happens if a girl goes to the weaver at night is said only by implication, and the chorus is meant as a warning to other young girls:

> To the weaver's gin ye go, fair maids,
>   To the weaver's gin ye go,
> I rede you right, gang ne'er at night,
>   To the weaver's gin ye go. (I, 383)

As it is not the girl who speaks in it, it becomes the comment of a detached observer and recalls the function of the chorus in a Greek drama. The tune has an assertively rising melodic line in the major, before it falls into the minor in the last bar, which gives it that curiously sad twist at the end. Alexander Keith aptly describes the significance of this minor end thus: 'Sprightly enough through three-quarters of its length, it [the chorus] drops to the minor in the concluding bar, with an odd simulation of warning, a sort of admonitory, cautious finger wagged before the face of the lassie to enforce the prophecy of the dire consequences, "to the weaver's gin ye go".'[20]

'The rantin dog the Daddie o't' (80) is a song in which a young mother tries to grasp her situation with humour. It presents a young girl who enjoys life, love and sex and lets nothing depress her. She has a remedy for all the difficulties she might meet as an unmarried mother, and this is 'the rantin dog the daddie o't'. Her tune is cheerful and her attitude optimistic. She knows much more about life than the girl in 'To the Weaver's gin ye go', and she also knows how to meet it with both its hardships and its joys. The young weaver-lassie is filled with fear and shame after her introduction to sex, but this lassie thoroughly enjoys it, in spite of the fact that it puts her on the 'creepie-chair'. In a very female way she asks for protection ('O Wha my babie-clouts will buy') and attention ('O Wha will tent me when I cry'), and in a frank and open manner she sings out her passion ('Wha will mak me fidgin fain;/ Wha will kiss me o'er again').

The tune of the song consists of two sections (taking one stanza each) which are melodically built up in the same way. Each two-bar phrase corresponds to one line in the lyric. There is a shift between them from F major to E flat major back to F major. Finally, there is a refrain which is the same in both sections. For this air Burns has created a lyric with a very fine sense of structure and unity. The first three lines of each stanza are united at the beginning by the same word and at the end by the same rhyme. Each line is thought-contained as each two-bar phrase in the music is self-contained. The last line is the refrain and the answer to the questions:

> O Wha my babie-clouts will buy,
> O Wha will tent me when I cry;
> Wha will kiss me where I lie,
> The rantin dog the daddie o't. (I, 184)

Kinsley notes this structure and points out how well the air 'sustains the triple question and the energetic answer of Burns's stanza'. The repetitions suggest an urgency in the girl's

questions, and the nuances in her voice are brought about by
the variations provided by the tonal shifts between F and E flat
major and by the change of register between the two sections of
the tune.

A more reflective song is 'Bonie Dundee' (157). It has a wider
emotional range as it expresses affectionate love towards both
lover and child, and it conveys an almost holy stillness, yet also
the shivering of passionate love. The first half of the tune lies
low, whereas the second is more intense in the higher register. It
starts high, leaps down an octave but rises again in a very
expressive way. On the whole the intervals are dramatically
wider in the second half than in the first, which is more evenly
undulating. The triple rhythm has a lullaby-quality, which
finely sustains the tenderness of the lyric and creates an image
of the young mother rocking the child in her lap.

The first stanza, which is traditional, perceptively responds
to the difference of expression between the two halves of the
tune. The first half-stanza (for the low part of the tune) is an
objective presentation of the situation. It introduces the theme
of the girl who has been made pregnant by 'a young brisk
Sodger Laddie', whereas the second half-stanza takes us straight
into the emotional life of this girl:

> O gin I saw the laddie that gae me 't!
> Aft has he doudl'd me upon his knee;
> May Heaven protect my bonie Scots laddie,
> And send him safe hame to his babie and me.   (I, 339)

With the intensive lifts in the tune her thoughts seem to
wander away to the laddie she is in love with, and they merely
touch upon the child. On the return to the low part of the tune
in the first four lines of the second stanza, all her attention now
turns to the baby, the music being illustrative of an action
almost—from having wistfully looked away, she now looks
down at the baby in her lap. To the rocking tune she gives him
her blessings: 'My blessins upon thy sweet, wee lippie!/ My
blessins upon thy bonie e'e brie!' The music gives variation to
the repeated blessings as the second lies a fifth higher than the
first. From 'my blessins' she moves to 'Thy smiles are sae like
my blyth Sodger laddie', which prepares for the switch of
attention in the last four lines (for the high part of the tune).

Here Burns makes the girl react in the same way as she did in the first stanza: she turns away from the baby, her thoughts are still centred round it, but they are now also circling round the 'dadie dear'. They are the proud but affectionate thoughts of a mother, who has great dreams for her son. Best of all he will be like his father and remind her of him. The transition from the low part of the tune to the more dramatic and intense second half is marked in the text by the word 'but':

> But I'll big a bow'r on yon bonie banks,
>   Whare Tay rins wimplin by sae clear;
> And I'll cleed thee in the tartan sae fine,
>   And mak thee a man like thy dadie dear.   (I, 339)

As we have seen the girls in the songs discussed are fully-fledged characters, capable of deep emotions and intelligent thinking. They are caught in various life-situations, acting and feeling, something which makes them and their emotions seem very real. They also come alive through the fact that they speak for themselves in the songs—life is viewed through their eyes and described in their own words. But their characters and emotions are only given their full gamut of expression in conjunction with the tunes. The restlessness and impatience of the girl in 'Tam Glen', the anguish of 'Ay waukin O' and the girlishness of 'I'm o'er young to Marry Yet', for instance, would not be as palpable without the tunes. In some songs even, the emotions behind the words lie wholly in the music, and a song like 'Jamie come try me' means little without its tune. The language of the girls is conversational and the poetic diction limpid, and, as always, Burns is at his best when he bases his songs on the folk-song tradition with its simplicity of both poetical and musical style as well as of thought. The wedding of text and tune in these songs is perfect, and through this medium Burns has created a type of woman whose character, thoughts and emotions are universal and modern. She does not only link up with the old Scotland but also has her sisters in the emancipated women of the twentieth century.

95

NOTES

1. *Robert Burns's Commonplace Book 1783–1785*, ed. James C. Ewing and Davidson Cook (Glasgow, 1938), p. 3.
2. The term 'song' in this essay refers to the whole composition, consisting of both lyric and tune. Burns wrote his songs for specific tunes, and he never conceived of them as being only read. They are units of poetry and music and should be treated as such. For a systematic textual-musical study of the songs in the *Scots Musical Museum*, see my *The Songs of Robert Burns: A Study of the Unity of Poetry and Music*, diss., Studia Anglistica Upsaliensia, 30 (Uppsala, 1977). The present essay is based on Chapter III of this study.
3. Christina Keith, *The Russet Coat: A Critical Study of Burns' Poetry and of Its Background* (London, 1956), p. 147.
4. Ibid., pp. 205–6.
5. Ibid., pp. 198–99.
6. The songs are referred to by their titles and numbers in *The Poems and Songs of Robert Burns*, ed. James Kinsley, 3 vols. (Oxford, 1968). References in the text to critical comments made by Kinsley are to be found in Vol. III under the number of the song. The musical examples are given from *The Scots Musical Museum Originally Published by James Johnson with Illustrations of the Lyric Poetry and Music of Scotland by William Stenhouse* (*SMM*), Vol. I, 1853, facs. ed. (Hatboro, Pennsylvania, 1962).
7. The shape of a melody is important for the expression of the song and for the impact of the words. Rising melodic lines as well as upward skips are more energetic and assertive than falling lines, which are more passive. Words on the top of a melodic line or a skip are emphasized. See Deryck Cooke, *The Language of Music* (Oxford, 1959), pp. 105–6.
8. Keith, *The Russet Coat*, p. 147.
9. There is a difference of expression between dotted and undotted (even) rhythms. Cooke, p. 100, observes that the latter has an effect 'of a smooth, unimpeded flow of any particular emotion', whereas the former allows for more tension.
10. Thomas Crawford, *Burns: A Study of the Poems and Songs* (Edinburgh, 1960), p. 304.
11. A snap is a rhythmic figure in which the accented beat is shorter than the unaccented (see example 8, 'Hárry', 'gállant'). The heavy accent on the first beat tends to affect the pronunciation of the initial consonant of the word and give it more energy.
12. Crawford, p. 295.
13. Cooke finds (p. 97) that there is an intrinsic difference of expression between duple (two- and four-beat) and triple (three-beat) time: 'As a general rule we may take it that duple rhythm is more rigid and controlled, triple rhythm more relaxed and abandoned.'
14. The lack of an upbeat gives a certain energy to a song through its 'direct attack' on the first beat of the bar. See Julia P. Dabney, *The Musical Basis of Verse: A Scientific Study of the Principles of Poetic Composition* (New York, 1901), p. 47.

15. Robert D. Thornton, *The Tuneful Flame: Songs of Robert Burns as He Sang Them* (Kansas, 1957), p. 10.
16. Crawford, p. 300.
17. Gavin Greig, *Folk-song in Buchan and Folk-song of the North-east* (Hatboro, Pennsylvania, 1963), p. 34.
18. Ibid.
19. Crawford, p. 305.
20. Alexander Keith, *Burns and Folk-song* (Aberdeen, 1922), pp. 25–6.

5

Burns and Bawdy

by R. D. S. JACK

1

This is a touchy subject and a difficult one, but it must be openly discussed by critics if they ever hope to come to a full understanding of Burns as poet and, secondarily, as man. The first certainty is that Burns was himself attracted towards bawdry, albeit in that mixed spirit of abandonment and guilt which marks the sensual individual brought up within the precepts of Calvinism. When he enclosed 'The Case of Conscience' to Provost Maxwell of Lochmaben, he wrote:

> I shall betake myself to a subject ever fertile of themes, a Subject, the turtle-feast of the Sons of Satan, and the delicious, secret Sugar-plumb of the Babes of Grace . . . in short, may it please Your Lordship, I intend to write BAUDY![1] (I, 377)

Burns never freed himself either from the enjoyment he felt in writing or recording bawdy verse, nor from the fear he felt, that in some way such activities endangered the future of his immortal soul:

> There is, there must be, some truth in original sin.—My violent propensity to B––dy convinces me of it.—Lack a day! if that species of Composition be the Sin against 'the Haly Ghaist', 'I am the most offending soul alive.' (II, 213)

Unfortunately, it would appear the same fear seems to have beset most assessors of his work, anxious either to deny its bawdy element entirely or seriously to underestimate the importance it held for the poet. The present essay is an attempt to redress the balance.

The researches of DeLancey Ferguson, Goodsir Smith, Kinsley, Legman and others have firmly established that Burns did compose a fair number of the songs contained in the first known edition of *The Merry Muses*[2] and that he was also responsible for the refurbishing of other 'indelicate' songs in the collection. David Daiches provides us with a fair assessment of the situation:

> As a matter of fact, the majority of the poems in *The Merry Muses* are traditional, or improvements of traditional pieces, and it would thus be true to say that a minority of them are Burns's own. But a fair number are by Burns himself, and his hand can be suspected in many of the others.[3]

Why then do we continue to ignore this extremely important aspect of the poet's work? Undoubtedly the first reason is non-literary. Despite Legman's efforts overtly erotic literature tends still to be shielded from the eyes of the public. Even the photostat copy of the 1800 edition of *The Merry Muses* in the National Library of Scotland is gratuitously preceded by a letter anonymously written to the Editor of the 'North British Daily Mail'. The author, perhaps unconscious of his own Freudian imagery, fulminates that:

> . . . Those who connect the name of Scotia's bard with such a work do not deserve to be called countrymen of him who spent the last ten years of his life in purifying the stream of Scottish song and widening its channels.

One is, therefore, chided before one starts reading. The present writer, on the other hand, sides with Maurice Lindsay, when he remarks:

> *The Merry Muses* cannot be regarded as 'obscene', except by those who regard sex itself as 'obscene'.[4]

Let us, therefore, accept the bawdy element within the songs and verse of Burns and see what this acceptance implies for our evaluation of him as poet or folk-song collector, rather than attempting a moral whitewash which goes against all the evidence.

The second reason for shying away from the bawdy side to Burns is more understandable. Many of these verses are not the finest examples of the poet's art. Yet Burns was at all times an uneven writer and there seems to me the same mixture of genius and lack of inspiration in his original bawdy works as in his less contentious contributions to literature. No one was more conscious of this unevenness than Burns himself. Yet poems and songs like 'For a' that and a' that' and 'Mary Morison'—both damned with faint praise by the poet (correctly in my opinion)—appear in all the editions of his work, while his weaker erotic verse is often used as an excuse for excising all of it. The criterion, however concealed, is still moral rather than literary.

Finally, even those who remain unaffected by the first two difficulties are faced by more genuine problems. Fitzhugh noted that the:

> textual, bibliographical, editorial and historical problems relating to Burns and bawdy songs are riddling, perplexed and labyrinthical in the extreme.[5]

The triple activity of Burns as original writer, refurbisher and copyist has raised similar problems in the less controversial areas of his work, but the idealizing tendencies of the Burns cult, stretching even to falsification and omission of some of the poet's letters, has indeed made the situation more complex in the case of bawdry.[6] Now, however, we have Kinsley's excellent edition and Legman's facsimile of the 1800 text of *The Merry Muses*.[7] This allows a literary critic objectively to assess Burns's contribution to the extensive and often inspired bawdy literature of Scotland. In the following study, I have followed Kinsley's attributions and texts. Citations from *The Merry Muses* follow Legman. Any instances where I have departed from these principles are indicated.

My major reason for analysing Burns's bawdry is my belief that many of his finest songs and verses are of that type. This contention will, I hope, be borne out in the course of the essay. I have, however, concentrated on four aspects in particular. First, there is the crucial question of the poet's treatment of older folk songs. Then I have analysed two areas of his original bawdry—those with a religious topic and those which parody recognized literary forms. Finally, and on a more general level, I have tried to indicate the ways in which his verse was influenced by folk erotica, while retaining its own thematic and imagistic originality. Clearly, such an approach does not cover the whole range of the poet's contribution to bawdry, but it does pinpoint some of the major problems involved and highlights some of his best work.

2

We are constantly reminded that, as folk-song refurbisher, Burns often expurgated the bawdy material, converting overt sexual references into romantic ones and moving the various tones employed for the presentation of erotic topics in the direction of pathos or sentimentality. Usually, the resultant song, though markedly different from the older folk version, proves a triumph of his art. Such is the case with 'John Anderson my jo, John'. Burns's text for Johnson's *Musical Museum* is a masterpiece of controlled sentimentality, depicting with great sensitivity the continuation of love in old age after passion has died. The wife contrasts her husband's hair, once as black as the raven, with its present snowlike whiteness; his youthful, unwrinkled forehead with his present baldness, yet ends with a tender judgement:

> But blessings on your frosty pow,
> John Anderson my Jo.   (II, 529)

In *The Merry Muses* we have the undoubted source for this poem, a work already widely known throughout Scotland. When we compare the two, what immediately impresses is the boldness of the Burnsian metamorphosis, which nonetheless retains, in markedly different contexts, some of the original ideas and imagery. For example, the opposition between youthful attraction and the wrinkles of old age, focused in the *Musical Museum* song on the forehead, had in the folk song been applied to sexual prowess:

> But now its waxen wan, John,
> And wrinkles to and fro;
> I've twa gae-ups for ae gae-down,
> John Anderson, my jo.   (Legman, p. 53)

The snow imagery, applied in almost benedictional tones to the husband in the expurgation, is also present in the original, but used by the wife, when expatiating on her continued beauty and availability:

> Frae my tap-knot to my tae, John,
> I'm like new-fa'n snow;
> And it's a' for your convenience
> John Anderson, my jo.   (Legman, p. 54)

The popularity of the older song was deserved, and as Goodsir Smith has pointed out, it also has a strong element of pathos.[8] Tonally and psychologically it is more complex than Burns's version. The woman in her frustration at John's disinterest in sex moves from direct castigation to protestations of her continued faithfulness; from descriptions of her beauty (wasted only in being unused) to fond memories of those past occasions when John's 'chanter-pipe' had thrilled her. But she does end with a clear threat. Either he comes to bed:

> Or ye shall hae the horns, John,
> Upon your head to grow;
> An' that's the cuckold's mallison,
> John Anderson, my jo.   (Legman, p. 55)

This example serves to show how extreme Burns's expurgations often are. Both songs are successful but in very different ways. Often, inevitably, the work of the trained poet far surpasses the rough material with which he is dealing. (Compare for example the versions of 'Duncan Gray' or 'Eppie McNab'.) Yet, there are occasions when Burns's version does not fare so well in the comparison. Such a one, I believe, is 'As I cam o'er the Cairney Mount'. In his manuscript notes Burns refers to his song as 'original' and with 'humour in its composition'. Professor Kinsley rightly remarks that this humour will only be apparent to someone who already knew the bawdy original and thus could understand the meaning of the asterisks after the chorus and pick up the mock pastoral tone of the second stanza:[9]

> Now Phebus blinkit on the bent,
> And O'er the knowes the lambs were bleating:
> But he wan my heart's consent,
> To be his ain at the neist meeting.   (II, 863)

Standing on its own, the song presents an unhappy mixture of rustic realism, Highland romanticism and mythological paraphernalia.

This overall lack of unity contrasts markedly with the version preserved in *The Merry Muses*. Here the conventional concept of love as warfare is developed with some ingenuity. The penis becomes a 'durk' sheathed in the woman's 'leather'; foreplay is 'warlike pranks', copulation likened to a military attack moving on two flanks but pushing most 'fiercely in the centre'. The woman, though being struck three times to every one, bravely(!) holds her ground and receives the man's fire. Even the resolution to continue the affair, rather weakly presented in the expurgated version, maintains the central metaphor:

> But our ammunition being spent,
> And we quite out o' breath an' sweating,
> We did agree with ae consent,
> To fight it out at the next meeting.   (Legman, p. 45)

A thorough reading of *The Merry Muses* thus serves to demonstrate that Burns did not always improve through purifying, while it also helps the reader to pick up innuendoes in the 'respectable' versions, undreamt of by those who have not looked at the sources.

So far I have dealt with songs which Burns altered radically, but on occasions the differences between the texts of the *Musical Museum* and *The Merry Muses* are slight, albeit important. This indicates the care Burns took when handling folk material and trying to present it to a different audience. A good example is 'Gat ye me, O gat ye me', which appears in the *Musical Museum* as 'The Lass of Ecclefechan', and in *The Merry Muses* as 'O Gat Ye Me Wi' Naething'. Both poems belong to the mediaeval 'estrif' form. In each case there are only two stanzas, the second being to all intents and purposes identical. The evidence suggests that Burns heard the first stanza as preserved in *The Merry Muses* but considered it too 'indelicate' for publication so altered it and then added the second stanza intact, although other possibilities do exist.

Both versions begin with the wife's complaint that her bodily attractions are more than enough for a useless husband,

103

although in the *Musical Museum* edition she lays more stress on her personal possessions and those of her family. To this the husband replies that he has remained faithful until marriage. After that he has wandered, now longing intensely for his wife's death and the freedom it implies. In 'The Lass of Ecclefechan' Burns provides us with a neat balance, giving a stanza to each. In 'O Gat Ye Me Wi' Naething', the husband breaks in to the first stanza with the barbed couplet:

> Indeed, o'er muckle far gudewife,
> For that was ay the fau't o't.   (Legman, p. 74)

The reference here is to the size of the woman's vagina about which she had earlier boasted:

> A rock, a reel, a spinning wheel,
> A gude black c––t was ae thing.   (Legman, p. 74)

Burns excises this explicit comment with its implications of promiscuity. Instead the wife concentrates on the theme of property and particularly her grandfather's possession of a house on two floors. In so doing, he has, perforce, to lose some of the scurrilous wit present in the original, but he does not allow his readers to miss the ironical message of the folk song. In the *Musical Museum* version only, the woman refers to herself as 'The toss of Ecclefechan', a phrase which can mean either that she is the toast of the village or an easy 'lay'. Burns's expurgations very often merely substitute covert for overt bawdry and exhibit a careful poetic judgement, aware at once of its duty to folk song integrity and to the realities of publication with the more rigorous moral strictures implied by the presentation of such material in print.

A study of Burns in relation to folk bawdry, however, does strongly emphasize another side to the poet's activities. Expurgator he may have been, but as Legman and others have demonstrated, he had two audiences and two motivations. There was not only Johnson, Thomson and the presses. There was also the conviviality of groups such as the Crochallan Fencibles and the pressure on the 'poet' in their midst to elaborate upon rather than emasculate the earthy songs, which were so much appreciated by Smellie, Hay, Cleghorn, Ainslie and others. Burns, therefore, did not only dilute bawdry, he also made an important positive contribution to that side of Scottish verse which Hugh MacDiarmid, in regretting its omission from his *Golden Treasury of Scottish Poetry*, termed 'this most essential and exhilarating and important element of our poetic corpus'.[10]

The clearest proof of this resides in his original bawdy songs and verse. Before leaving his contribution as folk song refurbisher, however, one should note that the evidence strongly suggests that he added stanzas to the end of such songs or occasionally may have inserted stanzas. Equally, it seems probable that he sometimes produced different versions of the same song, each intended for a different audience. The problems involved in pinpointing such activities are accentuated by Burns's own admission, that he tried to imitate the roughness and metrical irregularity of the 'old Scotch Songs', when acting in this capacity.[11] Thus Legman and Randall but not Kinsley are persuaded that the additional two stanzas to 'The Reel o' Stumpie' found in *The Merry Muses* are original Burns:

> Lang kail, pease and leeks,
> They were at the kirst'nin' o't,
> Lang lads wanton breeks,
> They were at the getting o't.
>
> The Bailie he gaed farthest ben,
> Mess John was ripe and ready o't;
> But the sherra had a wanton fling,
> The sherra was the daddie o't.   (Legman, p. 27)

Again, the stanza

> Wry-c————d is she,
> Wry-c————d is she,
> Wry-c————d is she,
> And pishes gain' her thie.   (Legman, p. 60)

which appears in *The Merry Muses* version of 'Saw ye my Maggie' but not in the Abbotsford MS is held by Goodsir Smith, Legman and Randall to be a Burnsian insertion. Kinsley is more cautious. There is a similar division of opinion when it comes to attributing credit for the four versions of 'Green Grow the Rashes O'. Clearly, Burns was responsible for the purest version (Kinsley No. 45). It also seems likely that he extensively revised the bawdy song on which it was based, when composing the 'Fragment', which he sent to Richmond in September 1786. This is, in itself, evidence that he enjoyed bawdy composition:

> I dought na speak—yet was na fley'd—
> My heart play'd duntie, duntie, O;
> An' ceremony laid aside,
> I fairly fun' her c—ntie, O. (I, 294)

Yet it does not solve the question of what part, if any, Burns played in composing the two, even more explicit, versions to be found in *The Merry Muses*.

Having looked at all the evidence, I tend to side with Legman in the first case, with Kinsley in the second and would suspect that only the second version of 'Green Grow the Rashes O' in *The Merry Muses*[12] is unaffected by some Burnsian revision. But no matter how critics may divide on particular cases, the certainty remains that Burns, while working as a folk song collector with a special wallet for his 'walkers',[13] expurgated Scottish bawdry for one audience in various ways but enlarged upon it (again in various ways) for other more private groups or for individuals.

3

When one comes to examine those bawdy songs, which are probably the poet's own composition, it is striking how many of the best deal with sex in relation to religion. Goodsir Smith has argued that the reaction from Calvinism in large measure accounts for the popularity and the wit of such verse in Scots.[14] Burns himself was ever conscious both of the needs of the flesh and (usually later) of the horrors of hypothetical spiritual vengeance:

> If there be any truth in the Orthodox faith of these churches, I am damned past redemption, and what is worse, damned to all eternity. (II, 12)

Certainly, he often places bawdry within a religious context and in a manner which betrays his inability to escape either from the attraction of the one or the combined promise and

threat of the other. This tension produced some of his finest
indecent verse, which may for the present purposes be divided
into three broad classifications.

First of all, and especially in his younger days, there are
works which cock a snook at conventional religion but with a
fieriness of tone which argues for more real religious concern
than the poet wishes to confess. Such a one is 'The Fornicator',
in which he addresses a male audience ('Ye jovial boys') and
asks them in confidential tones to 'lend an ear', while he
recounts the outcome of his latest affair. On the surface there
is little indication of conscience. Indeed, he rather naïvely
boasts of his continued determination to prove a lover despite
the efforts of the constituted Church. He and his Betsy
(Elizabeth Paton) are upbraided in front of the congregation
but even in that moment the poet's eyes chance to glance
down at

> Those limbs so clean where I, between,
> Commenc'd a Fornicator. (I, 101)

Scarcely are they out of church, than they are making love
again. Yet, while Burns glorifies his sensuality and seems even
to gain an extra thrill from contravening the set theological
order of his day, it is important to note that (less stridently) he
analyses his conduct in terms consistent with Christian teaching and suggestive of a need to excuse his actions even to
himself. Thus, he is anxious to distinguish between his own
natural passions and the unnatural ones of those who seek out
whores or need the artificial stimulus of drink to whet their
sexual appetite. In almost Pauline fashion he stresses that
procreation should be the end of sex, a conclusion somewhat
at odds with the persistent boast of the refrain:

> But a bony lass upon the grass
> To teach her esse Mater,
> And no reward but for regard,
> O that's a Fornicator. (I, 102)

He also emphasizes that his goods are to be shared with Betsy
and his 'roguish boy' even in the greatest extremes of poverty.
The Christian concept of sharing one's possessions in a spirit
of charity is therefore advanced within a poem which on

another level glorifies the flouting of religious teaching. Finally, he finds comfort in the thought that great men such as Caesar and Alexander had shared this weakness. Critics, rightly, have pointed out that this final stanza seems incongruous in its sudden raising of the level of application from rural Ayrshire to classical history, but Burns so often draws the names of the great into the 'lists' of fornication that one is forced to conclude that the psychological need to find heroic precedents for his inclinations may, at times, have obliterated his sense of poetic proportion.

It was Byron who most succinctly summed up the extremes to be found in Burns:

> What an antithetical mind!—tenderness, roughness—delicacy, coarseness—sentiment, sensuality—soaring and grovelling, dirt and deity—all mixed up in that one compound of inspired clay![15]

To a large degree any study of his bawdry emphasizes the roughness, coarseness and sensuality, while showing that these elements in his personality could also find inspired poetic expression. Yet, whatever the bias, the two sides usually find joint expression in some form or other. Nowhere is this more obvious than in his bawdy 'religious' verse. 'The Fornicator' on one level is quite a successful, lighthearted poem written for a group of men and flouting conventional morality. Yet the poet seems also anxious to convince a rather different audience that his definition of fornication is also a definition of love; that he is aware of his moral responsibilities and that Caesar fell into the same category! This schizophrenic vision lies behind most of his religious bawdry and usually contributes to its wit and complexity in more subtle fashions than in 'The Fornicator'.

Certainly, schizophrenic vision of a rather different kind lies behind the second class of Burns's bawdy religious verse— that which attacks Puritan hypocrisy. This had proved a fertile subject for more respectable Kirk satires such as 'Holy Willie's Prayer' and 'The Holy Fair'. In both 'Godly Girzie' and 'The Case of Conscience' we see the same control of comic incongruity as reality is set against appearance, spiritual protestation against physical motivation. But while the bawdy context permits even more outrageous humour, it also prevents the drawing of rigorous moral judgements. As a result, although the puritanical figures who hold the centre of the stage in each are rigorously satirized for falling away from the ideals they purport to hold, there is some sympathy for them, drawn from the fact that their lower selves mirror that very victory of sensuality over all other forces, which forms the central tenet of most bawdry.

Initially Girzie appears to be the archetype of piety, a fact which the narrator comically underlines in the first stanza by repeating the word 'haly' in connection with her three times and adding a 'godly' for good measure. She is, therefore, raised on to a pedestal of purity from which, we presume, she looks down at the 'man o' sin', who encounters her on Craigie Hills as she returns from her day of religious meetings. Skilfully, her extreme holiness is countered by a similar emphasis on his strength and sexual impatience:

> The chiel' was wight, the chiel' was stark,
> He wad na wait to chap nor ca'. (II, 901)

If we have been taking this dramatic preparation at face value, we can only see the matching of implacable extremes—evil opposing good; lust facing Christian virtue. The comic anti-climax is perfectly achieved. Instead of violence and perhaps rape, Girzie gives way without a murmur. The narrator, whose sincerity has been suspect from the outset, takes on himself the role of excusing sexual readiness in terms consistent with his earlier portrait and so adds to the humour by inadequately excusing her:

> And she was faint wi' haly wark,
> She had na pith to say him na. (II, 901)

The obvious fact that spiritual contemplation provides no excuse for physical weakness and indeed should, in such a context, have had the opposite effect underlines both Girzie's hypocrisy and the narrator's ambivalent position.

The latter's role in the drama is all important. As he determinedly apologizes for his 'haly' heroine, he actually underlines just how far she falls away from the piety of her outward appearance. Yet, although we may suspect that he is throughout being ironic, he at all times maintains a surface seriousness. Thus, when we read the next couplet, which describes, with inspired attention to comic detail, the manner in which Girzie succumbs, the humorous incongruities become even more complex:

> But ay she glowr'd up to the moon,
> And ay she sigh'd most piouslie.　　　　　　　　　(II, 901)

A whole variety of comic interpretations are possible here. Girzie may actually be glowering while yielding, as a sop to her Calvinist conscience. On the other hand, this may be the narrator's ironic way of interpreting her expressions of sexual abandonment. Equally, she may be pretending to sigh with martyrly resignation or (more probably) the narrator chooses to interpret her sighs of real passion in this way.

What is most interesting of all is that Burns chooses to drop the narratorial voice in the last couplet, giving Girzie a forceful and witty last word:

> I trust my heart's in heaven aboon,
> Whare'er your sinfu' p————e be.　　　　　　　(II, 901)

In a sense, therefore, the poet has gained humour from two divergent ways of looking at the same incident. From a moral viewpoint he has set the pretensions of Girzie against her true sensuality, moving her down from the pedestal of holiness. Using verbal and narratorial ambiguity, however, he has also suggested that in falling as 'deity' she actually rises as woman, gaining the sensual pleasure she craves, while retaining her mental superiority and spiritual façade. The audience for whom Burns wrote such verses could appreciate both sides of this comic coin.

'The Case of Conscience' presents a rather similar duality. Once again we have a religious woman with strong sexual longings, who gives way with little difficulty. The major difference is that her seducer is not a bold blade but the very preacher whose spiritual consolation she seeks. It is as if we were seeing worked out in some detail the implications behind stanzas 7 and 8 of 'Holy Willie's Prayer'. There can be no doubt that on one level the 'priest' in particular is powerfully satirized. He carefully disguises his lustful intent in Christian terms. He shows quite blatantly the usual Antinomian hatred towards those rejected by God:

> Were ye o' the Reprobate race
> Created to sin and be brunt. . . .   (I, 497)

He moves from the heights of the theological high style to the depths of colloquialism in a fashion which parodies the prevalent techniques of eighteenth-century auld-licht preaching and he does take advantage of an old woman of obviously lower intelligence.

Yet I would uphold that the bawdy context of this poem and in particular the audience for whom it was intended, guaranteed that this latter day Holy Willie should not be so consistently vilified as his predecessor. In fact we are encouraged at times to laugh with him as he manipulates, with a skill reminiscent of Tartuffe, the materials of religion in order to gain the ends of the flesh. He manages to convince the old woman of the ludicrous sophistry that her promiscuity is in fact a sign of purity:

> It's naught but Beelzebub's art,
> But that's the mair sign of a saunt,
> He kens that ye're pure at the heart,
> Sae levels his darts at your ──. ──   (I, 497)

He uses the Calvinist belief in faith's superiority to works and the Antinomian tenet of predestination to prove that innocence and promiscuity can co-exist for her and, by implication, for him. His wit and sexual desire reach their diverse climaxes in his explication of copulation as a means of renewing the Covenant:

> And now with a sanctify'd kiss
> Let's kneel and renew convenant:
> It's this—and it's this—and it's this—
> That settles the pride o' your ──. ──   (I, 498)

The ironies involved in this conclusion are as obvious as they have been carefully prepared for. The woman, anticipating spiritual consolation for promiscuity gets further physical proof of it, but one which claims to cure the 'pride' of her offending member. She comes for the sort of satisfaction which one associates with the confessional but comes away with an entirely different type, which satisfies her even more.

Much bitter satire is levelled against this lascivious 'priest' but it is lessened, not only through the narrator's constant focus on his Machiavellian skill but also through the characterization of the woman with whom he is dealing. In a way, she represents an ideal in Burnsian bawdry—more than sixty years old, inhibited by Calvinism, she is still unable to resist that one passion which was honoured by all the Crochallan Fencibles. In her naïvety and religious gullibility she too becomes a comic butt within the poem, yet her sensuality is throughout treated with good-humoured sympathy.

And what is the conclusion? The 'priest' proves a good lover; she goes home rejoicing and the narrator asks his listeners to charge their glasses both to her and to those who rejoice in the sexual act:

> Then high to her memory charge;
> And may he who takes it affront,
> Still ride in Love's channel at large,
> And never make port in a—!!!   (I, 498)

Thus, a study of Burns's religious bawdry uncovers the same range of comic techniques; the same ability to draw ludicrous portraits of extreme Calvinism; the same sensitivity to double-entendres and verbal detail, which are found elsewhere in his satires. Yet these poems are designed for a more private audience and seek to glorify sex above all. The clearcut contrasts between an accepted theological or moral ideal and the comic falling away from it, which lie at the centre of his 'respectable' Kirk satires are blurred in the bawdry, dealing with similar themes. The methods used to achieve this include greater ambiguity of narratorial stance; careful attention to characterization and conclusions which tend to undercut any firm moral standpoint towards which the reader may have been working. In these ways Burns guarantees that his cronies may gain mirth from all aspects of the 'puritanical' situation.

Before examining the third type of Burns's religious bawdry, one should remember that, in one of his letters to Clarinda, the poet had protested:

If you have, on some suspicious evidence, from some lying oracle, learnt that I despise or ridicule so sacredly important a matter as real Religion, you have, my Clarinda, much misconstrued your friend. (I, 153)

Admittedly his letters to this source are not always free from exaggeration or posturizing. Yet, the evidence even of his most indecent religious verse does not wholly controvert this remark. True, he could be a bitter enemy to 'false friends' of Christianity, yet there was always a need within him to find comfort in the loving doctrine of that Bible in which he was so deeply versed.

As a result, even in his 'respectable' work he delighted in finding Biblical examples of heroes, writers and prophets who had shown leanings towards promiscuity. Only too well aware of the Biblical attitude to adultery he took comfort in the thought that Jacob, Solomon, David and others had achieved a laudable place in the overall divine scheme, while scarcely remaining chaste or faithful. Two of his bawdy songs, 'The Bonniest Lass' and 'The Patriarch', carry this line of thought to its poetic extreme.

Kinsley is uninclined to attribute 'The Bonniest Lass' to Burns and its omission from early editions of *The Merry Muses* is indeed a major problem. But there are so many details, such as the 'a' that' refrain, the use of particular phrases such as 'mim-mou'd' or 'clever chiel' and the reducing of Biblical figures to the level of lustful humanity, all of which appear elsewhere in Burnsian originals, that I am inclined to disagree in this instance.[16] King David's love for women had been a source of poetic comfort for Burns in 'What ails ye now?' Here it becomes grounds for superiority. The warm-hearted narrator openly castigates the Biblical character for not accepting when desire has outdone performance. He extends his sympathy instead to those young girls brought to the bed of a monarch able to arouse their passion but not satisfy it:

> Wha wadna pity thae sweet dames
> He fumbled at, an' a' that,
> An' raised their bluid up into flames
> He couldna drown, for a' that.[17]

Even more interestingly, he focuses on King Solomon whom he had designated his 'favourite author' in his letters.[18] Solomon

113

was an ideal figure for Burns to identify with—a man of accepted holiness, of exceptional literary ability, whose life and writings bore open witness to sexual vulnerability. I, therefore, see stanza 9 of 'The Bonniest Lass' as at once a yoking of that King into the body of bawdry and a rather more serious attempt to justify, through divine associations, the poet's similar outpourings:

> For a' that an a' that,
> Tho' a preacher wise an' a' that,
> The smuttiest sang that e'er was sung
> His Sang o' Sangs is a' that.   (Barke and Smith, p. 9)

The technique here employed of placing hallowed figures within a context of realism and sexuality produces a necessarily comic effect through incongruity. It is even more powerfully handled in 'The Patriarch', where the story of Jacob as told in *Genesis* XXIX–XXX becomes the basis for a hilariously imagined bedroom conflict between the Jewish leader and his wife.[19] The very first stanza brings us face to face with an entirely new Jacob. Gone is the exalted leader and in his place we see a husband attempting in inadequate and perfunctory fashion to satisfy his wife:

> As honest Jacob on a night,
> Wi' his beloved beauty,
> Was duly laid on wedlock's bed,
> And noddin' at his duty.   (II, 899)

It should be noted that the comic force of this stanza does not reside solely in the conflict between exalted personage and sexual circumstance.[20] Within that framework Burns adds delightful contrasts between the idealism of 'beloved beauty' and Jacob's obvious disinterest in that beauty; between the normal sexual initiative of the male and the implied passivity of 'duly laid'. This sets the standard for a song, which deserves to rank as one of Burns's finest farcical works.

The central contrast is underlined in many ways; first of all simply by making both Jacob and Rachel speak in the foulest of language:

> 'How lang, she says, ye fumblin' wretch,
> 'Will ye be f—————g at it?'   (II, 899)

114

or by using the flyting of one to visualize the other in a ludicrous and bestial light:

> 'Ye pegh, and grane, and groazle there,
> 'And make an unco' splutter.' (II, 899)

More subtly, Burns may juxtapose the language of bawdry with specifically Biblical imagery:

> Then Rachel calm, as ony lamb,
> She claps him on the waulies, (II, 899)

or set the admission of Christian 'debt' within the context of a 'mow'.

The tale is also full of ironic reversals. Jacob, from his initial position of weakness turns the tables on his wife. Nor does he achieve this by pleading faithfulness and age in reply to her jibes. Instead he details the extent of his sexual activities:

> 'I've bairn'd the servant gypsies baith,
> 'Forbye your titty Leah.' (II, 899)

Having thus established his potency he protests that for every 'mow' each of them has received, she has got 'a dizzen'. In terms of Christian morality, one might have expected this argument to have led Rachel into a diatribe on adultery.[21] In fact she reacts with the appreciation usually shown by women in Burns's bawdry for men of proven sexual power. As readers, we bring into the poem Christian expectation encouraged by the Biblical topic. At every turn Burns allows his characters comically to frustrate these expectations through reacting as sensual, imperfect individuals rather than holy caricatures.

Finally, as in 'Godly Girzie', he permits his creations to have their own sense of humour. Particularly fine is Rachel's justification of her barrenness in terms of the time it takes her spouse to become sexually active:

> 'My eldest wean might die of age,
> 'Before that ye could get it.' (II, 899)

At no time in this poem does Burns contravene the evidence of the Bible. Jacob was linked to Leah; he did lie with Bilhah and Zilpah and their fertility did highlight the barrenness of Rachel, whom he loved most (Genesis, XXIX, 30). Indeed, the strength of Burns's poem in part derives from the accuracy of its Biblical base and from the way in which he develops the sexual implications of his text. But he also manages, finally, to suggest a highly imaginative, bawdy reason for the conception of Joseph. Comforted by his wife's forgiveness, Jacob

> . . . soon forgat his ire;
> The Patriarch, he coost the sark,
> And up and till't like fire!!!   (II, 900)

The most basic passions are, thus, by implication drawn into the highest scheme of all.

I therefore believe that a study of Burns's religious bawdry is necessary on three major grounds. It opens up a further area of Burnsian satire and confirms the already overwhelming evidence of his varied talents in that mode. Yet it also highlights the fact that the 'bawdy' Burns wrote for a different audience than the 'respectable' Burns (if so simplistic a distinction may be permitted) and that the humorous techniques, the characterization and, above all, the poet's moral and theological position are consequently affected. Finally, the dual vision, obvious in so many of these works, gives the clearest possible literary expression of that conflict between spirituality and sensuality, Calvinism and promiscuity which accounts for so much that is glorious in his writings yet proved traumatic in his personal life.

4

A second division of Burns's original bawdry, much smaller but equally worthy of serious attention, comprises his parodies. Generally, these are skilful examples of 'obscenity used ironically for purposes of literary criticism',[22] but sometimes they also employ the chosen mode to intensify humour directed against a central character.

The most obvious example is the 'Ode to Spring'. A mock-pastoral, it was sent to Thomson in January 1795, accompanied by a letter in which Burns sets out his aims clearly. A friend had challenged him to write 'originally' on this traditional topic. Burns accepted and

> . . . pledged myself to bring in the verdant fields,—the budding flowers,—the chrystal streams,—the melody of the groves,—& a love-story into the bargain, & yet be original. (II, 283)

116

Sidney Goodsir Smith, whose critical opinion is to be respected, dismisses the resultant product as 'too obviously written to order, the Muse is not in it.'[23] One can see why he came to this conclusion. The rigid demands of the challenge do involve a somewhat analytical movement through the characteristics of the pastoral. One can almost see Burns ticking off in turn the '*locus amoenus*', the mythological apparatus, the traditional pastoral lovers and so forth. Yet, in a sense this is the essence of parody, that it clinically exaggerates the features of any given mode, while, as here, introducing wholly incongruous elements.

The 'Ode to Spring' is no masterpiece but it is a fairly successful 'jeu d'esprit'. In a variety of ways bawdry invades the idealized pastoral grove. The first couplet sets the scene in more ways than one:

> When maukin bucks at early f———s,
> In dewy glens are seen, Sir.   (II, 761)

Thus one word undercuts the traditional presentation of natural setting, animal innocence and the fertility of spring. In this opening stanza the poet moves from animal life to bird life to the creatures of myth, in conventional fashion. But instead of an indirect presentation of love as the governing natural power, we are told that the birds 'm—w' and Apollo is anxious to 'r—ger' Thetis.

This is not the only source of humour. Burns mercilessly parodies the introduction of mythological apparatus by introducing it at every excuse and in the most high-sounding fashion possible. We do not have Apollo but 'Latona's sun', accompanied by *Dame* Nature and *Madame* Thetis. This extreme presentation of mythological figures serves to highlight the comedy of incongruity when regularly set against the language of obscenity, but it also serves as a wry comment on writers in the decadent pastoral tradition, who used such excesses quite seriously. Their love of complex rhymes is also effectively parodied, when Dame Nature is provided with an 'impètus', presumably solely to find a rhyme fit to match that great enemy of all rhymesters, 'Madame Thetis'.

If the first stanza announced its parodic intent at once, the second works on a different comic principle. Until the very last line, despite its conventional drawing in of all the necessary springtime details (hills, flowers, Damon and Sylvia), it could be taken for a genuine, if insipid, piece of pastoral verse. But that last line with its sudden drop from pastoral innocence to sexual endeavour wholly redefines the idealized definition of harmony encouraged until then:

> The wild-birds sang, the echoes rang,
> While Damon's a—se beat time, Sir.   (II, 761)

This allows Burns in the third stanza, while continuing the natural thematic progression of his poem, to indulge in sexual double-entendres throughout:

> First, wi' the thrush, his thrust and push,
> Had compass large and long, Sir;
> The blackbird next, his tuneful text,
> Was bolder, clear and strong, Sir;
> The linnet's lay came then in play,
> And the lark that soar'd aboon, Sir;
> Till Damon, fierce, mistim'd his a——,
> And f——'d quite out o' tune, Sir.   (II, 762)

Beyond the ingenious use of words and phrases capable of applying both to musical and sexual harmony, two further points are worthy of comment. Burns sets one level against the other. What is musically the complement of four-part harmony, is sexually a competitive proof of potency. This permits the poet to present in the last couplet a hilariously novel interpretation of the age-old theme of man standing outside the natural order, while implicitly questioning whether that order exists other than in his own idealizing imagination.

I am not making excessive claims for the poetic merit of this song but I do oppose Goodsir Smith on three grounds. The clinical approach which he condemns is a necessary part of the poem's parodic effectiveness. Further, Burns as a parodist manages to make both obvious and subtle critical comments on the pastoral form, its literary techniques and the philosophy underlying it. Finally, he achieves within the space of three stanzas a wide variety of comic effects. The work is more complex than might at first appear and the 'muse' certainly not absent.

Although Burns did compose other pieces of bawdry such as 'Libel Summons' ('The Court of Equity') and 'Act Sederunt of the Session', which parodied the language or conduct of particular groups in society, setting them within an obscene context, his finest full parody of a literary mode is 'Grim Grizzle', a twenty-stanza poem in ballad form, celebrating the inevitable downfall of a proud landowner, who wished her cows to defecate to order. As Kinsley points out, this theme survives today in many a rural joke,[24] but Burns in an appended note to the text in the Rosebery MS would have us believe that the immediate inspiration for his version was an epitaph he stumbled on in the ruins of Dunblane Abbey:

> Here lyes with Dethe auld Grizzel Grimme
> Lincluden's ugly witche.
> O Dethe, an' what a taste hast thou
> Can lye with siche a bitche![25]

And while one may well suspect that both occasion and epitaph came from the poet's invention, such damning epitaphs can still be found in Scottish kirkyards.

Of course, Burns did use the ballad form for a variety of topics, some verging on bawdry. But only in 'Grim Grizzle' do we have a low theme linked to an exaggerated use of all the rhetorical techniques of heroic balladry. In accordance with this tradition both Grizzle and her herdsman are given formulaic titles. She is regularly referred to as 'a mighty Dame', while he is always 'John o' Clods'. Their confrontation over cowshit is also characterized by the frequent use of heroic formulae, including 'O' meikle fame and pride' and the celebrated threat 'Now wae betide thee.'

It is true that the main function of such literary apparatus is to render Grizzle herself more ludicrous by contrast but the parody of the ballad is throughout maintained.[26] Burns rejoices in introducing all the well-worn stylistic characteristics of the mode. There are the repeated phrases:

> And she has ca'd on John o' Clods,
>   Of her herdsmen the chief,
> And she has ca'd on John o' Clods,
>   And tell'd him a' her grief: (II, 819)

syntactic repetitions with variation: 'Ye claut my byre, ye sweep my byre' (II, 819); reinforcements: 'But she had skill, and meikle skill' (II, 818); and parenthetic stop-gap phrases: 'As she was wont to do.' The list could be continued but if anyone still doubts whether part of the poet's intention was to highlight, through exaggeration, the mechanical nature of balladry which relied excessively on such techniques then he need only read those two wonderful stanzas, where John o' Clods, like the warrior leaders of old prepares to launch on his verbal defence:

> Then John o' Clods he lookèd up
>   And syne he lookèd down;
> He lookèd east, he lookèd west,
>   He lookèd roun' and roun'.
>
> His bonnet and his rowantree club
>   Frae either hand did fa';
> Wi' lifted een and open mouth
>   He naething said at a'.   (II, 819)

To give a description built up from carefully observed details was of course the conventional way of introducing a moment like this in balladry. But to check every possible direction of vision; note things falling not from one hand but two; to lift the eye and open the mouth only to end with the anticlimax of nothing issuing from the latter must be parodic.

It is, however, somewhat artificial to separate this parodying of the ballad form from the humorous way in which Burns destroys Grizzle herself. In the first four stanzas the ballad techniques are used to raise her on to a pedestal of pride and power. Yet, even at this stage, little touches suggest that she is not really so noble or mighty as is being claimed. After all, is it desirable for a lady of the nobility to be 'loudest' in the hall? And when she is striding unharmed through scenes, where 'Beauty durst na gang', is it bravery or ugliness which is her major protection? It is, perhaps, characteristic of the subtly ironic tone of this opening movement that it ends with a couplet, which in overtly seeking to extend her domains actually cuts her down to size:

> But she had skill, and meikle skill,
>   In barn and eke in byre.   (II, 818)

From now on the rhetorical trappings of heroic balladry ludicrously contrast with the figure of this domineering small landowner, whose avariciousness, smallmindedness and vindictiveness are first revealed in her own prolonged complaint to the herdsman. She falls further when her absurd notions and flyting tone are unfavourably contrasted with his commonsense and quiet dignity:

> 'Your kye will at nae bidding sh——,
>   Let me do what I can;
> Your kye will at nae bidding sh——
>   Of onie earthly man.   (II, 820)

Finally, she sinks into farcical impotence, as she disappears from the poem manipulating the cow's tail like a pump, while vainly screeching 'Sh——, sh——, ye bitch'. The narrator then adds the final poignant touch by indicating that her roars reach Lincluden Abbey. In so doing, he reminds us of that power, which alone determines such things.

The success of the poem lies first in the linking of literary parody to the humorous presentation of a central character's fall from pride. Yet, the work is also very carefully structured. One moves from the narratorial introduction effortlessly into Grizzle's flyting; from John's brave reply (winning its way out of silence through hesitation into defiance) to the beautifully visualized dénouement. During each of these different stages, the tension between low theme and the higher associations conjured up by the form and the rhetorical patterns is differently handled but always effectively and sometimes in a manner which introduces subtle ironies.

5

Having now considered Burns's expurgations and adaptations of particular folk songs as well as two groups of his own original verse, I should like to end this study on a more general note. If we look at those bawdy songs and poems, which most editors accept to be Burnsian originals or to contain substantial passages by the poet, it becomes clear that they do fit into the general pattern of eighteenth-century Scottish folk bawdry. Yet within that tradition, Burns does show a consistent prefer-ence for particular themes and approaches, while obviously relishing the poetic challenges posed. This is obviously a large topic and I can only scratch the surface but the attempt seems worthwhile, especially when research in the area is so limited.

Inevitably eighteenth-century folk bawdry, as preserved in *The Merry Muses* and elsewhere, focused on sensual rather than chaste womanhood. Burns, however, chose to celebrate two types of heroine in particular—either the sexually voracious woman, who longs for the passion as fiercely as any male, or the vulnerable girl, who cannot say 'No' but remains in need of her seducer's protection. The redoubtable Muirland Meg clearly belongs to the first class:

> Love's her delight, and kissin's her treasure;
> She'll stick at nae price, an' ye gie her good measure.
> As lang's a sheep-fit, and as girt's a goose-egg,
> And that's the measure o' Muirland Meg.   (II, 898)

So is the heroine of 'The Trogger', who despite her token refusal obviously rejoices in the pedlar's sexual forwardness and afterwards appreciates first the beer and then the memories of their casual encounter.

This poem is told, using a female *persona* and some critics, notably Randall and Legman, have stressed that, proportionally, Burns used this technique more frequently than is usual in Scottish folk bawdry. That is true, but it is fallacious to argue from this to a deeper involvement with the female predicament. Burns in his erotic verse is writing for an audience of men and the vision of women he presents is essentially a masculine vision, usually presenting them as sexual objects, mirrors of his own longings or a means of bolstering the male ego. In 'Muirland Meg' and 'The Trogger' we see Burns's own fierce sex drive translated into female terms.

In both 'Here's his health in water' and 'The Rantin' Dog the Daddie o't', we have the other type of heroine. But as Burns allows the two girls to lament their state of pregnancy and the social trials they are having to endure, he also indirectly celebrates the man's potency and charm, factors which result in their still adoring him. He therefore uses their lament indirectly to glorify man's power over woman. In the second instance, the identity of the male lover is in no doubt:

122

> When I mount the Creepie-chair,
> Wha will sit beside me there,
> Gie me Rob, I'll seek nae mair,
> The rantin dog the Daddie o't.[27]   (I, 184)

And when he is not indirectly glorifying his own sexual prowess through the voice of his conquests, he may suggest it through the occupations or activities he bestows upon his heroes—the bard in 'The Jolly Beggars', 'The Jolly Gauger', 'The Ploughman' and (possibly) the freemason in 'A Masonic Song'.[28]

If Burns's presentation of women in his erotic verse is at once traditional and personal, so is his attitude to sex generally. One notices, for example, the frequency with which he relates it to social divisions of one sort or another. This again was a common folk theme but Burns looks at the problems in rather more detail. Thus, sex may be seen as the obliterator of all class distinctions:

> Amang the broom he laid her; amang the broom sae green,
> And he's fa'n to the beggar, as she had been a queen.
>   (II, 902)

or even humorously invert the usual hierarchy in some situations. We are told that 'nine inch will please a lady',

> But for a koontrie c−nt like mine,
> In sooth, we're nae sae gentle;
> We'll tak tway thumb-bread to the nine,
> And that's a sonsy p−ntle.   (I, 457)

Yet, in other more poignant verses, such as 'Wha'll m−w me now', he suggests that promiscuity is still easier for the lady than the peasant lass:

> Now I maun thole the scornfu' sneer
>   O' mony a saucy quine;
> When, curse upon her godly face!
>   Her c−−t's as merry's mine.   (II, 903)

Such melancholy touches are few, however, in a selection of bawdry, which generally banishes serious considerations and regularly proclaims sex as the unifier of all factions. It is a pastime which, though it may be the sole consolation of the poor, proves much more enjoyable and less wasteful than the more celebrated activities of kings, princes and politicians:

> When Br—nsw—ck's great Prince cam a cruising to Fr-nce
> Republican billies to cowe,
> Bauld Br——nsw—c's great prince wad hae shawn better sense,
> At hame with his Princess to mowe. (II, 668)[29]

In the comparative seriousness of literary analysis, we should not forget that Burns's bawdry is, above all, a joyful praising of the animal side to human nature. He probes the place of sex in society and politics but generally the viewpoint is that of sexual optimism rather than philosophical profundity. There is a time and a place for more sober considerations of bastardy and republicanism but not in this mode, not for this audience, not now.

Finally, one must remember that all successful bawdry must, by definition, be imagistically ingenious. To avoid literary boredom, the act round which most of it centres has to be poetically transmitted via a variety of metaphors. Burns found many of these to hand in the folk poetry which he collected and his own erotic verse relied on striking imagery for its effect much more than does his more respectable work. At times he seems to rejoice in finding as many diverse ways of presenting the act as possible. In 'Brose and Butter' the penis is compared variously to a gardener's dibble, a mouse, a mole and a rolling pin, while the vagina is likened to the pouch which holds the dirk.[29] Sometimes, however, as in the 'Act Sederunt of the Session', there is a controlling theme into which the sexual associations have to fit. In this case the context is legal and the humour centres on standing penes being found guilty of high transgression. Burns, therefore, uses an image which at once suggests legal punishment and sexual satisfaction:

> And they've provided dungeons deep,
> Ilk lass has ane in her possession;
> Until the wretches wail and weep,
> They there shall lie for their transgressioun. (II, 719)

The evidence provided by the non-bawdy writings of Burns suggests a genius more readily given to rhetorical than imagistic ingenuity, as Carlyle had remarked. It is only in his bawdy verse that one regularly discovers this sort of 'metaphysical' daring, and the poet seems to have enjoyed the challenge. Certainly, he takes care that the imagery he employs is consistent with the *persona* chosen to carry out the seduction. Thus, in 'Wha'll m−w me now', the soldier's testicles become 'bandileers' (cases holding musket charges), while his cooper copulates as if he were hooping a barrel:

> The Couper o' Cuddy cam here awa,
>   He ca'd the girrs out o'er us a';   (II, 848)

Occasionally, as in 'Wha is that at my bower-door', the key image is carried throughout. Bower, door, gate, rising and entry all refer on surface level to the lover's apparently innocent desire to come into his lady's house. But each and every reference is to sexual entry:

> In my bower if ye should stay,
>   Let me stay, quo' Findlay;
> I fear ye'll bide till break o' day;
>   Indeed will I, quo' Findlay.—   (II, 617)

I would suggest to those readers who admire poetry which metaphorically yokes together apparently irreconcilable elements through metaphor and who have found Burns wanting in this respect, that they turn to his bawdy verse. But they should do this, aware that many of these images, however striking, already had a wide currency in Scottish folk bawdry. Nonetheless, Burns's erotic verse once more introduces us to an artist with a wider poetic range than that ascribed to him by many critics.

NOTES

1. All quotations from the *Letters* are from the DeLancey Ferguson edition, 2 vols. (Oxford, 1931).
2. The 1800 Rosebery edition. A photostat exists in the National Library of Scotland.
3. David Daiches, *Robert Burns* (London, 1958), p. 311.
4. Maurice Lindsay, *Robert Burns* (London, 1954), p. 252.
5. R. T. Fitzhugh, *Robert Burns: The Man and the Poet* (Chapel Hill, 1943), p. 333.

6. See Daiches, op. cit., p. 311; J. Kinsley, 'Burns and the Merry Muses', *Renaissance and Modern Studies*, IX (1965), pp. 5–6.

7. *The Poems and Songs of Robert Burns*, ed. James Kinsley, 3 vols. (Oxford, 1968); *The Merry Muses of Caledonia*, ed. G. Legman (New York, 1965). These texts are used throughout.

8. Sidney Goodsir Smith, 'Robert Burns and *The Merry Muses of Caledonia*', *Hudson Review*, 7 (1954–55), 346.

9. Kinsley, *Poems*, III, p. 1511.

10. *Golden Treasury of Scottish Poetry*, ed. Hugh MacDiarmid (London, 1946), p. xxxvii.

11. See *Letters*, II, p. 129; *Robert Burns's Commonplace Book 1783–85*, ed. J. C. Ewing and D. Cook (London, 1965), p. 37.

12. See Legman, op. cit., pp. 28, 29. He comments (p. 159) that, 'the "Older Edition" of the *Merry Muses* is in all probability the real folk-song.'

13. 'Walkers' = bawdy songs. See Legman, op. cit., p. xxvii.

14. Goodsir Smith, op. cit., p. 333.

15. Cited in *The Merry Muses of Caledonia*, ed. J. Barke and S. Goodsir Smith (London, 1970), p. 39.

16. But see Kinsley, *Poems*, III, p. 1522.

17. Barke and Smith, op. cit., p. 91.

18. See Letters No. 191 and 125.

19. For further background, see Legman, op. cit., pp. 147–50.

20. See Daiches, op. cit., p. 315.

21. These events did take place before the commandments. Jacob was also married to Leah, while he went to the handmaids at the wish of Rachel.

22. Daiches, op. cit., p. 313.

23. Goodsir Smith, op. cit., p. 347.

24. Kinsley, *Poems*, III, p. 1493.

25. *The Poetry of Robert Burns*, ed. W. E. Henley and T. F. Henderson, 4 vols. (Edinburgh, 1896), II, p. 459.

26. Kinsley, *Poems*, III, p. 1493, refers to it as 'The parody of the ballad. . . .'

27. It is possible that 'Here's his health in water' also refers to one of Burns's bastards with Jean Armour being the mother in this case.

28. Kinsley is most unwilling to accept that Burns had any hand in the composition of 'A Masonic Song'.

29. Legman regrets (pp. xiii–xiv) that in this poem ('Why should na poor folk mowe') Burns appears to be forsaking his earlier Republican sympathies. In part this is true. He did grow less enthusiastic as the Revolution took its course, as did many others. But he is also writing bawdry and in bawdry, sex, not politics, reigns supreme. Anyway, the only stanza which really compromises Republican principles is that in which the health of King George and Queen Charlotte is proposed. Interestingly, it is omitted from *The Merry Muses'* version.

6

Robert Burns: The Image and the Verse-epistles

by G. SCOTT WILSON

'From the deserts of Sudan,
From Japan to Yucatan. . . .'

So sings a modern British singer to indicate, albeit allusively,
the universal range of the sexual impulse, but such a popular
and panoramic vista might equally apply to the fame of Robert
Burns.

Exiled Scots have made his name, if not his poetry, famous
world-wide. In honour (?) of Robert Burns, a haggis wilts in
the steaming heat of Lagos or, like a small, wet boulder,
glistens in the beery conviviality of Canadian 'rumpus rooms'.
Robert Burns, 'Caledonia's bard', is now as universally recognizable an image as Muhammad Ali.

Softened by the cosmetic erosion of commerce, Burns's
features loom out at us from shiny tins of shortbread, bottles of
whisky, even from packets of Edinburgh 'rock'. They appear
on anything, indeed, that will profit from being marketed as
Scots, Scottish, Scotch, or 'frae Bonnie Scotland', the variety
of adjectival forms eloquently testifying to commercial vague-
ness about the 'Scotland' which Burns so omnipresently
endorses.

However, Burns is not just an inspired commercial creation,
although his importance in this respect is considerable.[1] He is

most profitably seen as a great figure of Scottish popular culture, equivalent in his totemic potency for Scots to Muhammad Ali for blacks in America and elsewhere. To regard Burns as 'just a poet' is to see Ali as a mere fighter, which he never was. A visible embodiment of Black Power, a threat to W.A.S.P. culture by his 'uppity' behaviour, he carried the hopes and aspirations of many blacks who were to see, in his treatment by the American draft authorities, the inevitable fate of one who maintained too high a profile; it confirmed their expectations of white American society.

Burns has served a similar purpose in Scotland. As an integral part of Scottish popular culture, Burns has been used and abused by Scotsmen of all historical periods since his first leap to fame in 1786–87. Whole generations of Scots have re-made him in their own sentimental, or political, or nostalgic image. Scotsmen have used Burns as a charm, as an icon to be cherished and proudly displayed. Around Burns has been built a myth that would appear to minister to some need in the Scottish popular psyche, for, at various periods, it has provided solace in times of personal and national despondency, acted as a commercial shorthand for all Scotland, and has been an emotional crutch in much the same way as Elvis Presley was created through and accepted by the Official Elvis Fan Club. That officially approved image was, and remains, preferred to the true, or 'unofficial' man whose rather sordid and all too fallible reality, if known, would have robbed a generation of its willing self-delusions.

In what follows, my concern will be with the 'image' of Robert Burns. Although the vicissitudes of Burns's image throughout Scots history is a fascinating topic—from the appropriation of him by an enfeebled literary establishment in Edinburgh to bolster that city's status as the equal of England in producing prodigies and curiosities, social and literary; through his nineteenth-century incarnation as one who offers succour to the most lamentable clutch of poetasters Scotland has ever produced; through his role, in MacDiarmid's eyes, of alluring Siren who led Scots poetry down the primrose path to effeteness; to the present where snatches of his songs and mistaken notions of his typical behaviour are to be heard and seen during the Scottish football fans' invasion of London, or, alternatively, where worthy small-town burghers celebrate his birthday as a cautionary tale of country boy ruined by urban sophistication, but finding ultimate happiness in the arms of his wife—the *Sunday Post/Daily Record* version, this. Although, as I say, these changes of image are fascinating, I do not intend to make them the subject of this essay.

Rather, I propose to examine Burns's conscious creation for himself of an 'image'—that is to say, a view of himself sustained through such means as dress, action within social groups, controlled selection and release of autobiographical 'information', choice of literary associates, etc. His reasons for fashioning these 'images' I shall examine as the need arises but, essentially, I shall argue that they were twofold—financial, and psychological. Such a way of looking at Burns's life is novel, I believe, and requires a degree of speculative imagination. However, I have chosen to examine Burns in this manner because of the insights it can provide and because there is sufficient 'hard' evidence in the form of letters, action and facts to justify an approach which sees him as a social and literary performer in the same tradition as the popular celebrities of our own age.

Two things remain to be said about Burns and his image-building. Firstly, that he was not the first to do so. Pope is an obvious earlier example, as are Johnson and Boswell, of men who used their position within society, and the promptings of their personality and taste to create, for public consumption, 'images' of themselves that served a purpose other than mere self-expression. Nor was Burns the last literary figure to realize the benefits, psychological, social, and financial, that could accrue through the careful presentation and exaggeration of elements of one's own personality; one can readily think of Byron, Wilde, Hemingway, and many others. Secondly, the fact that one of Burns's main reasons for the creation of his 'image' was financial should not be regarded, I believe, as a reason for censure. Burns's prime purpose in publishing the Edinburgh edition in 1787 (and it is with this edition that most of his image-building was concerned) was financial, but desire for money need not invalidate artistic creativity. Money becomes a corrupting factor when those who provide the money are no longer satisfied with the created artefact in isolation, but require the 'presenter' to accommodate himself to their standards of behaviour, or when they perceive an excessive discrepancy between the presenter and the significance of what it is he presents. Burns encountered this crisis in Edinburgh (and Dumfries) where the poetry required to maintain there an image created by other means was alien to his creative talent or, at least, did not permit him to develop a satisfying self-image by means of that poetry, as he had been able to do in Ayrshire.

Burns's making of an image for himself would not merit inclusion in a collection of predominantly literary essays were it not for the way in which he used poetry, and, unsurpassedly, the verse-epistle as the means of creating, at a crucial point in his development as man and poet, a richly symbolic 'image'. That technique produced poetry of a very high order and I propose to examine the verse-epistle as Burns's image-building technique in the second part of this study. Before that, I shall examine the non-poetic means which Burns employed, and I shall turn first to the 'autobiographical' letter to Dr. John Moore.

Repeatedly, in his prose letters, Burns quite confidently expresses his self-knowledge:

> I have long studied myself, and I think I know pretty exactly what ground I occupy, both as a Man and a Poet; and however the world, or a friend, may sometimes differ from me in that particular, I stand for it, in silent resolve, with all the tenaciousness of Property. (I, 59)

He has looked at himself calculatingly and, as a mature adult, knows himself; he has taken stock of himself, and has not found himself wanting. A similarly calculating self-awareness is evident in the letter to Moore, far too long to quote, but an essential document for the understanding of Burns's technique of image-building. In that letter, Burns abandons a straightforwardly chronological account of his life, choosing instead to present the 'facts' in an emotionally telling order; he falsifies and dramatizes his account of the publication of the Kilmarnock edition and its effect on his decision to remain in Scotland; knowing Moore's interest in the social customs of less civilized societies (as expressed in his 'View of Society and Manners in France, Switzerland, and Germany' (1779) where he writes patronizingly of the poor), Burns gives realistic and 'sentimental'[3] detail of the life of a tenant-farmer; he produces deliberately showy writing which takes a cliché, 'The only two doors by which I could enter the fields of fortune' (I, 109), and elaborates it with an enthusiasm that owes more to contrivance than to any sense of what is witty or idiomatic—the 'door' becomes a 'contracted' 'aperture' and, then, a 'contaminated' 'threshold'; and, finally, he lays a pungent trail of literary influences from 'tales . . . concerning devils . . . witches . . . spunkies . . .' to Addison, Locke and Sterne. All this reeks of conscious image-building and is done with a desire to please that is reminiscent of an underwriter stuffing a rights issue prospectus with all the attractions that will tempt a canny investor in a remote country. Such self-presentation goes beyond mere wishing to make a good impression.

The letter to Dr. Moore shows a man who is creating himself anew for consumption by a literary audience whose desires and taste he has quickly assimilated and judged. Burns was quick to realize that he could succeed by giving prominence to his host nation's or culture's preconceived view of the Scots character and personality.

A similar image-making process can be seen at work in such letters as those Burns sent home from Edinburgh to Gavin Hamilton and other Ayrshire notables whose good opinion Burns had won and whose friendship, especially that of Hamilton, was financially and socially important to him. Although one cannot 'prove' the argument, the parallel between Burns and the early Ali is irresistible. The latter was originally bankrolled by local white businessmen who saw him as a means to a fast buck or, more generously, as a valuable Public Relations exercise which would demonstrate just how liberal the 'good ole boys' of the South could really be. The tone of Burns's letters to Hamilton, Ballantine, Robert Muir, Aiken and the Earl of Eglinton, written in late 1786/early 1787, suggest a similar proprietary relationship, with Burns aware of the need to present an image of grateful recipient to his generous patrons. In these letters, Burns is assuring them he had not let the side down, had committed no horrible gaffes, had repaid their 'investment' and, by his success in the capital, had confirmed their wit, their taste in spotting so early one destined for greatness, and, by implication, *their* claim to the attention of the 'high heid yins' in the capital.

Of Burns's many backers, the most fascinating in terms of their mutual relationship is Gavin Hamilton. Although Burns cannot be fairly called a kept man, there is evident in the correspondence between the two a desire to please, on Burns's part, that goes beyond the ordinary.[4] This is even more noticeable in his poetry where, at times, Burns writes as if he were apologist for Hamilton. Certainly, it must be admitted that the relationship between Burns and Hamilton was beneficial to both. Burns obtained legal advice, patronage, and the introduction to a wider circle of influential acquaintances. In return, Hamilton, as part of his long-running battle with a local church authority of wide-ranging powers, could attack that institution without direct implication through his highly skilled and indebted protégé, Burns the poet.

If, from afar, Burns could present an uncomplicated image of gratitude and local patriotism to his Ayrshire backers, the task of creating an image to suit Edinburgh society was not so simple. Burns knew that the presentation of himself to Edinburgh society required delicate balance. On the one hand, the earthy independence and uprightness to be expected of one who had had no more civilizing influence than rude nature itself, yet, on the other hand, gratitude at having been selected for the full treatment by an Edinburgh thirsting for celebrities and stimulated by curiosity. One could cite the several contemporary accounts of the impression of manly independence that Burns made on the ladies and gentlemen of the Edinburgh salons, but that would not *prove* Burns's *choice* of this image. More telling, as proof, is the prefatory portrait to the 1787 Edinburgh edition. This was a costly extra to Burns in what was already a dangerously speculative venture, but it was one which would sell his book by providing visual confirmation of the statements by which that literary pandar, Henry Mackenzie, had chosen to introduce their latest thrill to an Edinburgh audience of played-out *literati*, and jaded ladies. The Beugo engraving of Nasmyth's painting confirmed what was already whispered among the ladies, that the new poet was

132

very handsome. His independence was reflected in the clothes he is shown wearing, 'like that of a farmer of the better sort',[5] and in his refusal to look at the purchaser—the engraving shows him assuredly gazing into the distance. In short, the portrait confirms and highlights those qualities of insight, manliness, and physical presentability which were implied in the early reviews of the Kilmarnock edition by Mackenzie and others, and which were remarked on by so many of Burns's contemporaries.

Further evidence for the cultivation of this image of sturdy, rustic independence is to be found in Burns's petition to erect a tombstone over the grave, then unmarked, of Robert Fergusson. The act satisfied an ever present need in Burns to link himself with what he took to be his poetic tradition. A similar motivation can be seen at Mauchline where, in his verse-epistles to Lapraik and Sillar, he can be seen claiming membership, indeed leadership, of an Ayrshire poetic brotherhood, and, at Ellisland and in Dumfries, where, by his activity in reconstituting, rescuing, and reviving the corpus of the Scottish song tradition, he was associating himself with all former Scottish poetry. Burns did not enjoy isolation. His art thrived in the midst of an intimate audience. That audience could be receptive and familiar, like his cronies and fellow-thinkers at Mauchline, or, equally productive, an audience whose collective personality he knew so inwardly as to be sure of antagonizing them. Edinburgh, however, left him floundering, and it is not too far-fetched to see his claim for the recognition of Fergusson as a reaching-out, on his part, for the one man who could have given him the responsive, attentive ear he required. However, a more important and immediate calculation in his petition was the knowledge that it would confirm him as a 'character', a man who showed that keen independence which Edinburgh expected of him and half-feared. (The tone of the reply to his request, especially the use of the word 'disinterested', appears to reveal how Burns, knowingly, had touched a raw nerve of guilt or gentility.)

If Burns knew, instinctively, how to present an image that signified independence, he could also show gratitude in his acceptance of the role, thrust upon him, of 'Caledonia's bard, brother Burns'. This is most evident in the decision to print a subscription list to the 1787 Edinburgh edition, and in the Preface to that volume where, despite lip-service to his independence, he lavishes effusive praise on the 'Noblemen and Gentlemen of The Caledonian Hunt', presenting himself as the mere vehicle, the conduit, for 'The Poetic Genius of my Country'. There is no irony in these words:

> I come to congratulate my Country, that the blood of her ancient heroes still runs uncontaminated; and that from your courage, knowledge, and public spirit, she may expect protection, wealth, and liberty.

This is the prose equivalent of his verse-epistle to Robert Graham of Fintry.[5] Burns is performing, giving his audience what it wants, even if, at other times, as in 'The Twa Dogs, A Tale', he would treat the 'Gentles' with crushing irony. To ask when he is genuine is to be irrelevant and historically and socially naïve.

Such a conscious moulding of one's image is a strain, but Burns could find relief in the company of men like Smellie, Ainslie, Nicol and others with whom he indulged a taste for bawdry and low-life. Those critics who would see in this division evidence of an unbridgeable gulf between a 'high' English literary tradition and a debilitated, even frivolous native tradition are, I think, incorrect. Instead, such a compartmentalization in Burns's life in Edinburgh is the inevitable adjunct of a man who has a public image to maintain. A man, such as Burns, who had been adopted as the 'official' representative of the hopes and values of a social group, had to keep his displays of independence and his relish for a Scots tradition within the bounds licensed by the Court by whom he had been chosen to play Fool. Burns's separation of his Edinburgh life into these two parts was merely the sensible discretion of a man who needed an outlet for that part of his life which his 'officially' conferred image would not permit him to show.

However, the neatness of this scheme offends, and certainly nothing about Burns's stay in Edinburgh was uncomplicated. There is some evidence to suggest that for men such as Ainslie, Burns was consciously purveying an image of himself in the Crochallan Fencibles and, at other times, as distorted as that he acted out for Edinburgh's 'official' arbiters of taste. The prime source here is the notorious letter which Burns sent to Ainslie on 3 March 1788 soon after his return to Mauchline and Jean Armour, part of which I give below:

> I have been through sore tribulation, and under much buffet-ing of the Wicked One, since I came to this country. Jean I found banished like a martyr—forlorn, destitute, and friend-less; all for the good old cause: I have reconciled her to her fate: I have reconciled her to her mother: I have taken her a room: I have taken her to my arms: I have given her a mahogany bed: I have given her a guinea: and I have f————d her till she rejoiced with joy unspeakable and full of glory. . . . I took the opportunity of some dry horselitter, and gave her such a thun-dering scalade that electrified the very marrow of her bones. O, what a peacemaker is a guid, weel-willy p——tle! It is the mediator, the guarantee, the umpire, the bond of union, the solemn league and covenant, the plenipotentiary, the Aaron's rod, the Jacob's staff, the prophet Elisha's pot of oil, the Ahasuerus' sceptre, the sword of mercy, the philosopher's stone, the horn of plenty, and Tree of Life between Man and Woman. . . . (I, 199–200)

What sort of man writes a letter like this to an acquaintance of a few months only? Although no manuscript of the letter is known, Ferguson accepts it as genuine, and rightly so, in my view. Entirely typical of Burns is the malicious enjoyment of combining sacred and profane, the accretive listing, evident in the verse-letters, his inevitable casting of himself in the role of embattled fighter, the use of predictable euphemism in 'the good old cause', and the ambiguously religious vocabulary of 'martyr', 'rejoice', 'joy', and 'glory'! However, more disturbing than any confirmation of its genuineness is the fact that all of the above indicators could equally be evidence of the con-scious artistry of Burns in writing the letter. I say 'more dis-turbing' because that would suggest that Burns was using himself and his wife-to-be to present to Ainslie an image of himself that accords with the interests and pleasures of the Crochallan Fencibles. That Burns actually had intercourse with a woman visibly pregnant and only one month or less from the end of her term, under the conditions he describes, is doubtful. As a farmer with a knowledge of animal physiology, even if in no other capacity, he must have been aware of the dangers in such 'love-making'. (The twins who were born did survive only days.) Whatever the facts, it remains true that in the letter we see Burns writing to his fellow fornicator in Edinburgh to boast of his sexual prowess in the most callous way. This is the Burns who chooses to present himself as a Scottish Tom Jones, an earthy son of the soil, a worthy Fencible. With this letter, Burns becomes the country boy with a fund of dirty stories previously unheard in the city, titillating his salon solicitor's taste for smut.

Although the image Burns fashions for himself above is not typical, it is nonetheless not the most false image he adopted. That doubtful accolade must be reserved for his version of the 'panting swain' in what De Lancey Ferguson rightly calls Burns's 'hothouse' relationship with Clarinda, Mrs. McLehose. His adjective is well chosen for the 'affaire' reeks of the atmosphere of an orchid house. Artificial, protected from the cold blasts of reality by the wilful blindness of each participant, sustained in a prose of posturing mannerism and florid exclamation, their relationship has all the cloying scent and exaggeration of blooms raised under peculiar conditions.

Burns's willingness to play this role is further evidence of how corrupting the acting out of an image can be. When one is forced to adopt the audience's expectation of one's self to an extent that is so far removed from one's own experience or natural tendency, the effect on one's personality can only be grossly distorting. (Boxers, practitioners of a brutal skill, are, when successful, often now converted into 'media creations' who are expected to sing, dance, and appear on chat shows where they may be taken up by fashionable society to the detriment of their real talent.) Burns, in his Sylvander costume, could be equally embarrassing; unfortunately, he left many examples to choose from. Let this brief extract suffice:

> I believe there is no holding converse, or carrying on correspondence, with an amiable woman, much less a *gloriously-amiable fine woman*, without some mixture of that delicious passion whose most devoted slave I have, more than once, had the honour of being. But why be hurt, or offended on that account? Can no honest man have a prepossession for a fine woman, but he must run his head against an intrigue? Take a little of the tender witchcraft of love, and add it to the generous,

the honourable sentiments of manly friendship, and I know but one more delightful morsel, which few, few in any rank, ever taste. Such a composition is like adding cream to strawberries: it not only gives the fruit a more elegant richness, but has a peculiar deliciousness of its own.[7]

This low point, artistically, of Burns's image-making should, to obtain a true picture, be contrasted with Burns's creation of an image for himself at Mauchline between 1784 and 1786. Here, his creation of a public image assumes real importance, psychologically and artistically. While he did not eschew such means as dress,[8] association with prominent minority groups, and acts of defiance, some minor, some major, which would loom larger still in the magnifying lens that is a village community, he did use poetry as his major method of projecting his image and used, most gloriously, the verse-epistle.

The verse-epistles which Burns wrote between 1784 and 1786 are, with the possible exception of Pope's Horatian epistles, the finest examples of the style in Scots or English. Pope's epistles are among his greatest poetry for, although his claim to be a scourge of bad taste may seem arrogant and presumptuous, he writes with a passionate concern and urgency of purpose that springs from his awareness of the precariousness of his status and from his conviction that lapses in 'taste' are symbolic of a greater spiritual blindness in the dominant ethos of his time. So it is with Burns. To criticize him as merely egocentric or his ideas as derivative is foolish. Each epistle should be seen as a performance by a masterly performer who knows that it is not enough to win, but to carry on the fight in defiant, exuberant style.

In the verse-epistles of Burns, we see a man discovering a talent, revelling in it, and elevating the practice of it to a style of living—combative, cocky, independent, fiercely alive. To read the verse-epistles is to see a man raising himself to the status of an image. That image was created out of personal necessity like most great popular images, and that need, and the power of the image, may still be felt today in these poems.

In what follows, I have space to choose only one poem out of the many fine epistles which Burns wrote during these years to illustrate his purpose and incomparable skill in image-making, throughout the verse-epistles. My analysis of the 'Second Epistle to Lapraik' (I, 89–93) will, I hope, reveal Burns's understanding of his totemic significance to Scots then, as now.

The roles which Burns adopted in his early prose letters and the literary types and characters with whom he identified in his early verse had been defence-mechanisms in which to take refuge, or a form of compensatory activity for one who lacked a fixed aim. Now, in Mauchline, Burns could begin to give memorable expression to what his experience of society and books had taught him. He was working within a genre which encouraged the adoption of roles and was writing from a situation in the village which must have seemed like the actualization of the themes of much of his early poetry—the conflicts between youth and age, prudence and abandon, wealth and poverty.

He regarded his situation and the stance he took as emblematic. It had a symbolic significance for others. This tendency is early revealed by the deliberate way in which he links his fate with the plight of larger historical or fictional characters whose fortunes were known to all, such as Tom Jones and William Wallace. It becomes especially prominent in his epistolary verse. He firmly believes that the treatment he receives as man and poet from the society in which he lives is an indicator of that society's moral, political, and religious well-being. That is the significance of the quotation from Ramsay's epistolary verse which accompanied his *Proposals, for Publishing* . . . :

> Set out the brunt side o' your shin,
> For pride in Poet's is nae sin;
> Glory's the Prize for which they rin,
>   And Fame's their jo;
> And wha blaws best the Horn shall win:
>   And wharefore no?[9]

As the outcome of local religious controversies in Mauchline and Ayrshire had, in Burns's eyes, consequences for every parish in Scotland, so the treatment of the poet himself was a microcosm of the fate of all free spirits in a repressive and retributive society. The conviction that his verse and his actions are in the nature of test-cases lends power and pressure to the epistles. This explains the intense egocentricity of the verse-letters. 'I, Rob, am here' (I, 91) is a defiant, triumphant challenge to Fate, to Authority, and to all the dull, dismal forces in opposition. This image is a vibrant affirmation of the power of life itself.

One convention of epistolary verse, the conscious adoption of different *personae* or roles, often within the same poem, allowed Burns to be different men without insincerity or contradiction. The very freedom of the epistolary form gave ample room for expression to Burns's wish to form an image of himself suited to differing correspondents. The different, occasionally conflicting, elements of his personality could co-exist happily within the ill-defined bounds of such verse.

The verse-epistles written in Mauchline were Burns's underground communications system and he used it for many and varied purposes. With it, he could broadcast to selected listeners material which would entertain or instruct. They formed the medium in which he could strut, vaunt, and challenge before an audience of one (his correspondent), of several (those sympathetic members of the circle who, though not directly addressed, would almost certainly hear of the message), or of many (his clerical and lay opponents in Mauchline who, though excluded from the actual performance, could hear the derisory laughter engendered by it—they form a distant, but none the less essential audience for Burns to consider). Alternatively, the epistle could be the small room in which Burns confided his inmost hopes and desires to his closest acquaintances. Then, the very act of confiding was evidence of friendship, an act of faith in the shared principles of their alternative morality.

The verse-epistles are both private and public. They can give cathartic release in the joy of artistic creation, or can be a challenge to other poets and poetasters in the district to match Burns's skill. He uses the epistle to link the scattered forces which he wished to marshal against his dull, leaden foes in the Church, in politics, and in life. To its recipient, a verse-epistle from Burns could be a lifeline, a challenge, a source of humour, an appreciative thump on the back, or a considered appeal for support. His tone in these poems varies from the sentimental to the bawdy, and includes all emotional stops between. The choice of appropriate voice is superb, and quite unparalleled in the literature of his time. Few poets, indeed, have ever managed so well the bewildering range of voices we hear in the epistles.

John Lapraik received, in all, three epistles from Burns between April and September 1785. In this group of verses, Burns appears as a man who was seeking the companionship and approval of other poets because he regarded them as sympathetic and convivial individuals, and because he believed they had a unique insight and capacity for truth. In these epistles, poetry preserves a vision of the world which is closed to prose. Burns is pre-eminently the poet, encouraging poetry because it has become for him a symbol of an alternative social order.

Unlike most of Burns's other correspondents in Mauchline, Lapraik was of Burns's father's generation. He had trusted the Ayr Bank of Douglas, Heron and Co., the collapse of which in August 1773 heavily implicated and ultimately ruined him. Although he struggled for several years to repay his own debts and those for which he had stood surety, his creditors insisted on his being jailed, largely to provoke recalcitrant 'friends' to act as security for remaining sums owed. This strategy had the desired effect, and Lapraik was soon released, but not before his experience had prompted him to write poetry in earnest. One consequence of this was that his *Poems, On Several Occasions* were published in 1788.[10] Like Sillar and others, he was exploiting the taste for vernacular poetry which Burns's success had aroused, but it is unfair to ascribe all his beliefs to servile copying of Burns. The similarity of outlook in Lapraik and Burns is more correctly traced to their common status and shared experience of life.

Lapraik describes his poetry as 'merely the effect of his own observations, on nature, men, and things, and these huddled together without any order or method' (p. 3). This observer of men and their ways takes great delight in the relief from labour which conviviality brings, and can face Fate with the support of loyal friends. He scorns the blind pursuit of wealth which he knows, from bitter personal experience, destroys the common humanity which ought to join men together:

> Mankind a common system is,
>   And should support
> Each other, in their stations here,
>   And them comfort.[11]

Having established friendly contact with this local poet in his first, Burns's second verse-letter to Lapraik was written in reply to an epistle which Lapraik had sent him and which is now lost. This is unfortunate since we cannot now know how far the development of Burns's epistle was determined by the contents of Lapraik's poem. However, one epistle which Lapraik addressed to Burns, though written at a later date, gives some idea of the effect which Burns's correspondence had on the older man:

> When sitting lanely by myself,
> Just unco griev'd and wae,
> To think that Fortune, fickle Joe!
> Had kick'd me o'er the brae!
>
> . . . .
> Till your kind Muse, wi' friendly blast,
> First tooted up my fame,
> And sounded loud, through a' the Wast,
> My lang forgotten name.
>
> Quoth I, 'Shall I, like to a sumph,
> 'Sit douff and dowie here,
> 'And suffer the ill-natur'd warld
> 'To ca' RAB BURNS a liar.'[12]

This was what Burns intended. Not only that Lapraik should be urged to write poetry and so add to the fame of Ayrshire (a subject close to Burns's heart at this point in 1785 as his next epistle to William Simson makes clear), but also that he should cultivate that attitude to life, the poetic spirit, which is the central theme of this epistle. In it, Burns casts himself essentially as poet like Lapraik and contrasts their opportunities in life with other, more prestigious occupations. His conclusion is that their values, as represented by the image of the poet, are infinitely superior to those typified by such representative figures as the merchant or the Baillie. But, it is not merely the poet who is presented as the example. It is, significantly, *Burns* as poet. The man becomes the totemic image. He offers *his* actions, *his* behaviour, *himself*, as the symbol of the values he urges and as an example of the struggle to be waged. Like the leader of a band of guerillas, he tells his history and shows the scars of battle. In this way, he raises morale, boosts the confidence of the newly enlisted and proves, by his very presence, that the cause in which he fights has God on its side. 'After all', Burns says, '*I've* survived.'

In no other epistle do we sense that the speaker is so immediately before us. This is quite deliberate, for one of the many contrasts which create the tension of the poem is that between spontaneity and calculation, between the impulsiveness of the poet's emotion and the way in which the mercantile spirit doles out its approval or disapproval according to its assessment of the profit to be gained from the bestowal of a wintry smile. Burns seems to be only one step ahead of us as we read. He sought to give the impression of writing the epistle as we watch, for that was proof that what we read is genuine and unaffected, the promptings of his heart transferred to paper as they rise.

The graphic image of the farm which opens the epistle reveals a man weary from sowing, but determined to take the time to repay a debt of friendship. The introduction of financial imagery with 'debtor' is deliberate. Lapraik, ruined in the Ayr Bank scandal, would no doubt smile ruefully at the idea of his being owed anything, but Burns also uses the term to make the contrast between this kind of debt of friendship (which ought always to be honoured), and those financial transactions, alluded to in ll. 79–84, which corrupt and even deny the possibility of friendship. He described, in frank detail, all the drudgery of farm life which Lapraik the farmer would recognize, for he wishes his advice about the cathartic value of composition to have the force of a real solution, arrived at in the real world. It must be seen as no mere poetic cliché, but as a claim which his experience had substantiated. The slow movement of the stanza reflects the drudgery and also plays its part in the larger structure of the epistle. The claim which Burns will make for the re-animating power of poetry is verified by the increasing tempo of the poem which, from this lethargic opening, speeds up to the dazzling rapidity of stanza 6 where, refreshed, he begins to compose.

142

The argument with the Muse is conventional but Burns uses it for quite specific ends. She is presented, firstly, as part of that conspiracy which tries to prevent him repaying his debt to Lapraik. However, the tussle with the Muse also allows him to distance, tactfully, his praise of the older poet and permits the introduction of set-piece dialogue which varies the pattern of the verse, cutting across Burns's narrative to give the effect of a dramatic interlude. This epistle combines much of the best of Burns's inheritance from English and Scottish traditions. There is the moral conviction of Augustan epistolary poetry, the belief in the necessity of poetry and poets as exemplified by Ramsay in his verse and action, and, not least, the superb technical skill of Fergusson. This last is particularly evident, and especially in these stanzas which introduce the whining, resentful Muse and describe Burns's disagreement with her. The expressive neologisms of 'The tapetless, ramfeezl'd hizzie' (l. 13) concentrate his dislike, but he allows the complaining figure to reveal her own character in direct speech which, by careful placing of the pauses, reads like the true voice of a lazy, nebby woman:

> . . . 'Ye ken we've been sae busy
>   'This month an' mair,
> 'That trouth, my head is grown right dizzie,
>   'An' something sair.'   (I, 90)

This skill in construction and in poetic technique is apparent throughout and is to be explained by Burns's shaping his presentation for an audience who would read his poetry closely and would be alert to its many nuances. For example, the image of Burns, the stern moralist, urging the Muse to obey her conscience is deliberately exaggerated for the sake of incongruity. Lapraik's knowledge of Burns's character, as he chose to present it in the first epistle, meant that he would see the humour in this contradictory role. Yet, the determination to write is genuine, and he makes this plain by acting out the business of composition before our eyes. The effect of stanza 6 is complex. We know, of course, that Burns has written the epistle so far but, having been drawn closer to the poet as he narrows the physical scope of the poem, we now willingly succumb to the illusion he creates of being at his shoulder,

143

looking on, as he converts his vow to write into action. His resolve contrasts with the Muse's lackadaisical spirit, and the determined energy and immediacy of this stanza is his challenging response to all those forces trying to stop his writing to Lapraik:

> Sae I gat paper in a blink,
> An' down gaed *stumpie* in the ink:
> Quoth I, 'Before I sleep a wink,
>   'I vow I'll close it;
> 'An' if ye winna mak it clink,
>   'By Jove I'll prose it!'   (I, 90)

One can see and hear the plash of the pen as it thrust into the bottle, because Burns has so constructed the poem to bring this poet before us as living proof of the efficacy of his philosophy of cathartic and restorative composition. This is the first climax of the poem. He has honoured his debt to Lapraik by beginning (or so it seems, although the poem is already thirty lines old) to write; he has entertained and encouraged his correspondent and has, with some conviction, presented himself as proof of the values he advocates.

In the next four stanzas Burns is not concerned, as he was in the first epistle, to define the true poetic spirit. Instead, by vivid presentation of the 'poet' image, he urges on Lapraik the importance of that outlook on life as a valid response to the misfortunes which men in their situation must inevitably encounter. His growing isolation in Mauchline society, which he found increasingly stifling and inimical, convinced him that his role was that of an Opposition. His epistles are his Parliamentary chamber, for there, like the leader of a minority party, he attacks, castigates and theorizes, proposing solutions and visualizing New Jerusalems if only his ideas are accepted. Unlike most Parliamentary oppositions, however, he can justify his claims. His proof? Simply his actions in the village, his existence as an alternative, his very survival, as poet. The advice of ll. 43–8 is confident and skilfully expressed but it gains enormously from the two stanzas which follow. In ll. 49–54, Burns can look to a future for himself, and this alone is sufficient to justify his defiant dismissal of capricious and malevolent Fortune in 'Ne'er mind how Fortune waft an' warp; She's but a b–tch' (ll. 47–8). Like Lapraik and others in their situation, he has been buffeted by Fate, but his response is a determination to enjoy laughter, song, and dance, all of which suggest activity and sociability. The infectious confidence of stanza 9 balances the more rhetorical and considered statement of ll. 73ff. Its informality may mask the serious intent, but Burns knows that this throwaway tone is appropriate as he addresses Lapraik directly.

Fate, however, is always ready to deal an awkward blow, as the hint of dogged persistence in 'Still persecuted by the limmer/ Frae year to year' (ll. 57–8) suggests. Yet, by recalling the inevitability with which the seasons return, the first two lines of stanza 10 allow Burns to link himself with all the energy and potential fecundity of Spring and also to suggest that *his* survival has a similar inevitability. 'I, Rob, am here' crowns his persuasive argument. Despite everything, the poet has survived and, therefore, triumphed. The conviction that his fate at the hands of society is of importance as a measure of that society's well-being rings throughout this and his other epistles from this period. Mauchline was Burns's battleground. There, his opponents were clearly visible as was his opposition to them. His existence constituted a threat to the established authority of the Kirk and to the douce sensibilities of the conservative villagers. His life in Mauchline was one long test-case. If he survived, he had not only won a victory for himself, but had enlarged the scope for freedom of all who wished to disagree with or dissociate themselves from the dominant orthodoxy. That is the significance of 'I, Rob, am here', and that is the combative, visionary spirit which informs these Mauchline epistles. Burns has stepped out of the poem and spoken directly to Lapraik and all who read the epistle. Now, the poem becomes more of a dramatic monologue which builds to a heightened climax. Lapraik is still addressed, but the following stanzas have all the restless self-questioning and daring speculation of a man testing his philosophy aloud and finding it triumphantly intact.

It is typical of the antithetical quality of Burns's mind that, when he is most physically present as a positive force, the spectral, negative forces begin to crowd round. So far, Burns has presented only his philosophy. Now, to demonstrate to all its validity, he offers what might, at first sight, appear to be alternatives but which, on closer examination, prove to be insubstantial, mere treasures upon earth. Ought we to envy the 'city-gent', the 'Baillie', or 'the paughty, feudal Thane', all symbols of worldly success, figures to whom respect is due? Burns's answer is in two parts—the affirmation of ll. 73ff., and the damning manner in which he poses the questions. The phrasing and construction of stanzas 11 and 12 demand a negative answer to each question as it is posed. The tawdry, modish abbreviation of 'city-gent' reveals Burns's contempt for the breed, while 'lie an' sklent' captures the shifty, greedy glance of the merchant who has his eye on the main chance and nothing else. The same precision lays bare the Baillie. The swelling self-importance which accompanies wealth is well caught in '. . . big wi' cent per cent', and it also conveys the man's overweening pride. He considers such wealth to be a natural growth, for the association of 'big wi' ' and 'muckle wame' makes an implicit comparison between his bulk, puffed with pride and good living, and that of the pregnant woman. However, the sneer of 'some bit *Brugh*' pricks this pursy balloon; it suggests an area of influence and power which is positively Lilliputian. In stanza 12, the respect which the externals of dress and manner demand is withheld. Instead, with the folk-phrase, 'nae sheep-shank bane', Burns dismisses the haughty lord and the notion that his 'ruffl'd sark an' glancin cane' should be envied.

He completes his rejection of their value-system in the apostrophe of ll. 73–8. There, he makes a plea for the individual spirit and for the indomitability of each man who has a capacity for self-reliance, independence, and natural talent. Given these, one needs nothing else—neither wealth nor position. Without the latter, the respect one meets must be genuine, the friendships, sincere. Why flatter a man who can bestow nothing but friendship in return? This reflection is the base on which Burns builds to his climax. The emotional pulse of the poem, like the manner of address, has fluctuated with the ebb and flow of Burns's anger. Now, however, he progresses steadily to a final statement which reaches upwards to the light.

Burns offers a set of values, different from those which have brought conventional respect to the 'city-gent', but which are truer and, ultimately, more socially responsible. They are best exemplified in the image of 'The social, friendly, honest man' (l. 87) and 'The followers o' the ragged Nine' (l. 92). The former are at one with the Christian view of the world as a universal brotherhood and the latter resemble those 'blessed fools' who, by their refusal to take thought for the morrow, escape the curse of inhumanity in their personal relationships— a curse which Burns believes is necessarily visited on those wheeler-dealers and calculating social climbers. For them, thought for the morrow is thought for themselves. Burns has seen a saner, better world which he tries to describe in this final section. Its moral norms are very different from those which prevail in the world of the Baillie and the trader.

The contrast between their world and that which Burns envisages is concentrated in the word 'state' (l. 79) where he deliberately exploits its ambiguity of meaning. The word could have two interpretations—'condition', or 'organized society'. If the former, then ll. 78–80 mean that man's natural state is to be 'rich an' great' and that those who are not are doomed:

> Damnation then would be our fate,
> Beyond remead. (I, 92)

This convenient perversion of Christian teaching would suit the 'sordid sons o' Mammon's line' admirably. Alternatively, the postulation, 'Were this the charter of our state,/ "On pain o' hell be rich an' great"' (ll. 79–80), invites the thought that this is, in fact, the sort of society in which we live and, to the rich and powerful, we *are* damned. Our poverty marks us as outcasts from society as they understand it. Such packing of meaning into a small space is not a skill usually associated with Burns or with 'Standart Habby'. The reason for this is that the verse flows with such ease in the hands of a master that one falsely assumes one is listening to witty conversation and nothing more.

Burns and Lapraik choose to live by another set of rules which have a greater sanction than any man-made 'charter'. Their 'creed' is based on the 'royal mandate' and is of greater antiquity. It is relevant in any society and to every man who will recognize it. Three great Burnsian positives are celebrated in ll. 85–90: friendship, honesty of heart, and a common humanity. The poem has been building to this definitive statement of the values he cherishes, and they are expressed in terms of religious conviction. The language of the stanza is simple, the tone elevated, the commitment, total. All-inclusive phrases such as 'Whate'er he be' and 'none but he' are used to reflect the democratic appeal. On this basis, Burns and Lapraik can accept their condition without succumbing or flinching. Song, dance, and laughter are innocent pursuits and fruitful sources of happiness. Their very 'thoughtlessness' holds out hope of a joy which the 'sordid sons o' Mammon's line' can never know. Their inhumanity is revealed as Burns compares them to some frenetically grubbing animal. They 'scrape, an' squeeze, an' growl' to prosper at the expense of others in a cut-throat world, only to meet with due reward after death:

> Their worthless nievefu' of a *soul*,
> May in some *future carcase* howl,
>   The forest's fright;
> Or in some day-detesting owl
>   May shun the light.   (I, 93)

For Burns and Lapraik, the prospect is very different. The vision of their paradisaical existence cannot compare with Dante's contemplation of ineffable light, nor should it in an epistle to a friend. There is, nevertheless, a similar strength of conviction behind Burns's less majestic, more personal vision:

> Then may L*****K and B**** arise,
> To reach their native, kindred skies,
> And *sing* their pleasures, hopes an' joys,
>   In some mild sphere,
> Still closer knit in friendship's ties
>   Each passing year!   (I, 93)

The movement is upwards towards friendship and song, for the poetic spirit, Burns's antidote to the poisonous morality of 'catch-the-plack', is presented here as the ultimate positive force.

The Mauchline epistles remain among the most innovative, exciting, and important poetry of the century. The imagery of freedom and release and the vigour and zest of the language implies a commitment to imaginative freedom worthy of comparison with Blake or Dickens. They express Burns's insight into the insidious mechanization of the spirit and his distaste for rigidity and excessive formality in relations between people. He has the same unerring nose for hypocrisy as Byron and, like the later poet, has the happy knack of seizing on the telling physical image and exactly the right note of parody to convey his scathing anger. His best epistles succeed because they allow and encourage Burns to invent and prolong an image which has all the power found in a creation that springs from the need of the creator and matches the need of his audience. In Mauchline, such image-making was Burns's greatest work. He fashioned for his audience then, as for his audience now, an 'image' so convincing, so perfectly conceived for its purpose that it still inspires today. To remain indifferent to the overwhelming style presented in these stanzas is to deny one's humanity, as the following lines from the epistle 'To J. S****' demonstrate:

> An anxious e'e I never throws
> Behint my lug, or by my nose;
> I jouk beneath Misfortune's blows
> As weel's I may;
> Sworn foe to *sorrow*, *care*, and *prose*,
> I rhyme away.
>
> O ye, douse folk, that live by rule,
> Grave, tideless-blooded, calm and cool,
> Compar'd wi' you—O fool! fool! fool!
> How much unlike!
> Your hearts are just a standing pool,
> Your lives, a dyke!
>
> Nae hare-brain'd, sentimental traces,
> In your unletter'd, nameless faces!
> In *arioso* trills and graces
> Ye never stray,
> But *gravissimo*, solemn basses
> Ye hum away.
>
> Ye are sae *grave*, nae doubt ye're *wise*;
> Nae ferly tho' ye do despise

The hairum-scairum, ram-stam boys,
                The rattling squad:
I see ye upward cast your eyes—
                —Ye ken the road—

Whilst I—but I shall haud me there—
Wi' you I'll scarce gang *ony where*—
Then *Jamie*, I shall say nae mair,
                But quat my sang,
Content *with* You to mak a *pair*,
                Whare'er I gang.   (I, 183)

NOTES

1. Proof of his prominence was furnished by Murray and Barbara Grigor's exhibition at the Edinburgh Festival, 1981, 'Scotch Myths . . . '.
2. *The Letters of Robert Burns*, ed. De Lancey Ferguson, 2 vols. (Oxford, 1931), I, p. 59. All quotations come from this edition.
3. The word is Burns's own—he tells his voluminous correspondent, Mrs. Dunlop, who has stressed the value of Dr. Moore's good opinion, that he is about to write 'a letter of sentiment' to him. See William Wallace, *Robert Burns and Mrs. Dunlop* (London, 1898), p. 7.
4. See, especially, the letter of 7 December 1786 to Hamilton (Ferguson, I, p. 55).
5. The remark is quoted in *The Poems and Songs of Robert Burns*, ed. James Kinsley, 3 vols. (Oxford, 1968), III, p. 1536. All quotations from Burns's poems follow this edition.
6. See Kinsley, op. cit., II, pp. 585–89.
7. *The Life and Works of Robert Burns*, ed. Chambers and Wallace, 2 vols. (Edinburgh, 1896), II, p. 228.
8. 'He wore the only tied hair in the parish; and in the church, his plaid, which was of a particular colour . . . he wrapped in a particular manner round his shoulders. . . .' David Sillar recollecting Burns in Tarbolton. Cited in Chambers/Wallace, op. cit., I, p. 68.
9. 'Familiar Epistles between Lieutenant William Hamilton and Allan Ramsay', No. 2.
10. John Lapraik, *Poems, On Several Occasions* (Kilmarnock, 1788).
11. Ibid., p. 118. 'On the Distressed Conditions of Honest Farmers', ll. 3–6.
12. Ibid., pp. 36, 37. From 'Epistle to R****/ B***S'.

7

The Impulse of Wit: Sterne and Burns's Letters

by K. G. SIMPSON

The keeness of satire was, I am almost at a loss whether to say his forte or his foible; for though nature had endowed him with a portion of the most pointed excellence in that dangerous talent, he suffered it too often to be the vehicle of personal, and sometimes unfounded, animosities. It was not always that sportiveness of humour, that 'unwary pleasantry', which Sterne has depictured with touches so conciliatory, but the darts of ridicule were frequently directed as the caprice of the instant suggested, or as the altercations of parties and of persons happened to kindle the restlessness of his spirit into interest or aversion. This however, was not invariably the case; his wit (which is no unusual matter indeed) had always the start of his judgment, and would lead him to the indulgence of raillery uniformly acute, but often unaccompanied with the least desire to wound. . . . ' 'Twas no extravagant arithmetic' to say of him, as was said of Yorick, 'that for every ten jokes he got an hundred enemies'.[1]

Maria Riddell also deemed Burns 'a good hater', but added that 'the warmth of his passions was fortunately corrected by their versatility.' Her judgement of Burns is relevant to this paper in three major respects. She identified, rightly, Burns's

151

satirical vigour as 'that dangerous talent'. In Burns it was the result of the union of acute personal responsiveness and a tradition of vigorously expressive satire, a tradition endemic in Scottish literature and typified in the flyting.[2] Epitomized in Burns is the Scottish capacity for convincing utterance, be it of what the speaker believes or of anything but what he believes. This talent for ironic voice characterizes earlier Scottish literature, but it seems likely that it drew renewed force from the bias of Scottish Enlightenment activity in the direction of rhetoric. With Burns, personality, ability, and circumstances combined to give it an added edge. Certainly Maria Riddell is justified in regarding Burns's satire as more acerbic than that of Sterne, but there are many points of similarity with Sterne, and this essay will be concerned with establishing that Burns's versatility of voice and tone derived much from the example of Sterne. Further, as Maria Riddell claimed, that very facility in Burns was a mixed blessing in that time and again it led to his wit taking precedence over his judgement.

J. De Lancey Ferguson observed that 'the biographers of few modern authors are so completely dependent upon their subject's letters for knowledge of the details of his life as are those of Burns.'[3] Not only is it the case that, as Thomas Crawford has stated, Burns 'was brought up on the epistolary dogma that one should suit one's style to the needs and personality of one's correspondents',[4] but it is equally true that in many of his letters Burns, to meet the needs of his own personality, assumed distinctive voices. Catherine Carswell's claim that 'to a unique extent the man and his work are one'[5] acquires a certain poignant irony, given the complexity of the man's personality and the nature of his circumstances: the diversity of voices which Burns's letters reveal is a direct reflection of the fragmentation of the self. In this Sterne was a major, and not altogether salutary, influence.

To Dr. John Moore he wrote:

> My life flowed on much in the same tenor till my twenty-third year.—Vive l'amour et vive la bagatelle, were my sole principles of action.—The addition of two more Authors to my library gave me great pleasure; Sterne and McKenzie.—Tristram Shandy and the Man of Feeling were my bosom favourites.
>
> (I, 111–12)[6]

To such a personality as that of Burns access to the *persona* of the sentimentalist at this stage of his life was to have great significance. Despite his acute eye for the comic, it was with the pathetic rather than the risible elements of sentimentalism that Burns was to find a strong affinity. Moreover on one occasion Burns wrote of *Tristram Shandy* in such a way as to suggest that he shared the view of Cowper and Jefferson that the book was a force for good.[7] Burns wrote:

> If Miss Georgina McKay is still at Dunlop, I beg you will make her my Compliments, and request her in my name to sing you a song at the close of every page, by way of dissipating Ennui; as David . . . playing on his harp chased the Evil Spirit out of Saul.—This Evil Spirit, I take it, was just, long-spun Sermons, & many-pag'd Epistles, & Birth-day Poetry, & patience-vexing Memorials, Remonstrances, Dedications, Revolution-Addresses, & c. & c. & c. while David's harp, I suppose was, mystically speaking, Tristram Shandy, Laugh & be fat, Cauld Kail in Aberdeen, Green grow the rashes, & the rest of that inspired and inspiring family. (I, 278–79)

As often with Burns, comic reduction cloaks a serious point: good is on the side of the individual man, but the whole man; it is life in its private, personal, witty, bawdy dimensions. The phrase, 'mystically speaking' is telling: that *Tristram Shandy* held for Burns this mystique—essentially celebratory of life in its fullness—perhaps explains his omission of Sterne from his projected comparative evaluation of the novelists, Moore, Fielding, Richardson, and Smollett (II, 29).

Amongst Burns's letters the earliest sustained echoes of Sterne occur in the letter to John Arnot, written late in 1785, in which Burns offers an account of how he 'lost a Wife' (Jean Armour). In a manner distinctly Shandean the tone vacillates between genuine, if at times maudlin, self-pity and jocular self-dramatization. The prefatory 'story of the letter' includes an attack, which might have been written by Sterne, on Prudence. In the letter a formal preamble gives way to an increasingly ironic tone, and then, in the following, the voice becomes unmistakably that of Tristram:

> You have doubtless, Sir, heard my story, heard it with all its exaggerations; but as my actions, & my motives for action, are

153

peculiarly like myself, & that is peculiarly like nobody else, I shall just beg a leisure-moment & a spare tear of you, untill I tell my own story my own way.—[8]

I have been all my life, Sir, one of the rueful-looking, long-visaged sons of Disappointment.—A damned Star has always kept my zenith, & shed its baleful influence, in that emphatic curse of the Prophet—'And behold whatsoever he doth, it shall not prosper!'—I rarely hit where I aim: & if I want anything, I am almost sure never to find it where I seek it. (I, 27–8)

The direct address; the appeals for sympathy and licence to relate in one's own way; the belief in a personally hostile providence; and the awareness of one's failure to match intention and realization: all of these clearly echo Sterne's 'small HERO'.[9]

The letter proceeds to what is, in effect, a brilliantly contrived debate between instinct and conventional morality. In terms closely imitative of Sterne at his most sensual, Burns relates that his 'mouth watered deliciously' to visualize the consummation of a marriage. Then he launches, with unconcealed relish, into a lengthy piece of bawdry which, in terms of linguistic energy and sustained metaphorical invention, matches anything in Sterne ('I was well aware . . . more total defeat' (I, 28–9)). The use of military metaphor for the expression of sexual activity owes much to the example of Sterne (e.g. Widow Wadman's courtship of Uncle Toby, and the account of how Tristram came to be circumcised by the window, in *Tristram Shandy*).[10] Burns's innate sensuality has found expression in a highly skilled use of a derivative literary manner—the comic-epic. Burns gives an account of the rise and the frustration of his passion in a remarkable passage where the verbal dynamism and the correlation of formal and referential aspects of the prose may again stand comparison with Sterne (See 'How I bore this . . . another wife'). After this account of what he calls 'this fatal era of my life', Burns asserts that he will evade 'the holy beagles, the houghmagandie pack' that are already on to him; and the letter ends in this characteristically Shandean manner:

I am so struck, on a review, with the impertinent length of this letter, that I shall not increase it with one single word of apology; but abruptly conclude it with assuring you that I am, Sir, Your, & Misery's most humble serv^t. (I, 30)

The Sternean features of this relatively early letter recur across the whole range of the letters. For instance, the defiant proclamation of the writer's entitlement to be whimsically himself is a favourite strategy of Burns. Echoing Tristram's preoccupation with the way in which experience will not readily submit to the systematic ordering of chronology, Burns writes: 'I have no idea of corresponding as a clock strikes; I only write when the spirit moves me' (I, 128). Above all else the validity of individual experience is to be upheld, and it includes the writer's freedom to wander off 'in this rhapsodical tangent' (I, 298). (Compare Tristram's description of his book as 'this rhapsodical work' (*Tristram Shandy*, I, Ch. 13).) The right to be oneself, indeed the inevitability of being oneself, come to be expressed in terms of Sterne's 'hobby-horse'. 'Ballad-making', Burns wrote to Thomson, 'is now as completely my hobby-horse, as ever Fortification was Uncle Toby's; so I'll e'en canter it away till I come to the limit of my race' (II, 166).[11] Here the very phrase 'I'll e'en canter it away' mimics Sterne's manner.

But Burns, like Tristram, falls foul of the difficulty of achieving freedom of expression by means of an artificial medium; hence the writer's heightened awareness of both his role as writer and the limitations of his medium. For both Burns and Sterne letter-writing is an art-form and the writer is a self-conscious artist who can exploit the artificiality of his medium for comic purposes. For instance, Sterne begins a letter to Mary Macartney thus:

> An urn of cold water in the driest stage of the driest Desert in Arabia, pour'd out by an angel's hand to a thirsty Pilgrim, could not have been more gratefully received than Miss Macartny's Letter—pray is that Simile too warm? or conceived too orientally? if it is; I could easily mend it, by saying with the dull phlegm of an unfeeling John Trot, (*suivant les ordinances*) *That Yrs of the 8th Inst came safe to hand*. (*Letters*, 117)

To Cunningham Burns wrote:

> It is not that I *can* not write you: should you doubt it, take the following fragment which was intended for you some time ago,

and be convinced that I can *antithesize* Sentiment & *circumvolute* Periods, as well as any Coiner of phrase in the regions of Philology (II, 12),

and he proceeds to write in the most formal and inflated of modes. Burns is capable too of a Shandean blank space: 'I should return my thanks for your   hospitality' (I leave a blank for the epithet, as I know none can do it justice) (I, 198); and a letter in the mock-sublime to Wilhelmina Alexander has, by way of postscript, a dialogue between writer and reader that begins: 'Well, Mr. Burns, & *did* the Lady give you the desired 'Permission'?—No! She was too fine a Lady *to notice* so plain a compliment' (I, 51).

Burns's stylistic dynamism has clear affinities with that of Sterne. The vigorous account of the horse-race with the Highlander alongside Loch Lomond owes something to Tristram's description of Dr. Slop's fall (*Tristram Shandy*, II, Ch. 9). And the same letter includes this statement which has, as well as a reference to *Tristram Shandy*, a distinctly Shandean cadence: 'But I am an old hawk at the sport, & wrote her such a cool, deliberate, prudent reply, as brought my bird from her aerial towerings, pop, down at my foot, like Corporal Trim's hat' (I, 100). To Mrs. Dunlop Burns was to describe Francis Grose not only in terms of Dr. Slop but in prose whose rhythms and cadences reproduce thus those of their original: 'if you discover a cheerful-looking grig of an old, fat fellow, the precise figure of Dr. Slop, wheeling about your avenue in his own carriage with a pencil & paper in his hand, you may conclude, "Thou art the man!"' (I, 346).[12] The following owes much to Tristram's comic correlation of physical and mental states:

> Well, Divines may say what they please, but I maintain that a hearty blast of execration is to the mind, what breathing a vein is to the body: the overloaded sluices of both are wonderfully relieved by their respective evacuations.—I feel myself vastly easier then [*sic*] when I began my letter, and can now go on to business. (II, 52)

There are, too, a few letters where Burns writes blatantly and at length as Tristram (e.g. to Provost Maxwell of Lochmaben (I, 377–78)).[13]

The love of pattern, which Kurt Wittig noted as a characteristic of the poems,[14] is a feature of the conscious artistry which informs the letters. The interplay of formal manner and comically commonplace detail is carefully managed. Burns writes, for instance, to Maria Riddell: 'On the conditions & capitulations you so obligingly make, I shall certainly make my plain, weather-beaten, rustic phiz a part of your box furniture on Tuesday' (II, 216).[15] The repeated use of ironic juxtaposition, comic-heroic, and mock-sublime may give rise to the suspicion that the formulaic use of literary modes is being made to serve the purpose of diverting, restraining, or sublimating within a process of style, something which is intensely and emotionally personal. It is as if by fixing the stylistic extremes of the sublime and the banal Burns hopes, or perhaps *needs* in terms of his own psychic health, to shed or conceal somewhere between them the serious concern— personal, emotional, or political—which has stimulated him to write.

That granted, it can be recognized that there is a further area of affinity with Sterne. In the habitual use of the reductive mode the grand generalization often gives way to, and is undermined by, the bizarrely particular. This exemplifies Sterne's and Burns's shared cry for freedom, the defence of the individual's right to be—both personally and stylistically (and with each writer Buffon's 'le style c'est l'homme' holds good)— splendidly, riotously himself. Thus the flux of language mirrors the flux of the writer's thought.

Yet in a letter of advice to his brother William, Burns questioned the adequacy of language as a vehicle for the expression of mental activity, and he proceeded to advocate proof by individual experience, in terms of which any orthodox empiricist might be proud. Burns wrote:

> There is an excellent Scots Saying, that 'A man's mind is his kingdom'.—It is certainly so; but how few can govern that kingdom with propriety.—The serious mischiefs in Business which this Flux of language occasion, do not come immediately to your situation . . .
> . . . Whatever you read, whatever you hear, concerning the ways and works of that strange creature, MAN, look into the living world about you, look into Yourself, for the evidences of the fact, or the application of the doctrine. (I, 313–14)

Later, in a letter to Mrs. Dunlop, he stated:

> The most cordial believers in a Future State have ever been the Unfortunate.—This of itself; if God is Good, which is, I think the most intuitive truth in Nature; this very propensity to, and supreme happiness of, depending on a Life beyond Death & the Grave, is a very strong proof of the reality of its existence.— Though I have no objection to what the Christian system tells us of Another world; yet I own I am partial to those proofs & ideas of it which we have wrought out of our own heads and hearts.—The first has the demonstration of an authenticated story, the last has the conviction of an intuitive truth. (II, 26)

Here the term, 'intuitive truth', is plainly significant. Seeing its origin in the Common Sense School of thought, perhaps as communicated to Burns by Dugald Stewart, Fairchild claims that 'its usefulness in rationalizing the cult of feeling is obvious.'[16] Perhaps this is to assume a degree of success which Burns never realized: what can be said is that on occasion he *attempted* to rationalize the cult of feeling.

Burns's use of the term represents, like much else in his thought, a somewhat uneasy compromise. If he felt at times the need to attempt to rationalize experience into truth, equally he exemplified, and upheld the importance of, the flux of the mind. It is no accident that Locke is mentioned in his letters on several occasions (e.g. I, 109, 168), or that Burns refers to the association of ideas (I, 179–80; II, 293). 'We know nothing, or next to nothing, of the substance or structure of our Souls, so cannot account for those seeming caprices in them' (I, 283), Burns wrote to Mrs. Dunlop. In similar vein, and in terms even more reminiscent of Sterne, he informed William Dunbar:

> In vain do we talk of reason, my dear Sir; we are the offspring of Caprice, & the nurslings of Habitude. —The most pleasurable part of our existence, the strings that tie heart to heart, are the manufacture of some hitherto undescribed and unknown power within us. (I, 300)

To the offspring of Caprice and nursling of Habitude the temptations of Wit are irresistible. Thus to Mrs. Dunlop he admitted: 'Politics is dangerous ground for me to tread on, & yet I cannot for the soul of me resist an impulse of any thing like Wit' (I, 321). That Burns had clearly before him as fore-

most example of the impulse of wit the work of Laurence
Sterne is substantiated by this letter to Ainslie where the
Shandean legacy is blatant:

> I recd your last, & was much entertained with it; but I will not
> at this time, nor at·any other time, answer it.—Answer a letter?
> I never could answer a letter in my life!—I have written many a
> letter in return for letters I have received; but then—they were
> original matter—spurt—away! zig, here; zag, there; as if the
> Devil that, my grannie (an old woman *indeed*) often told me,
> rode on Will-o'-wisp, or, in her more classic phrase, SPUNKIE,
> were looking over my elbow.—A happy thought that idea has
> ingendered in my head! SPUNKIE—thou shalt henceforth be my
> Symbol, Signature, & Tutelary Genius! Like thee, hap-step-&-
> lowp, here-awa-there-awa, higglety-pigglety, pell-mell, hither-
> &-yon, ram-stam, happy-go-lucky, up-tails-a'-by-the-light-o'-
> the-moon, has been, is, & shall be, my progress through the
> mosses & moors of this vile, bleak, barren wilderness of a life of
> ours . . .
>
> . . . I feel myself vastly better.—I give you friendly joy of
> Robie Waters' brother.—'Twas a happy thought his begetting
> him against a *Book press*.—No doubt, as you with equal sagacity
> & science remark, it will have an astonishing effect on the
> young BOOK-WORM'S head-piece. (II, 174)[17]

Wit becomes a welcome refuge in a world where experience
is complex, response is ambivalent, and both resist language's
attempts to render them. To Mrs. Dunlop Burns acknowledged:

> . . . the word, 'Love', owing to the intermingledoms of the good
> & the bad, the pure & impure, in this world, being rather an
> equivocal term for expressing one's sentiments & sensations, I
> must do justice to the sacred purity of my attachment. (II, 116)

Time and again in reading Burns's letters one encounters his
keen sense of the disparity between man's version of experience and experience itself. To Graham of Fintry he wrote:

> I have heard and read a good deal of Philanthropy, Generosity
> and Greatness of soul, and when rounded with the flourish of
> declamatory periods, or poured in the mellifluence of Parnassian
> measure, they have a tolerable effect on a musical ear; but when
> these high sounding professions are compared with the very act
> and deed as they are usually performed I do not think there is
> any thing in or belonging to Human Nature, so baldly dis-
> proportionate. (I, 348)

At its widest the gulf for Burns exists between the ideal and the actual. 'Like many other fine sayings', he remarked of some lines from Thomson's *Alfred*, 'it has, I fear, more of Philosophy than Human-nature in it' (II, 26). For Burns, as for Sterne, the system which man erects out of experience, in an attempt to comprehend that experience, simply takes him ever further from it. 'Good God, why this disparity between our wishes and our powers?' (II, 164), he exclaimed, echoing both Sterne and Goethe;[18] and elsewhere (II, 36) he was to lament as additional constraints the poet's strength of imagination and delicacy of sensibility, the terms once more being redolent of Sterne.

If this is man's situation, thus severely circumscribed, what is more natural than that he should regard himself as ill-fated, the plaything of a whimsical and at times malign Providence? Burns is very close to Tristram when he writes of 'that evil planet, which has almost all my life shed its baleful rays on my devoted head' (I, 161); and he sees himself as 'a poor hairum-scairum poet whom Fortune had kept for her particular use, to wreak her temper on whenever she was in ill-humour' (I, 172). And the following owe something to the plaints of Tristram: 'A damned Star has almost all my life usurped my zenith, and squinted out the cursed rays of its malign influences' (I, 333); 'I have not yet forgiven Fortune for her mischievous game of Cross Purposes that deprived me of the pleasure of seeing you again when you were here' (I, 375–76); 'However, Providence to keep up the proper proportion of evil with the good, which it seems is necessary in this sublunary state, thought proper to check my exultation by a very serious misfortune' (II, 70). At various points in his life Burns was abused by 'Fate, or Providence, or whatever is the true appellation for the Power who presides over & directs the affairs of this our world' (II, 48). Equally incontrovertible, however, is the facility with which he adopted the *persona* of victim, the model for which he found in Tristram.

In both Sterne and Burns the awareness of man's limitation leads to a defiant and compensatory assertion of individuality (in Sterne's terms, the hobby-horse is ridden all the harder). It leads, too, to fierce attacks on the artificial restraints which man imposes upon himself. While Blake lamented 'the mind-forg'd manacles', Sterne demonstrated, especially through the figure of Walter Shandy, the absurdity of slavish adherence to rationalism. Burns's innate anti-rationalism, which could occasion his writing that 'with all reverence to the cold theorems of Reason, a few honest Prejudices & benevolent Prepossessions, are some of the utmost consequence' (I, 342), found endorsement in Sterne. Burns attacked rationalism's Presbyterian manifestation as Prudence.

It was because of the deep division within Burns that he persisted in pleading for instinct and intuition in an almost plaintive manner. To Mrs. McLehose he wrote: 'Some yet unnamed feelings; things, not principles, but better than whims, carry me farther than boasted reason ever did a Philosopher' (I, 144). In terms distinctly Shandean he wrote to Brown:

> I have always found an honest passion, or native instinct, the trustiest auxiliary in the warfare of this world. —Reason almost always comes to me, like an unlucky wife to a poor devil of a husband—just in time enough to add her reproaches to his other grievances. (I, 206)

The following extract from a letter written on the same day as the above reveals Burns grasping at revealed religion:

> . . . a man, conscious of having acted an honest part among his fellow creatures; even granting that he may have been the sport, at times, of passions and instincts; he goes to a great unknown Being who could have no other end in giving him existence but to make him happy; who gave him those passions and instincts and well knows their force. (I, 207)

This is worthy of Tristram's Uncle Toby himself. But Burns's hold on revealed religion was altogether more precarious. Two years later he was to write to Mrs. Dunlop:

> Still the damned dogmas of reasoning Philosophy throw in their doubts; but upon the whole, I believe, or rather I have a kind of conviction, though not absolute certainty, of the world beyond the grave. (II, 118)

The result of such doubts was, in addition to a defiant assertion of self, a spirited attack on 'that cardinal virtue' (I, 318), Prudence, and its practitioners. For Burns (with unmistakable echoes of Rousseauism):

161

> We come into this world with a heart and disposition to do good
> for it, untill by dashing a large mixture of base Alloy called
> Prudence alias Selfishness, the too precious Metal of the Soul is
> brought down to the blackguard Sterling of ordinary currency.
> (I, 242)

In much of this, as in most of Burns's letters, there is an
element of attitudinizing along with more than a grain of
truth. When he struck attitudes he was aware of it. A letter to
Mrs. McLehose ends:

> If you send me a page baptised in the font of sanctimonious
> Prudence—By Heaven, Earth & Hell, I will tear it into
> atoms!—. . .
>   . . . I need scarcely remark that the foregoing was the fustian
> rant of enthusiastic youth. (II, 156)

Burns shares with Sterne a benevolent emotionalism and
offers the heart as source of positive good (or as much good as
can be man's, given his condition). 'Almost all my religious
tenets originate from my heart' (II, 58), he proclaims, with a
certain degree of scarce-concealed satisfaction; and since his
heart is that of a poet it has a 'bedlam warmth' (I, 123). Again
sounding like Uncle Toby, he claims, for the benefit of
Clarinda, that his is 'the Religion of the bosom' (I, 161).
Quoting *Tristram Shandy* (III, Ch. 10), he tells Maria Riddell:
'If it is true, that "Offences come only from the heart";—
before you, I am guiltless' (II, 230). To Mrs. Dunlop he
affirms: 'The heart of the Man and the fancy of the Poet are
the two grand considerations for which I live' (I, 276); and to
the same lady he was to extol 'a heart glowing with the noble
enthusiasm of Generosity, Benevolence and Greatness of Soul'
(I, 343). The primacy of feeling bears upon his rare excursions
into literary criticism: amongst his 'few strictures on Miss
Williams Poem on the Slave Trade' is: 'Verse 46th I am afraid
is rather unworthy of the rest: "to dare to feel", is an idea that
I do not altogether like' (I, 353).

For Burns and Sterne the heart is life; it is the source of
good; and in it originates any consolation that may be man's
for his victimization by Providence, to which limitation he
adds by creating the constraints of rationalist systems. To set
Burns on the subject of man (e.g. II, 235) alongside Sterne is

to be made aware of distinct similarities. Yet one is left after a reading of *Tristram Shandy* (though not, admittedly, Sterne's letters) with a strong sense of Sterne's genuine compassion for man, whereas too often with Burns the predominant response is one of sentimentality. In a profound essay on Sterne, Edwin Muir wrote that in his work 'the mind was free to consider every object in it . . . this ubiquity of interest is at the root of Sterne's humour.'[19] Was Burns's mind free in this sense? Did he possess this ubiquity of interest? Regrettably, the answers have to be that his mind lacked the imaginative range and freedom of Sterne's, being constrained both by personal needs and the cultural disorientation of his country. Moreover, Sterne's sentimentalizing is invariably part of an emotional flux or totality; too often Burns merely sentimentalizes, or sentimentalizes in isolation.

Hitherto I have been contending that the linguistic energy endemic in the Scots literary tradition is further strengthened in the instance of Burns by virtue of the poet's distinctive personality and his situation; that the post-Union cultural disorientation of the Scottish writer induced a compensatory emphasis on style; and that this is reflected in Burns's letters, which are the result of conscious artistry. They also reflect a considerable dramatic capacity in Burns. As early as December 1789 Burns wrote: 'I have some thoughts of the Drama' (I, 379); and three months later he was requesting copies of English and French dramatists from Hill, the bookseller (II, 15), (principally those of the major neo-classicists).[20] That the dramatic capacity found expression through the *personae* of the poems and the letters, rather than in a play, may be attributed in part at least to the cultural and religious bias against drama.

Before further consideration of the letters in terms of self-dramatization, and Sterne as a particular source of *personae*, it is worth anticipating one of several contradictions yet to be identified in Burns. Noting the 'dancing irresponsibility and the lashing whip of Burns's language', Kurt Wittig wrote of Burns's attack on Presbyterianism: 'Burns's attack . . . does not take the form of mere rational satire; it is in itself a liberating outburst of zest and vitality.'[21] Wittig is writing of the poetic satires, but the comment applies equally to the letters. The point is, however, that in the letters an antithetical process is in operation: the linguistic and satiric energy is temporarily liberating (as with Smollett), but the manifold self-dramatization is limiting and, ultimately, self-destroying. Thomas Crawford made the important point that 'the self-dramatizations of the epistles express a mind in motion.'[22] Precisely the same might be claimed for the letters with their fluctuations of tone, emotion, and *personae*. Byron, after reading certain of Burns's letters, exclaimed: 'What an antithetical mind!'[23] Perhaps the Burns of the letters was divided between the self, which was complex in itself, and the many alternative selves that it projected. This essay will argue that in time the self in effect *became* the various and fragmented substitute selves.

In his letters Burns manifests a heightened self-consciousness and a willingness for self-dramatization. In one letter he exclaims:

> God have mercy on me! a poor d—mned, incautious, duped, unfortunate fool! the sport, the miserable victim of rebellious pride, hypochondriac imagination, agonizing sensibility, and bedlam passions! (I, 172)

In another he comments: 'I am, just as usual, a rhyming, mason-making, raking, aimless, idle fellow' (I, 99). Probably the clearest indication that, at least earlier in his career, he was aware of the distinction between self and role occurs in the letter to Alexander Cunningham in which he relates thus the news of his marriage:

> I am, too, a married man. —This was a step of which I had no idea, when you & I were together. —On my return to Ayr-shire, I found a much-lov'd Female's positive happiness, or absolute Misery among my hands; and I could not trifle with such a sacred Deposite. —I am, since, doubly pleased with my conduct. —I have the consciousness of acting up to that generosity of principle I would be thought to possess; & I am really more & more pleased with my Choice. (I, 238)

In his edition of the letters of Sterne, Curtis observes of the reader's attitude to the writer that 'it is in the eighteenth century that we watch the transition of the public's attitude from one of decorous respect to one of prying curiosity', and he remarks of Sterne's letters that they 'were intended to be shown about' (*Letters*, xxiv; xxviii). Burns exemplifies the writer's responsiveness to this shift in public attitude, and he begins to dramatize, and offer versions of, himself. But some versions were for a strictly limited circle.

That Burns had the capacity to adopt many varied *personae* is undeniable. Maria Riddell commented:

> Many others perhaps may have ascended to prouder heights in the region of Parnassus, but none certainly ever outshone Burns in the charms— the sorcery, I would almost call it, of fascinating conversation, the spontaneous eloquence of social argument, or the unstudied poignancy of brilliant repartee.[24]

Burns devotees who take his every word literally would do well to ponder that 'sorcery'. Recent criticism, most notably that of John C. Weston, has recognized both the skill and the extent of Burns's use of ironic voice. Of the verse-satires Weston has noted:

> Nine of the eleven satires use, in several degrees of emphasis, the voice of the opponent. The other two . . . employ an irony which results from the poet's speaking in some degree other than what he means but not, as in the more typical, saying, more or less, the opposite of what he means.[25]

The ironic use of dramatic voice, the initial possibilities of which, as Weston suggests, Burns saw in Ramsay, bulks large in the letters. In some the 'opponent' is one of the poet's alternative selves, so that the letters as a whole may be regarded as a dramatization of the conflicts within Burns's own personality. Wittig notes that 'in Scots literature, it is often the feelings of others that are expressed, from inside their minds.'[26] In Burns's letters the 'others' are projections, or versions, of himself.

It is erroneous to see in Burns's Edinburgh period the origins of his internal divisions and self-fragmentation. Range and versatility of voice are evident from the earliest letters. At the age of twenty-one he wrote in formal Augustan prose to William Niven, a friend since early school-days, and even this early he was intent 'on presenting an image, or a version, of himself. To Niven he wrote: 'For my own part, I now see it improbable that I shall ever acquire riches, and am therefore endeavouring to gather a philosophical contempt of enjoyments so hard to be gained and so easily lost' (I, 3). The image of the self that he projected varied to suit the recipient. Accordingly he sent, as dutiful son, a letter from Irvine to his father in which he combines striking of noble attitudes with maudlin self-pity of this kind:

> Sometimes, indeed, when for an hour or two, as is sometimes the case, my spirits are a little lightened, I glimmer a little into futurity; but my principal, and indeed my only pleasurable employment is looking backwards & forwards in a moral & religious way—I am quite transported at the thought that ere long, perhaps very soon, I shall bid an eternal adieu to all the pains, & uneasiness & disquietudes of this weary life; for I assure you I am heartily tired of it, and, if I do not very much deceive myself I could contentedly & gladly resign it. (I, 4–5)

The question of how a warm-blooded young man of twenty-two could come to write in this way is answered by the post-script: having concluded 'I am, Honored Sir, your dutiful son, Robt. Burns', he adds: 'my meal is nearly out but I am going to borrow till I get more.'

In one of his earliest love-letters (probably to Alison Begbie) Burns proclaims:

> There is one rule which I have hitherto practised, and which I shall invariably keep with you, and that is, honestly to tell you the plain truth. There is something so mean and unmanly in the arts of dissimulation and falsehood, that I am surprised they can be acted by any one in so noble, so generous a passion, as virtuous love. (I, 9)

Professing virtuous love and acting for all he was worth, Burns could voice similar sentiments to Clarinda seven years later, asserting: 'The dignified and dignifying consciousness of an honest man, and the well-grounded trust in approving Heaven, are two most substantial [foundations] of happiness' (I, 202). Where the occasion demanded, Burns could readily proclaim the importance of sincerity (I, 147), or the validity of orthodox morality and religion (I, 184).

It is certainly not the purpose of this paper to argue that Burns was a hypocrite. The role-playing in which he engaged seems to have been typical of Scottish writers of the time. T. S.

Eliot wrote of Byron, in terms that apply equally to Burns: 'Hypocrite . . . except in the original sense of the word, is hardly the term for Byron. He was an actor who devoted immense trouble to *becoming* a role that he adopted.'[27]

Burns's letters may be seen as part of an enduring tradition in Scottish literature, that strain which C. M. Grieve described as 'tremendously idiosyncratic, full of a wild humour which blends the actual and the apocalyptic in an incalculable fashion'.[28] Viewed in this light the extravagances and contradictions of the multiple voices of Burns's letters are more readily understood and less readily reprehended. Burns possessed in large measure the rhetorical capacity and the tendency to fantasize which are characteristic of the innate Scottish response. Both of these qualities are epitomized in the flyting. The following description, by Wittig, of the flyting as an integral part of the Scottish tradition has acute relevance to the linguistic force of Burns's letters and its origin:

> True flyting . . . has little in common with satire and social criticism. It is essentially an act of revolt, primitive and un-ashamed, against all socially-imposed restraint; it revels in the sensuous as such; and in seeking to assert its own stubborn individualism it is quite prepared to let everything else 'gang tapsalteerie', or to the Devil if need be.[29]

Some of Burns's behaviour, both personal and literary, is explicable in terms of revolt against socially imposed restraint. His writing, including his letters (perhaps *especially* his letters where the restraining influence of form is less effective), serves as a medium at times for the expression, through diverse voices, of his frustration. The essence of the flyting may be observed in Burns's letters, but it has been set to the services of the individual psychological needs of the writer. Wittig also notes that the flyting and extravaganza are a strong feature of the literature of the Celtic fringe. Thus the extravagant and dynamic elements in Burns and Sterne are part of the one tradition. And Burns was, as Curtis said of Sterne, 'preoccupied with the absorbing drama of his own existence' (*Letters*, xxxii).

Of the fashionable *personae* available to Burns the one which had the greatest appeal for one of his temperament was that of the man of feeling. By Burns's day Europe had been pervaded by the belief in man's original natural benevolism, a belief for which Rousseau was the most eloquent and earnest spokesman. But by that time Rousseauism had bred various distorted forms: the sentimental comedies of Diderot who had claimed: 'If Nature ever made a sensitive soul, that soul, and you know it, is mine';[30] Goethe's *The Sorrows of Young Werther*, in which can be discerned a distinct distancing—sometimes ironic—of author from his hero; and Mackenzie's *The Man of Feeling*, where this is even more noticeably a feature. It is true that Burns was most attracted to the pathetic and sentimental aspects of the work of Mackenzie, 'the Man of Feeling, that first of men' (I, 191). But the duality in his values is reflected in the fact that, while extolling Harley's sentiments, he could yet warn of the impracticality of his behaviour. He wrote to Mrs. Dunlop:

> From what book, moral or even pious, will the susceptible young mind receive impressions more congenial to humanity and kindness, generosity and benevolence—in short, more of all that ennobles the soul to herself, or endears her to others—than from the simple affecting tale of poor Harley?
>
> Still, with all my admiration of McKenzie's writings, I do not know if they are the fittest reading for a young man who is about to set out, as the phrase is, to make his way into life. (II, 20)

Similarly, in another letter, he wrote: 'Sir, he is, without the least alloy, a universal Philanthropist; and his much beloved name is—A BOTTLE OF GOOD OLD PORT!' (I, 117).

Such qualification of the voice of feeling is rare, however. Burns and Sterne on the virtues of the honest heart sound remarkably similar. In one of his earliest letters Burns wrote to Niven:

> I shall be happy to hear from you how you go on in the ways of life; I do not mean so much how trade prospers, or if you have the prospect of riches, or the dread of poverty; as how you go on in the cultivation of the finer feelings of the heart. (I, 3)

The phrase is revealing: aged twenty-one, Burns was aware that the finer feelings of the heart required 'cultivation'. Benevolence he took care to project as one of his redeeming features. To James Smith he presented himself thus: 'For me, I am witless wild, and wicked; and have scarcely any vestige of the image of God left me, except a pretty large portion of honour and an enthusiastic, incoherent Benevolence' (I, 36).

In the letters the best exemplification of the way in which Burns capitalizes on the doctrine of the feeling heart is in the sequence of accounts of his encountering the wounded hare. The first mention of this includes an element of ironic awareness (and self-awareness). For Burns the sight of the hare

> set my humanity in tears and my indignation in arms.—The following was the result, which please read to the young ladies— I believe you may include the Major, too; as whatever I have said of shooting hares, I have not spoken one irreverend word against coursing them. (I, 324)

Within a fortnight he produced the following, much more formal and moralistic, version of the same incident:

> . . . I heard the burst of a shot from a neighbouring Plantation, & presently a poor little wounded hare came crippling by me.—You will guess my indignation at the inhuman fellow, who could shoot a hare at this season when they all of them have young ones; & it gave me no little gloomy satisfaction to see the poor injured creature escape him.—Indeed there is something in all that multiform business of destroying for our sport individuals in the animal creation that do not injure us materially, that I could never reconcile to my ideas of native Virtue & eternal Right. (I, 330)

After a further six weeks the incident inspired this highly sentimental account:

> . . . I heard the report of a gun from a neighbouring wood, and presently a poor little hare, dragging its wounded limbs, limped piteously by me.—I have always had an abhorrence at this way of assasinating God's creatures without first allowing them those means of defence with which he has variously endowed them; but at this season when the object of our treacherous murder is most probably a Parent, perhaps the mother, and of consequence to leave two little helpless nurslings to perish with hunger amid the pitiless wilds, such an action is not only a sin against the letter of the law, but likewise a deep crime against the *morality of the heart*. (I, 341)

Nothing demonstrates more tellingly the way in which Burns

worked at playing upon the feelings of his readers. Fairchild's comment that those of Burns's poems that are concerned with the 'sympathetic glow' reveal 'a mixture of genuine and fabricated feeling which suggests a lack of spiritual integration' applies equally readily to the letters; and the lack of integration encompasses personal and psychological dimensions.

Burns enacts the various roles which by his day were inseparable from the vogue of feeling. The following extract from an early letter suggests that the *persona* of the melancholic came easily to him:

> I have here likewise inclosed a small piece, the very latest of my productions. I am a good deal pleased with some sentiments myself, as they are just the native querulous feelings of a heart which, as the elegantly melting Gray says, 'Melancholy has marked for her own'. (I, 26)

Recalling the 'voluptuous enjoyment' of a blind grand-uncle in weeping while his mother sang 'The Life and Age of Man', Burns comments: 'It is this way of thinking, it is these melancholy truths, that make Religion so precious to the poor miserable Children of men' (I, 246). Habitually, then, Burns, as Sterne had done, offers melancholy as a component of an emotional compound. Awareness of the ambivalence, or the complexity, of feeling recurs. The birth of twins to Jean Armour led him to write: 'A very fine boy and girl have awakened a thousand (tender [deleted]) feelings that thrill, some with tender pleasure, and some with foreboding anguish, thro' my soul' (I, 42). One may compare Sterne's 'dined alone again today; and begin to find a pleasure in this kind of resigned Misery arising from this Situation, of heart unsupported by aught but its own tenderness'; and 'my Sentimental Journey will, I dare say, convince you that my feelings are from the heart, and that that heart is not of the worst of molds—praised be God for my sensibility! Though it has often made me wretched, yet I would not exchange it for all the pleasures the grossest sensualist ever felt' (*Letters*, 324; 395–96).

Burns shares with Sterne also the stylized and sentimental conception of the rural idyll. Burns made the following request of Peter Miller: '. . . fix me in any sequester'd romantic spot, and let me have such a lease as by care and industry I might live in humble decency, and have a spare hour now and then to write out an idle rhyme . . .' (I, 87–8). Sterne writes of 'a little sun-gilt cottage on the side of a romantic hill', and claims 'the loneliest Cottage that Love and Humility ever dwelt in' is preferable to the 'glittering Court' (*Letters*, 16; 333). In Burns there is again a certain duality in that he appears to relish both the romanticized domestic setting and the wild grandeur of the Highland landscapes (and its culture). Very much the tourist of sensibility, he enthuses: 'I have done nothing else but visited cascades, prospects, ruins, and Druidical temples, learned Highland tunes and pickt up Scotch songs, Jacobite anecdotes, &c. these two months' (I, 132–33). The dichotomy in Burns can almost be seen in geographical terms as he exclaims: 'warm as I was from Ossian's country where I had seen his very grave, what cared I for fisher-towns and fertile Carses?' (I, 125). The following union of wild untutored nature and man's creative fancy is even more revealing:

> My ready fancy, with colors more mellow than life itself, painted the beautiful wild scenery of Kilravock; the venerable grandeur of the castle; the spreading woods; the winding river, gladly leaving his unsightly heathy source, and lingering with apparent delight as he passes the fairy walk at the bottom of the garden. (I, 191)

This is almost Freudian, with the river representing Burns himself. His exemplification of sensibility reflects the uneasy union of wild scenery and fairy walk; and his attitude to the culture of the north is similarly ambivalent.

After the example of Sterne in his letters to Mrs. Draper, Burns, in his correspondence with Mrs. McLehose, plays the sentimental lover. Of Sterne's sentimentalism Curtis comments: 'His scene, to be sure, must contain the cherished room and tea-kettle and cat. But in addition to these it must contain a sweet and sympathetic woman to succour him' (*Letters*, xxxii). For Burns, by the winter of 1787 the sentimental relationship with 'Clarinda' fulfilled this function, while the prospect of domesticity became rapidly and inevitably inseparable from the figure of Jean Armour.

Such is the extent of the similarity that it seems almost

171

certain that Burns must have read the *Letters of the late Rev. Mr. Laurence Sterne*, published in London in 1775 by his daughter, Lydia de Medalle. Burns made specific reference to Sterne's letters to Eliza. To Thomson he wrote of the song, 'Craigieburnwood':

> The Lady on whom it was made, is one of the finest women in Scotland; and in fact (entre nous) is in a manner to me what Sterne's Eliza was to him—a Mistress, or Friend, or what you will, in the guileless simplicity of Platonic love. (II, 265)

Points of similarity abound: the worth of the honest heart; the pleasurable pain of love; the cruel providence which parts the lovers; the merits of solitude; and the stylization of Nature and love. Burns presents himself to Clarinda as the sentimental lover in the Sternean mould. 'Cannot you guess, my Clarinda', he wrote, 'what thoughts, what cares, what anxious forebodings, hopes and fears, must crowd the breast of the man of keen sensibility?' (I, 203). In the Clarinda letters, according to Fairchild, Burns was 'trying his hardest not to be his real self'.[32] This is less than true. Part of Burns's 'real self' was precisely the projection of *persona* in which he indulged in this correspondence.

In one of the earliest letters to Mrs. McLehose Burns wrote: 'I am determined to cultivate your friendship with the enthusiasm of Religion' (I, 144). Soon a clear division within his attitude became apparent. Within one letter he proclaimed both: 'I like the idea of Arcadian names in commerce of this kind', and, almost immediately after: 'I wish you to see me as I am.' Thereafter he embarks on the self-romanticizing that recurs throughout the Clarinda letters: 'I am, as most people of my trade are, a strange will o' wisp being; the victim too frequently of much imprudence and many follies.—My great constituent elements are Pride and Passion' (I, 149). For all the strong element of role-playing, Burns could yet assure Clarinda: 'You see I am either above, or incapable of Dissimulation' (I, 150), and: 'You are right . . . a friendly correspondence goes for nothing, except one write their undisguised sentiments' (I, 153).

Central to the relationship is the degree of emotional communion that is achieved, and especially the sharing of suffering or melancholy. But here the grandly emotional declamation sometimes descends into bathos or is undermined by reductively banal detail. It is difficult to believe that Burns was not conscious of the disruptive, even comic, effect of the intrusion of the particular in this:

> Did you, Madam, know what I feel when you talk of your sorrows!
> Good God! that one who has so much worth in the sight of Heaven, and is so amiable to her fellow-creatures, should be so unhappy! I can't venture out for cold. My limb is vastly better; but I have not any use of it without crutches. (I, 153)

Sterne's letters to Eliza contain a comparable fusion of elevated thoughts and sometimes bizarrely particular details (e.g. *Letters*, 314–16, where, on her departure for India, he warns her to beware of her shipmates and is deeply concerned that 'the fresh painting [of her cabin] will be enough to destroy every nerve about [her]').

From Mackenzie's Harley and from the example of Sterne's letters Burns adopts the formulaic use of weeping as proof of the feeling heart's empathic capacity. With Burns's 'You talk of weeping, Clarinda: some involuntary drops wet your lines as I read them' (I, 162) may be compared the following utterances of Sterne: 'I can never see or talk to this incomparable woman without bursting into tears' (*Letters*, 308); 'I wept my plate full, Eliza! and now I have begun, could shed tears till supper again' (*Letters*, 336); and he states (*Letters*, 325) that he cannot talk of Eliza without bursting into tears, which occasions outpourings of sympathy from his companion, Mrs. James. No more telling instance of Sterne's exploitation for effect of the processes of emotion can be found than the following: '. . . upon taking up my pen, my poor pulse quickened— my pale face glowed—and tears (ran [deleted]) stood ready in my eyes to fall upon the paper, as I traced the word Eliza' (*Letters*, 331–32). That substitution of 'stood' for 'ran' epitomizes the habitual striving after pathetic effect on the part of the self-projected man of feeling.

Sterne is the source too of self-dramatizing appeals for pity, as when Burns, describing his life as a ruined temple, exclaims: 'What strength, what proportion in some parts! what unsightly gaps, what prostrate ruins in others!' (I, 166). In Burns's 'I see you laughing at my fairy fancies, and calling me a voluptuous Mahometan' (I, 170) are clear echoes of Sterne's writing to Eliza as her 'Bramin' (*Letters*, 299). Common to each set of letters also is the sense of the torture of love. Burns writes: 'O Love and Sensibility, ye have conspired against My Peace! I love to madness, and I feel to torture' (I, 174); and Sterne, as well as writing in like vein, makes plain that his love for Eliza renders work, or anything else, impossible (*Letters*, 350, 351, 377). In each correspondence sensibility is a source of woe. Burns writes:

> Nature has been too kind to you for your happiness.—Your Delicacy, your Sensibility.—O why should such glorious qualifications be the fruitful source of woe! You have 'murdered sleep' to me last night.—I went to bed impress'd with an idea that you were unhappy; and every start I closed my eyes, busy Fancy painted you in such scenes of romantic misery, that I would almost be persuaded you are not well this morning. (I, 176)

With this may be compared Sterne's 'Remember how I Love—remember what I suffer' (*Letters*, 346) and a lengthy passage (*Letters*, 334) which is the quintessence of the suffering of the sentimental lover.

When Burns declares to Clarinda:

> You are the first, the only unexceptionable individual of the beauteous Sex that I ever met with; and never woman more intirely possessed my soul.—I know myself, and how far I can depend on passions, well. It has been my peculiar study (I, 181),

he is both playing a role and, in so doing, being himself. In this he is very much the modern—obsessively self-conscious, preoccupied with watching himself being himself in the variety of roles that comprise him, one of which is that of watcher.

The episode as sentimental lover revealed much about his personality. Once back at Ellisland he delivered in a letter to Mrs. Dunlop one of the most vituperative of his many attacks on the great and fashionable world (I, 311). The rush and expense of verbal energy was plainly therapeutic, venting, perhaps, his rage and dismay at finding himself playing such divergent roles ('To a man who has a Home, however humble or remote; if that Home is like mine, the scene of Domestic comfort; the bustle of Edinburgh will soon be a business of sickening disgust'). Noting that Burns resorts to satire to relieve the pressure of anger, John Weston observed that Burns 'always was a man of negative feelings, never a man of sweetness or compliance'.[33] In his lengthy autobiographical letter to Moore Burns wrote: 'My Passions when once they were lighted up, raged like so many devils, till they got vent in rhyme; and then conning over my verses, like a spell, soothed all into quiet' (I, 112). The vehement attack on 'the iron pride of unfeeling greatness' (Mrs. Oswald) (I, 296) fulfilled the same function. And an account of the attacks on Dr. McGill induced him to avow: 'I shall keep no measure with the savages, but fly at them with the faucons of Ridicule, or run them down with the bloodhounds of Satire, as lawful game wherever I start them' (I, 135–36). Such eruption of passionate feeling, frequently negative or hostile, into vigorous expression characterizes the work of several major Scottish writers of the period (Smollett, Burns, Byron, Hogg); so much so that one wonders if it amounts to an unconscious expression of the disorientation which the loss of nationhood occasioned.

Possibly this is one of the factors that contribute to a feature of Burns's letters which Burns devotees prefer to overlook: the recurrent assertions of his superiority may well be rooted in a deep personal (reflecting a national) insecurity. This is a characteristic of Burns which cannot be attributed to the Edinburgh sojourn since it appears in some of the earlier letters. On 17 November 1782 Burns wrote thus:

> I love to see a man who has a mind superiour to the world and the world's men, a man who, conscious of his own integrity, and at peace with himself, despises the censures and opinions of the unthinking rabble of mankind. The distinction of a poor man and a rich man is something indeed, but it is nothing to the difference between either a wise man or a fool, or a man of honor and a knave. (I, 12)

Burns as poet and man of feeling, for all the sympathetic glow, sees himself as a man apart, and certainly elevated above the rabble. 'Remember this', he enjoins Niven, 'never

175

blow my Songs among the Million, as I would abhor to hear every Prentice mouthing my poor performances in the streets' (I, 39). After his triumph he regretted, even resented, what he saw as slavish imitation by the inferior many, and complained: 'My success has encouraged such a shoal of ill-spawned monsters to crawl into public notice, under the title of Scots Poets, that the very term, Scots Poetry, borders on the burlesque' (I, 311–12).

Fairchild has claimed that the prime appeal of masonry to Burns was 'the combination of very hearty conviviality with a benevolism which hovered on the borderline between New Light religion and sentimental deism', while he also liked 'the democracy which enabled common folk to rub elbows with the gentry'. One suspects that, rather than the democracy, it was the union of brotherhood with exclusiveness which appealed. It is precisely the tension between these which issues out in the letters quoted above. Noting the ironies wherein Burns's 'artificially cultivated literary benevolism interfered with the true benevolism of his heart', Fairchild points out that he 'had spurned the antinomianism of the Evangelicals for antinomianism of a more attractive sort—the glorious freedom of the children of sensibility'.[34] In the fullest manifestation of that 'glorious freedom'—the Clarinda relationship—Burns evinces exactly the same paradox: such sentimental benevolism is inevitably contradictory since, aware of it, the sentimental lover recognizes his distinction from the majority. So to Clarinda Burns wrote:

> Coarse minds are not aware how much they injure the keenly feeling tie of bosom-friendship, when in their foolish officiousness they mention what nobody cares for recollecting.—People of nice sensibility and generous minds have a certain intrinsic dignity, that fires at being trifled with, or towered, or even too nearly approached. (I, 155)

Four days later the white-heat of such fire was beginning to take its toll of him, and he ended a letter to her: 'John Milton, I wish thy soul better rest than I expect on my pillow to-night. Oh for a little of the cart-horse part of human nature!' (I, 160). This is the less predominant note, however. On one, more typical, occasion, after enthusing on the luxury of his bliss and

176

noting how she has both stolen and refined his soul, he exclaims: 'What trifling silliness is the childish fondness of the every-day children of the world!' (I, 167).

Precisely this sense of the distinction that is inseparable from extreme sensibility also characterizes the letters of Sterne. To Eliza Sterne writes that only 'men of nice sensibility' can be touched by her 'bewitching sort of nameless excellence' (*Letters*, 313). He hopes she will read his letters 'when weary of fools and uninteresting discourse' (*Letters*, 316). 'Time and distance, or change of every thing wch. might allarm [*sic*] the little hearts of little men, create now uneasy suspence in mine' (*Letters*, 332), he avows. With echoes of Donne he exclaims: 'the Room will not be too little for us—but We shall be *too* big for the Room' (*Letters*, 367). The tone and style of the Clarinda letters owe much to such passages in Sterne's letters as:

> What a stupid, selfish, unsentimental set of Beings are the Bulk of our Sex! By Heaven! not one man out of 50, informed with feelings—or endowed either with heads or hearts able to possess & fill the mind of such a Being as thee, with one Vibration like its own. (*Letters*, 364–65)

The essential point of difference is that, unlike Sterne, Burns took with him far beyond the confines of sentimental romance the conviction of the superiority with which sensibility endowed one. To Alexander Cunningham he declared:

> Love is the Alpha and the Omega of human enjoyment . . . It is the emanation of Divinity that preserves the Sons and Daughters of rustic labour from degenerating into the brutes with which they daily hold converse. (I, 298)

Similarly, to William Dunbar he wrote: 'We are not shapen out of the common, heavy, methodical Clod, the elemental Stuff of the plodding, selfish Race, the Sons of Arithmetick and Prudence . . . in the name of random Sensibility then, let never the moon change on our silence any more' (II, 1–2).

Increasingly, however, there appears a realization that extreme sensibility is a questionable gift. The following typifies this sense:

> There is a species of the Human genus that I call the Gin-horse Class: what enviable dogs they are!—Round, and round, and

round they go—Mundell's ox that drives his cotton-mill, their exact prototype—without an idea or wish beyond their circle; fat, sleek, stupid, patient, quiet and contented:—while here I sit, altogether Novemberish, a damn'd melange of Fretfulness and melancholy; not enough of the one to rouse me to passion, nor of the other to repose me in torpor; my soul flouncing and fluttering round her tenement, like a wild Finch caught amid the horrors of winter and newly thrust into a cage. (II, 217)

This is no mere attitudinizing: here is the agonized, resentful awareness of the man who knows he is caught in a cage which he has helped to make. The thought of his soul 'in her wanderings through the weary, thorny wilderness of this world' induces the exclamation:

God knows I am ill-fitted for the struggle: I glory in being a Poet, and I want to be thought a wise man—I would fondly be generous, and I wish to be rich. After all, I am afraid I am a lost subject. (I, 139)

Paul Hazard noted the extent to which some of the greatest European minds of the eighteenth century are characterized by the union of contraries, and wrote: 'You might have thought about many and many a writer, that he was two men rolled into one.'[35] Burns exemplifies just such a union of contraries, but to it he lends a distinctly Scottish dimension. To the Earl of Buchan he dramatized the conflict within him in terms of Prudence v. Pride and Instinct, and situation v. aspirations (I, 73).

Reason and instinct coexisted in uneasy compromise in Burns. That he was aware of their contention within him is evident from this account of his father's death to his cousin James Burness:

On the 13th. Currt. I lost the best of fathers. Though to be sure we have had long warning of the impending stroke still the tender feelings of Nature claim their part and I cannot recollect the tender endearments and parental lessons of the best of friends and the ablest of instructors without feeling, what perhaps, the calmer dictates of reason would partly condemn. (I, 17)

Too readily reason and emotion became, respectively, a somewhat underhand practicality and sentimental gesturing. Two adjacent letters in Ferguson's edition make a telling juxta-position: in one Burns confides to Thomas Orr: 'I am at present so cursedly taken in with an affair of gallantry that I am very glad Peggy is off my hand as I am at present embar-rassed enough without her', while the next contains a highly stylized account of the heightened sensibility of the poet (I, 20–1). One is reminded of Fairchild's comment that 'the poetry of Burns is curiously divided between Fergusson and Mackenzie.'[36]

Goethe's Werther states that 'a man is a man, and the little bit of sense he may have plays little or no part at all when passion rages in him, and the limitations of humankind oppress him.'[37] Burns had more than a little bit of sense, but it was powerless in the face of passion, not least his passion for role-playing; and whilst the limitations of humankind may be said to have oppressed him, there is a sense in which he was oppressed most of all by himself. The divisions within himself oppressed him, and he was well aware of them and powerless to resolve them. On the most obvious level this led to the threat which his allegedly republican sentiments posed to his position in the Excise. The problems arising from his alleged political radicalism he explained to Erskine of Mar as his falling 'under the temptation of being witty [rather] than dis-affected' (II, 169).

Increasing pressures sundered even further the various con-flicting elements within Burns. Adding a poignancy to his situation is his capacity for self-analysis, which is evident in the following, albeit that there is the almost-inevitable exploitation of the point for the fullest effect:

> My worst enemy is Moimême. I lie so miserably open to the inroads and incursions of a mischievous, light-armed, well-mounted banditti, under the banners of Imagination, Whim, Caprice, and Passion, and the heavy-armed veteran regulars of Wisdom, Prudence, and Forethought, move so very, very slow, that I am almost in a state of perpetual warfare, and alas! frequent defeat. There are just two creatures I would envy, a horse in his native state traversing the forests of Asia, or an oyster on some of the desart shores of Europe. The one has not a wish without enjoyment, the other has neither wish nor fear. (I, 145–46)

179

Such a comment is difficult to reconcile with Ferguson's claim that 'Burns was conscious of no schizophrenia in himself, though he was well aware that a legend surrounded him.'[38] In Burns are clear indications of the conflict between Calvinist predeterminism and sentimentalism. Of man's condition Burns wrote to Ainslie: 'Whether he shall rise in the manly consciousness of a self-approving mind, or sink beneath a galling load of Regret and Remorse—these are alternatives of the last moment' (I, 232).

The dichotomies within Burns are further reflected in the various levels and styles of language which he uses in his letters. For instance, it is revealing to compare the language of 'Tam o' Shanter' with the prose account—in the formal prose of polite, educated society—of witch stories relating to Alloway Kirk which he sent to Francis Grose (II, 22). Increasingly there are signs that, in fact, Burns became trapped within the formal mode of writing. A letter to Alexander Cunningham, one of his closest friends, includes this tale of 'Charlie Caldwell, a drunken Carrier in Ayr':

> Charles had a Cara Sposa after his own heart, who used to take 'caup-out' with him till neither could see the other.—When those honest Genii of old Scotch Social Life—'REAMING SWATS'—used to transport the tender Pair beyond the bounds of sober joy, to the region of rapture; the ardent Lover would grapple the yielding Fair to his bosom—'MARGET! YE'RE A GLORY TO GOD, & THE DELIGHT O' MY SOUL!!'
>
> As I cannot in conscience tax you with the postage of a packet, I must keep this bizarre melange of an epistle untill I find the chance of a private conveyance. (II, 237)

Why did Burns employ a mode akin to the comic-epic, with its highly reductive connotations, when one side of him would almost certainly echo the carrier's sentiments? The answer must be that the *persona* which this mode expressed had become compulsive. On Burns more than any major Scottish writer since the Union did the cultural and linguistic dichotomy take its toll. The mask of the stylist in formal English prose would occasionally drop to reveal the depth of regret at the passing of a culture, some of the remnants of which he had permanized in song. 'These English Songs gravel me to death', he wrote, 'I have not that command of the language that I have of my native tongue.—In fact I think my ideas are more barren in English than in Scottish' (II, 268).

In the letters of the later years of Burns's life the divisions within his personality become more blatant, and the self-dramatization and self-distancing verge on the schizoid. He wrote to Gilbert from Ellisland early in 1790: 'My nerves are in a damnable State.—I feel that horrid hypochondria pervading every atom of both body & soul.—This farm has undone my enjoyment of myself' (II, 1). That phrase, 'my enjoyment of myself', exemplifies the extent to which his life had become meaningful in terms of self-drama: Burns was both cast and audience. Drink and bawdry offered some relief, but by late in 1791 he was writing to Ainslie: 'When I tell you even [Bawdry] has lost its power to please, you will guess something of my hell within, and all around me' (II, 99). At times despair mingled with something close to paranoia. A late letter to Mrs. Dunlop includes: 'I know not how to be the object of Pity.—My enemies may dislike (for they dare not despise me) & I can repay them in kind; but the Pity of a Friend is quite distressing' (II, 270).

The self-distancing and subterfuge became increasingly pronounced. In April 1793 a letter to Erskine of Mar contains this request:

> When you have honored this letter with a perusal, please commit it to the flames.—BURNS, in whose behalf you have so generously interested yourself, I have here, in his native colours, drawn *as he is*; but should any of the people in whose hands is the very bread he eats, get the least knowledge of the picture, it would ruin the poor Bard forever. (II, 171)

This epitomizes his condition: Burns *as he is* is presented in a verbal *picture*, but the self by which he is known is that of the 'poor Bard'—illusion and reality, roles and selves, have become interchangeable.[39] Burns might well be the forerunner of those whom Morse Peckham terms the Stylists—those who seek an answer to the dilemma of Romanticism in style. Stylism, as Peckham notes, 'degenerated into mannerism . . . Swinburne and Debussy ended up playing the roles of "Swinburne" and "Debussy" which they had invented and Hemingway ended

up playing the role of "Hemingway".' Burns ended up playing
the role of 'Burns', and as Hemingway *had* to commit suicide
(as Peckham notes) so Burns *had* to die the rustic bard.

Peckham observes, in terms acutely relevant to Burns
(though he is writing of the nineteenth century), that Stylism
offered no solution to 'the great Romantic problem of re-entry,
of commitment, of solving the paradox of entering into social
action without betraying one's selfhood or the selfhood of
others'. 'Stylism', he points out, 'could symbolize the self. But
how was one to be the self? It had separated itself from all but
one aspect of human life, but to the Romantic, sooner or later,
history must be encountered, for history is reality.'[40] Burns's
personae laid accretions of fantasy upon precisely that core of
reality.

In this light one can more readily understand the increasing
cultivation of solitude. When Burns begins a letter to Mrs.
Dunlop thus: 'Here in a solitary inn, in a solitary village, am I
set by myself, to amuse my brooding fancy as I may' (II, 246),
he is not merely playing the part of the extreme sentimentalist
whose acute sensibility isolates himself (cf. Sterne, *Letters*, 18,
331, 342, 345, 365): in himself he felt a growing isolation—
again the self *became* the role. Concomitant with solitude came
a heightened awareness of mortality which again, as the
following indicates, evokes Sterne:

> What a transient business is life!—Very lately I was a boy; but
> t'other day I was a young man; and I already begin to feel the
> rigid fibre and stiffening joints of Old Age coming fast o'er my
> frame. (II, 281)

Latterly the cumulative effect of simultaneously acting and
spectating wore him down. The following, from a letter written
less than a month before his death, exemplifies this:

> Alas, Clarke, I begin to fear the worst! As to my individual self,
> I am tranquil;—I would despise myself if I were not: but
> Burns's poor widow! & half a dozen of his dear little ones,
> helpless orphans, there I am weak as a woman's tear.—
> Enough of this! 'tis half of my disease! (II, 324)

As this shows, Burns is very far from tranquil; he knows it, and
indeed despises himself; but the disguise must be worn to the
last.

For all the humour and wit, the overwhelming note of the letters is a black one. Burns was only twenty-eight when he wrote: 'The great misfortune of my life was, never to have AN AIM' (I, 109). (Here there are distinct echoes of Tristram, who has an aim but appears to fail quite spectacularly in his attempts to realize it.) A year later Burns wrote of 'gloomy conjectures in the dark vista of Futurity—consciousness of my own inability for the struggle of the world' (I, 245). In February 1789 he wrote to Mrs. Dunlop: 'I am here more unhappy than I ever experienced before in Edinr.' (I, 309). To the same lady he wrote in October 1792: 'Alas, Madam! who would wish for many years? What is it but to drag existence until our joys gradually expire, and leave us in a night of misery' (II, 128). Early in the following year he was conceding to Thomson: 'It is impossible, at least I feel it in my stunted powers, to be always original, entertaining & witty' (II, 152). In respect of the sense of a loss of creative powers, as with regard to a despair of communing and a general feeling of alienation, there are in fact striking similarities between the utterances of Burns and those of Goethe's Werther. For instance, Werther writes: 'Suffice it to say that the source of all misery is within me just as I formerly bore within myself the source of all bliss . . . I suffer much, for I have lost what was my singular joy in life—the sacred, invigorating power with which I could create worlds around me', and: 'Thus I mock my pain. Were I really to let myself go, a whole litany of antitheses would be the result.'[41]

For the purpose of identifying the similarities and differences between Burns and Sterne, Muir's essay on Sterne is invaluable. Muir wrote of Sterne:

> By appearing only as his imaginative portrait in *Tristram Shandy*, he renounces the luxury of being himself; he never claims the reader's sympathies in the touching role of a human being. He is never a man, a gentleman, a husband, a father, a citizen, a clergyman. He is continuously encased in motley, and painted and wigged; every gesture and intonation is stylised; and Laurence Sterne is resolved into an imaginative sublimation of himself.

Such resolution of self into imaginative sublimation of self is what Burns in part attempted in his letters. Did he succeed, and with what results? The experience of Sterne helps towards providing the answer. In Sterne's case, says Muir,

> It not only enables us to do things which, with our own features presented to the world, we would not permit ourselves to do, or dare not do; it not only gives us licence to be irresponsible, undignified, outspoken: it sets free in us a new personality with a suppleness and daring of movement which seems to belong to a dream world.[42]

With Sterne this is enlivening and liberating, and it involves the comic held in balance with the tragic. In Burns that balance is disturbed, and the dream becomes nightmare; not simply because his reality has its nightmarish aspects, but because of the inability ever to shed the masks. It is hard to decide whether it is the case with Burns that actuality and roles fuse inseparably, or that actuality and version of actuality diverge irrecoverably. Either way, the result was anything but liberating.

Perhaps it was inevitable that the compulsive use of voice— so effective in the poems—with its concomitant emphasis on reductive vision, should come, in the letters, to reflect the overall limiting effect on the mind of the writer. The total effect of the habitual use of reductive *personae* must be to reduce— unless an alternative vision is offered. Burns could offer no such alternative. And perhaps the reason is not just in his own personality and circumstances but in the innate resistance of Scottish values to Romantic (as distinct from sentimental) vision and ideals. Calvinism, which was arraigned, by virtue of its discouragement of drama, for diverting Burns's dramatic energies into self-dramatization, is now doubly villain. By stressing man's flawed nature and the predetermination of human behaviour, Calvinism positively encourages a quasi-diabolism.

Against this background may be viewed such comments of Burns as this:

> By the bye, there is nothing in the whole frame of man, which seems to me so unaccountable as that thing called conscience. Had the troublesome yelping cur powers efficient to prevent a mischief, he might be of use; but at the beginning of the

business, his feeble efforts are to the workings of passion as the
infant frosts of an autumnal morning to the unclouded fervor of
the rising sun: and no sooner are the tumultuous doings of the
wicked deed over, than, amidst the bitter native consequences
of folly, in the very vortex of our horrors, up starts conscience
and harrows us with the feelings of the damned. (I, 77–8)

And to Clarinda he wrote: 'How wretched is the condition of
one who is haunted with conscious guilt, and trembling under
the idea of dreaded vengeance!' (I, 180).

In this light too may be seen the origins of his fascination
with Satan. To Mrs. Dunlop he wrote of his resolve 'to study
the sentiments of a very respectable Personage, Milton's
Satan—"Hail horrors! hail, infernal world!" '(I, 86). Reveal-
ingly, too, he cites the same to convey his response to the
behaviour of the Armour family (I, 95). Soon he was writing to
Nicol:

> I have bought a pocket Milton, which I carry perpetually about
> with me, in order to study the sentiments—the dauntless
> magnanimity; the intrepid unyielding independance; the des-
> perate daring, and noble defiance of hardship, in that great
> personage, Satan. (I, 96–7)

He then proceeds to give an account of his own situation in a
way that suggests a need to identify with Satan. A little later
he was to write to Mrs. McLehose: 'My favorite feature in
Milton's Satan is, his manly fortitude in supporting what
cannot be remedied—in short, the wild broken fragments of a
noble, exalted mind in ruins' (I, 156).

The basis of the attraction begins to become evident: Satan
conforms to one of Burns's sentimental images of himself.
Thus, on one occasion, he wrote to Mrs. Riddell 'from the
regions of Hell, amid the horrors of the damned' (II, 226); and
later to the same lady:

> No! if I must write, let it be Sedition, or Blasphemy, or some-
> thing else that begins with a B, so that I may grin with the grin
> of iniquity, and rejoice with the rejoicing of an apostate Angel.
>   —'All good to me is lost;
>   Evil, be thou my good!' (II, 323)

To Alexander Cunningham he described his life thus: 'The

resemblance that hits my fancy best is, that poor blackguard Miscreant, Satan, who, as Holy Writ tells us, roams about like a roaring lion, seeking, *searching*, whom he may devour' (I, 244). Burns sought, and devoured, alternative selves. In this there is a marked similarity with Byron. The comments of T. S. Eliot are acutely relevant to Burns. Having noted both that Byron's 'peculiar diabolism, his delight in posing as a damned creature' is related to his 'Scottish antecedence', Eliot proceeds thus:

> The romantic conception of Milton's Satan is semi-Promethean, and also contemplates Pride as a *virtue*. It would be difficult to say whether Byron was a proud man, or a man who liked to pose as a proud man ... His sense of damnation was also mitigated by a touch of unreality: to a man so occupied with himself and with the figure he was cutting nothing outside could be altogether real.[43]

'Nothing outside could be altogether real'—why this should be so true of Scottish men of letters in that period is difficult to determine. *Something* disrupted the balance of Scottish values in the course of the eighteenth century. Something distorted the Scottish ego. Something greatly exacerbated inherent tendencies to fantasy and self-drama. Probably it was a composite, but the extent to which, respectively, Calvinism, the after-effects of the Union, and the transient pre-eminence of Scotland as purveyor of the needs of European sentimental primitivism, contributed to this is impossible to determine with certainty. Undeniably, Burns was the first prominent exemplar of its effects.

If Burns admires the Devil as both hero and comedian, it is precisely because this is how he sees himself. In this may lie the reason for much of Burns's contemporary appeal beyond his own country. Scotland by-passed Romantic idealism and the traumas resultant from its disintegration, and in the later eighteenth century headed directly, though unwittingly, for that condition of alienation which now so characterizes the literature of Western man. There is, undeniably, much to admire in this, Burns's account of his aspirations:

> It [is] ever my opinion that the great, unhappy mistakes and blunders, both in a rational and religious point of view, of which

186

> we see thousands daily guilty, are owing to their ignorance, or
> mistaken notions of themselves.—To know myself had been all
> along my constant study.—I weighed myself alone; I balanced
> myself with others; I watched every means of information how
> much ground I occupied both as a Man and as a Poet: I studied
> assiduously Nature's DESIGN where she seem'd to have intended
> the various LIGHTS and SHADES in my character. (I, 114)

Self-knowledge, however, seemed invariably accompanied by
incapacity to act upon it, unless through *persona*, to the point
that one wonders if the claims to self-knowledge were not in
themselves the utterances of a *persona*.

The use of *persona* ultimately enslaved Burns. The ironic
mask became so compulsive that he ceased—irony of ironies,
given the claims for self-knowledge—to recognize it as such.
Such irony may well have been endemic within Scottish
values, but it also helps account for Burns's contemporary
appeal. Part of Burns's appeal to the twentieth century—
masks, and ironic use of voice—originates in what was to help
to reduce him to a multi-faceted, even schizoid, personality. It
is in precisely this respect that Burns was to encounter what
Muir, writing of Sterne, calls 'the inevitability of a maze'.[44]
This is the inevitability of the multiple surrogate selves of
modern man.

Muir writes feelingly that 'for a Scotsman to see Burns
simply as a poet is almost impossible ... He is more a personage to us than a poet, more a figurehead than a personage,
and more a myth than a figurehead.' Around Burns's diffusion
of self into roles there is a singular irony, given that he has
come to have this significance for Scotland. Personally cha-
meleon, he has become, nationally, static, a figurehead. Muir
continues:

> He is a myth evolved by the popular imagination, a communal
> poetic creation, a Protean figure; we can all shape him to our
> own likeness, for a myth is endlessly adaptable; so that to the
> respectable this secondary Burns is a decent man; to the
> Rabelaisian, bawdy ... He has the power of making any Scots-
> man, whether generous or canny, sentimental or prosaic,
> religious or profane, more wholeheartedly himself than he could
> have been without assistance; and in that way perhaps more
> human.[45]

187

Can it be that Burns, either unwittingly or else responsive to that popular imagination and its needs, assisted in the creation of the figure that is so Protean? Is it the case that this secondary Burns (in fact, these secondary Burnses) came into contention with, and finally overcame, the primary one? If so, it is poignantly ironic that, in having the power to make 'any Scotsman more wholeheartedly himself', Burns paid the price of surrendering that very capacity in himself.

Catherine Carswell wrote of Burns that 'there was in his fate a mingling of the tragic and the typical', and Muir saw him as 'a man indeed more really, more universally ordinary than any mere ordinary man could ever hope to be'.[46] Perhaps the corollary is that this is what is now the universally ordinary (which is also tragic)—the sacrifice of the self to roles or images. For Muir, Burns is 'an object-lesson in what poetic popularity really means'.[47] Auden has noted in the twentieth century an ever-widening gap between poet and readership.[48] Perhaps this is inevitable, unless the poet projects selves instead of self. Here, then, is the explanation for Catherine Carswell's observing that

> Had the still-earlier poetry of the *makars* . . . which was European as well as Scottish, continued its line down to Burns's day, Burns might have been, in a sense in which he is not now, a European poet. The extraordinary thing is that, as things are, he ranks as a world poet.[49]

'As things are', in a relativistic world, the emphatic bluff on the most fragile of bases is the best that man can achieve; hence the appeal of the *persona*. 'To lack sympathy with Burns', then, as Mrs. Carswell said, 'is to lack sympathy with mankind.' For Burns, as for Sterne, the impulse of wit is, given man's condition, the last remaining assertion of self, but it takes Burns away from self into roles and leaves him, irrecoverably, there.

NOTES

1. 'Character Sketch' in *Dumfries Journal* by 'Candidior' (Maria Riddell), *Robert Burns: The Critical Heritage*, edited by Donald A. Low (London and Boston, 1974), pp. 103–4.

2. See *The Letters of Robert Burns*, edited by J. De Lancey Ferguson (Oxford, 1931), II, p. 77, for an instance of Burns trying his hand at flyting.

3. J. De Lancey Ferguson, 'Some Aspects of the Burns Legend', *Philological Quarterly*, XI, No. 3, July 1932, 264.

4. Thomas Crawford, *Burns: A Study of the Poems and Songs* (Edinburgh and London, 1960), p. xiv.

5. Catherine Carswell, 'Robert Burns (1759–1796)', *From Anne to Victoria: Essays by Various Hands*, edited by Bonamy Dobree (London, 1937), p. 416.

6. See Crawford, *Burns*, p. 91, n. 31, for David Sillar's account of Burns's absorption in *Tristram Shandy* during a meal.

7. Cited in *The Letters of Laurence Sterne*, edited by Lewis Perry Curtis (Oxford, 1935), p. 92, n. 9.

8. Compare *Tristram Shandy*, I, Ch. 6: '. . . bear with me,—and let me go on, and tell my story my own way.'

9. *T.S.*, I, Ch. 5, where Tristram writes: 'I have been the continual sport of what the world calls fortune.' See also *T.S.*, I, Ch. 10: 'There is a fatality attends the actions of some men'; III, Ch. 8: 'Sport of small accidents, Tristram Shandy! that thou art, and ever will be!'

10. See *T.S.*, V, Ch. 19; II, Chs. 2–3; II, Ch. 6.

11. For further references to hobby-horses, see Burns, *Letters*, I, 280; II, 196; II, 275.

12. Compare *T.S.*, II, Ch. 9: 'a little, squat, uncourtly figure of a Dr. Slop'. Burns writes of 'one of our members, a little, wise-looking, squat, upright, jabbering body of a Taylor' (*Letters*, II, 175). That *Tristram Shandy* was set firmly in Burns's mind is confirmed by the appearance in his letters of specific phrases from the novel: 'the Chapter of Accidents' (II, 153); 'the Chapter of Chances & Changes' (II, 262); 'there is a fatality attends Miss [Peacock's] correspondence and mine' (II, 155).

13. Burns writes: 'Now that my first sentence is concluded, I have nothing to do but to pray Heaven to help me to another' (I, 377). Tristram claims: 'I begin with writing the first sentence—and trusting to Almighty God for the second' (*T.S.*, VIII, Ch. 2).

14. Kurt Wittig, *The Scottish Tradition in Literature* (Edinburgh, 1958), p. 219.

15. For further instances of the comic-epic or mock-sublime, see II, 76, 115, 150–51, 265.

16. Hoxie N. Fairchild, *Religious Trends in English Poetry* (New York and London, 1949), III, p. 58.

17. Compare Walter Shandy's concern with the risk of damage to his 'child's headpiece' at birth (*T.S.*, III, Ch. 16).

18. 'Inconsistent soul that man is!—languishing under wounds which he has the power to heal!—his whole life a contradiction to his knowledge!—his reason, that precious gift of God to him—(instead of pouring in oil), serving but to sharpen his sensibilities,—to multiply his pains and render him more melancholy and uneasy under them!' (*T.S.*, III, Ch. 21). 'What is man, this exalted demigod? Doesn't he lack power just when he needs it most?' (Goethe, *The Sorrows of Young Werther*, translated by Catherine Hutter (New York, 1962), p. 99).

19. Edwin Muir, 'Laurence Sterne', *Essays on Literature and Society* (London, 1965), p. 54.
20. Compare Sterne, *Letters*, p. 87: 'Half a word of Encouragement would be enough to make me conceive, and bring forth something for the Stage (how good, or how bad, is another story).'
21. Op. cit., pp. 208, 212.
22. Op. cit., p. 104.
23. *Works of Lord Byron* (London, 1898), IX, 376–77; cited Ferguson, 'Some Aspects of the Burns Legend', p. 263.
24. Op. cit., p. 102.
25. John C. Weston, 'Robert Burns's Satire', *Scottish Literary Journal*, I, No. 2, December 1974, p. 22.
26. Op. cit., p. 215.
27. T. S. Eliot, 'Byron', *On Poetry and Poets* (London, 1957), p. 205.
28. C. M. Grieve, *Albyn, or Scotland and the Future* (London, 1927), p. 22.
29. Op. cit., p. 210.
30. Cited Paul Hazard, *European Thought in the Eighteenth Century* (London, 1965), p. 409.
31. Op. cit., p. 49.
32. Ibid., p. 53.
33. Op. cit., p. 16.
34. Op. cit., pp. 42–3.
35. Op. cit., p. 254.
36. Op. cit., p. 50.
37. Op. cit., p. 61.
38. Op. cit., p. 264.
39. See also *Letters,* II, 181, 184, 220–21.
40. Morse Peckham, *The Triumph of Romanticism* (Columbia, S. Carolina, 1970), pp. 54–5.
41. Op. cit., p. 95.
42. Op. cit., pp. 52–3.
43. Op. cit., pp. 194–95.
44. Op. cit., p. 56.
45. Edwin Muir, 'Burns and Popular Poetry', *Essays on Literature and Society*, p. 58.
46. Op. cit., p. 416; op. cit., p. 59.
47. Ibid., p. 62.
48. W. H. Auden, 'The Poet and the City', *Modern Poets on Modern Poetry*, edited by James Scully (London, 1966), pp. 180–83.
49. Op. cit., p. 409.

8

Burns, Blake and Romantic Revolt

by ANDREW NOBLE

With the notable exception of Catherine Carswell, Scottish critics have been neither quick nor keen to detect a relationship between the work of Robert Burns and that of William Blake. While it has not been unknown for MacDiarmid to wax eloquent on what he considered the splendid spiritual anarchy present in Blake's programme, he was generally too obsessed with his vision of the debilitating effects of things English on Scotland to make the necessary connection. MacDiarmid's influence has been a pervasive one and a cause of considerable subsequent academic distortion in considering Anglo-Scottish literary relations. This has been particularly true in the case of Burns and been the cause of ignorance pertaining to his relationship to Blake and also his importance in the development of Romantic poetry in general.[1] MacDiarmid's basic testament of faith was that the spiritual essence, the language and, indeed, the very physiology of the Scot were different from the Englishman's. Like Melville's negroes, we are set to a different tune. Thus he wrote:

> A friend recently asked me to define the Scottish genius, and I answered, 'Freedom—the free development of human consciousness', and in the course of the argument I cited the misconceptions and difficulties that have risen through successive attempts to force Scottish history with its incomparably

chequered character, into the mould of English constitutionalism; the radicalism of Scotland in politics versus the conservatism of England . . . the extent to which the religious genius of Scotland had sought freedom until it became stultified and subverted.[2]

Such an attitude made it hard for MacDiarmid to grant stature to any English author, even one so radical as Blake. Also it provided him with a criterion to judge Scottish authors. In the case of Burns it is perfectly obvious that his rebellious and freedom-seeking poetry employs a language definably Scottish. From this observation, however, MacDiarmid made the fallacious conclusion that the servile imitation present in Burns's English poetry was not simply attributable to the malign influence of the decadent, sentimental verse present in a poet like Shenstone and belonging to the atmosphere of the latter part of the eighteenth century, but stemmed from the English tradition itself. To so see a tradition that embodies, as well as Blake, figures like Milton or Shelley is manifest nonsense. Blake consistently, and Burns at his best, were both poets preoccupied with human freedom. The differences between them of tongue and accent in no way detract from the remarkable affinity of their thought and poetry. Imaginative truth is not open to national annexation.

Not all the erroneous interpretation of the relationship of the work of the two poets is, however, traceable to the prejudices of Scottish national politics. Other modern political fallacies also distort the true literary and historical situation. An outstanding example of such distortion appears in the criticism of Robert Graves:

> Poetical ideas and poetical technique have always been class institutions, and poets born from the labouring or shop-keeping classes have with very few exceptions tried to elevate themselves by borrowing ideas and techniques to the enjoyment of which they were not born. Even revolutionary ideas are, by a paradox, upper-class ideas, a rebound from excesses of decorum. Burns's romantic sympathy with the French Revolution in its earlier stages could be read as a sign of natural good breeding, the gentlemanly radicalism of the literary jeunesse; the social gap between the crofters and the gentry was, moreover, not so wide in Scotland as in England, and he soon learned the trick of drawing room writing . . . Blake is the rare instance of a poet

192

who could afford not to learn a class technique: he was on intimate terms with the angels and wrote like an angel rather than like a gentleman. His radicalism was part of his personal religion, not, like Wordsworth's early radicalism, a philosophical affectation. If a man has complete identity with his convictions, then he is tough about them; if not, his convictions are a sentimental weakness, however strongly he may press them. The Romantic Revivalists were all spoiled as revolutionaries by their gentility. Blake was not one of them; he was a seer and despised the gentry in religion, literature and painting equally, which is why there is little or nothing of his mature work that could be confused with that of any contemporary or previous writer. He neither forfeited his personality by submitting to any conventional medium, nor complained of the neglect of his poems by the larger reading public.[3]

Graves's serious miscomprehension of Blake's actual pain at his non-recognition is not the least of his errors. If Mac-Diarmid distorts literature by subjecting it to a perverted national idealism, Graves causes it equal harm by projecting on it this kind of social cynicism. Class pressures are still heavy. In the late eighteenth century they were enormous. Burns surrendered to them more than Blake but not at all in the way that Graves asserts. Burns was, again more than Blake, tempted by social ambitions but his means of entry into the genteel world was through bad, Anglicized sentimental verse and not his vernacular poetry filled with harsh facts, comic satire, discontent and revolt. He may not have had Blake's degree of integrity. The regicidal sympathies of 'The Tree of Liberty' were kept hidden during his lifetime but, as Robert D. Thornton has recently shown, Burns paid a humiliating price for his admittedly erratic loyalty to the Republican cause.[4] Artists are not saints. They do not display complete congruence between thought and action. That congruence was arguably less in Burns than Blake. What the following essay argues, however, is that they were not at all the opposites Graves believes. If not identical twins, they were certainly spiritual kindred.

While Burns and Cowper both knew and admired each other's work, there is no evidence to suggest that Burns and

William Blake had the slightest knowledge of each other. With no Blakean influence acting on him, the fact that viable parallels exist between them strengthens the case for Burns's creative involvement in the new poetics. It is also a strong antidote to the argument that Burns's poetry is exclusively Scottish in both its manner and substance. Almost forty years ago Jacques Barzun considered these two poets the principal initiators of the Romantic Movement.[5] This movement, he believed, was characterized by a reaction against the established forms of eighteenth-century authority. This authority he further represented as sterile, even decadent, and the Romantic writers were therefore necessarily engaged in discovering new energies compatible with an increased search for greater individual freedom and responsibility. In an essay written some years prior to Barzun's book, Catherine Carswell had been more specific on the revolutionary element common to both poets:

> Blake, who was two years older than Burns, published no poems before 1783, and his 'Songs of Innocence' and of 'Experience' did not respectively see print until six and eleven years later. If Blake, until after his death in 1827, had any readers in Scotland it is unlikely that Burns was one of them. Neither is there any indication that Blake ever read a line of Burns. Yet these two have certain traits in common which are not to be found in any other of their contemporaries. Severed as they were in their characters, their traditions, their gifts and their expression, they shared identical qualities of heart, fundamental convictions and conceptions regarding the functions of poetry, which set them apart from other eighteenth-century writers and make of them blood brothers in retrospect. Both repudiate social restrictions of soul and body. Both add to this repudiation what Shelley lacks in his—a hard knowledge of the working-man's life. Unlike all who followed them, they are not gentlemanly nor romantic poets. Both are stoics as well as rebels. Blake and Burns were the only two men of their time who allowed themselves to be blithely instructed by the body. They gloried in the physical and the impulsive as against the ideal in living, and in the physical and the impulsive they perceived unending mystery. They were sweetly reasonable, but they suspected the dictatorship of the intellect to which all others bowed. They were not preachers but jocund partakers,

194

not reformers but prophets in action. They dared pit the 'light unanxious heart' against the sorry scheme of things as they found it, and if neither man saw his defeat with resignation he gave no quarter to despair. Without Utopian tincture, both of them—the one accepting his meed of neglect, the other never over-valuing his reward of unthinking praise—were consciously poets of a feasible future for humanity.[6]

Mrs. Carswell is, I consider, far nearer the truth of Burns here than is Graves. While, however, Graves inclined to scepticism, if not cynicism, regarding Romantic poetry and revolution, seeing Blake as the only Romantic of genuine integrity, Mrs. Carswell perhaps goes too far in the other direction. Deeply influenced by Lawrence's resurrectionary aspirations, re-birth before death, she is certainly correct in seeing much in Burns and Blake that more than foreshadows Lawrence's achievements but, given her commitment to the cause, she tends to overstress in this essay the positive side of the life and work of both men and to underestimate the external pressures and inner doubts that made life for them both profoundly problematic and far less than wholly success-ful. Read together, Blake's and Burns's letters spontaneously offer a series of highly relevant similarities. Both men suffered from miscomprehending neo-classic critics and patrons who could not respond to the imaginative virility of the new poetry because of their restricted aesthetic taste. This led directly to constant financial hardship for them both due to a lack of comprehending patronage. What sales they did have were commercially abused. Indeed Burns's estate and Blake during his lifetime suffered from the malpractices of the same publisher:

> Cromek loves artists as he loves his Meat
> He loves the Art, but 'tis the Art to Cheat.[7]

In both poets, too, we see the inevitable difficulties accruing to men of genius whose roots were in the common people. They were objects of either upper-class condescension, since, by definition, real art must pertain to the canons of refined taste, or fear. The fear, of course, was greatly intensified by not only their poetic endorsement of the American and French Revolu-tions but their active participation in sympathetic British pro-test. Burns sent carronades captured as a result of his excise work and was present in the Dumfries theatre during the sing-ing of revolutionary songs. Blake wore the Revolutionary cap as a member of the London crowd out in support of the French cause. This led both of them into trouble. Burns feared for his government post and Blake, over an altercation with a soldier, was on the brink of a charge for sedition. Inner fears as well as such outer pressures also tormented them. Both sets of letters record bouts of deep depression. Blake's 'I begin to Emerge from a Deep pit of Melancholy, Melancholy without any real reason for it, a Disease which God keep you from & all good men' finds ready echoes throughout Burns's letters. If we see in them spontaneity and joy, Mrs. Carswell's 'light unanxious heart', we also see its gloomy opposite. Their creative rhythm is characteristically Romantic in its combination of heights and troughs and its sense of the prolonged dark price to be paid for the luminous moment. What is perhaps most striking is their sense of isolation which, particularly with Burns as he grew older, intensified; both felt a lack of genuine response to what they essentially were, creative writers. Thus Burns wrote in 1788:

—I am here on my farm, busy with my harvests; but for all that most pleasurable part of Life called Social Communication, I am here at the very elbow of Existence.

—The only things that are to be found in this country, in any degree of perfection, are Stupidity & Canting. Prose, they know only in Graces, Prayers, & c. and the value of these they esti-mate, as they do their plaiding webs—by the Ell; as for the Muses, they have as much idea of a Rhinoceros as of a poet. (I, 251)

Blake wrote in a letter to Thomas Butts in 1803:

O why was I born with a different face?
Why was I not born like the rest of my race?
When I look, each one starts! when I speak I offend;
Then I'm silent & passive & lose every Friend.

Then my verse I dishonour, My pictures despise,
My person degrade & my temper chastise;
And the pen is my terror, the pencil my shame;
All my Talents I bury, and dead is my Fame.

> I am either too low or too highly priz'd;
> When Elate I am Envy'd, When Meek I'm despis'd.[9]

For Blake there is no viable middle ground between autism and creative self-realization. For Romanticism creativity is of the essence of self-hood. Blake constantly returns to the notion that if its energies are thwarted or repressed they turn inward and fester. For both men the risk of burning was far less than the certainty of the rotting produced by surrendering to fear. It is this sense of fundamental human wants, especially social and sexual wants, not simply unfulfilled by repressive authoritarianism but degraded and perverted by it which is fundamental to both poets. Though it would significantly diminish the imaginative potency of their assault to define it exclusively within the terms of class warfare, both are men of the common people, and a major element of their assault is against the institutions of the establishment and the alleged elements of moderation and prudence necessary both for neo-classic aesthetics and the gentility and respectability associated with it. Like it or not, for Blake and Burns, the lukewarm in life was to be spewed out.

Thus when we turn to their poetry we find that their creative empathy to the needs of their time caused both to body forth a poetry in which a pristine lyricism is frequently combined with an insurrectionary content. Blake, other elements of his genius apart, had the enormous benefit of being intellectually nourished by subterranean spiritual and metaphysical streams which had flowed through London for centuries as well as having access to more fruitful and provocative philosophic and aesthetic texts quite unknown to Burns. The imaginative proximity of Blake to Burns is, however, at times such as to make distinctions based on linguistic incompatibility fatuous. Hence, for example, Blake's—

> But if at the Church they would give us some Ale,
> And a pleasant fire our souls would regale,
> We'd sing and we'd pray all the live long day,
> Nor ever once wish from the Church to stray.

> Then the Parson might preach, & drink, & sing,
> And we'd be as happy as birds in the spring;
> And modest dame Lurch, who is always at Church,
> Would not have bandy children, nor fasting, nor birch.[10]

manifestly belongs in both its imagery and moral vision to a world profoundly similar to that of the Scotsman. Admittedly there is in Blake a metaphysical depth; a power of oblique, terrifying and infinitely suggestive symbolic resonance which lies quite beyond the horizon of even Burns's greatest poetry but they are undeniably kindred creative spirits.

Again and again in both of them we find an assault on the corrupt institutions of Church and State. Burns's—

> A fig for those by LAW protected,
>   LIBERTY'S a glorious feast!
> COURTS for Cowards were erected,
>   CHURCHES built to please the Priest.   (I, 208)

may not have the intensity of Blake's nightmare vision of—

> How the Chimney-sweeper's cry
> Every blackning church appals;
> And the hapless Soldier's sigh
> Runs in blood down Palace walls.[11]

but they have a shared sense of the total perversion of existent human institutions. They perceive human spontaneity and sexual vitality being devoured by a cancer of inverted spirituality, a Christless Christianity, the creation not of the divine but of the sick, repressed and resentful; Burns's 'holy beagles, the houghmagandie pack'. In both poets we have a sense of orthodox, 'respectable' virtue as being derived not from love but from a masked will to power; a resentment which achieves its most malign intensity in sexual relationships. To those who consider Burns in the context of Scottish repression merely a gay dog who enacts for us our fantasies of what we would all enjoy, this parallel with Blake's rage is salutary. For Blake 'as the caterpillar chooses the fairest leaves to lay her eggs on, so the priest lays his curse on the fairest joys'.[12] For Burns:

> As for those flinty-bosomed, puritannic Persecutors of Female Frailty, & Persecutors of Female Charms—I am quite sober—I am dispassionate—to shew you that I shall mend my pen ere I proceed—It is written, 'Thou shalt not take the name of the Lord thy God in vain', so I shall neither say, G—— curse them! nor G—— blast them! nor G—— damn them! but may Woman curse them! May Woman blast them! May her lovely hand inexorably shut the Portal of Rapture to their most earnest Prayers &

fondest essays for entrance! And when many years and much port and great business have delivered them over to Vulture Gouts and Aspen Palsies, *then* may the dear bewitching Charmer in derision throw open the blissful Gate to tantalize their impotent desires which like ghosts haunt their bosoms when all their powers to give or receive enjoyment, are for ever asleep in the sepulchre of their fathers. (II, 6–7)

It is of the essence of Romanticism to both radically question and discard prior definitions of the self. In consequence, the problem of creating an adequate definition for the self is the Herculean task it sets itself. What we see in both Blake and Burns is this search combined with a violent chafing against the decorous, societal vision of eighteenth-century man where, at least for the economically secure, there is a presumption of the manners and institutions of society as being appropriate to the deepest needs of the individual. In Jane Austen we can see the complex, indeed at times, harsh task, with a degree of reformulation, of accepting this compatibility between the self and the available social forms. In Blake and Burns, partly because of their class position, a voice emerges which will have no truck with what they see as this kind of enervated compromise. In Burns's letters we can thus at times find a voice remarkably similar in tone and imagery to that of Blake. Here, for example, his language is remarkably Blakean in its delineation of the creative self trapped in the meaningless routines of the complacent:

> —Sunday closes a period of our cursed revenue business, & may probably keep me employed with my pen until Noon.— Fine employment for a Poet's pen! There is a species of the Human genus that I call the Gin-horse Class: what enviable dogs they are!—Round, & round, & round they go—Mundell's ox that drives his cotton-mill, their exact prototype—without an idea or wish beyond their circle; fat, sleek, stupid, patient, quiet & contented:—while here I sit, altogether Novemberish, a damn'd melange of Fretfulness & melancholy; not enough of the one to rouse me to passion, nor of the other to repose me in torpor; my soul flouncing & fluttering round her tenement, like a wild Finch caught amid the horrors of winter & newly thrust into a cage.—(II, 216–17)

Thus we find in both poets an assault on the cautious,

sententious language, and selves of neo-classic aesthetics and society. Prudence as a form of life-restriction, if not a vice, is a term which resounds through their work. For example, Blake's 'Prudence is a rich ugly old maid courted by Incapacity' and 'Expect poison from the standing water' manifestly echoes Burns's:

> O ye, douse folks that live by rule,
> Grave tideless-blooded calm and cool
> Compar'd wi-you-O fool! fool! fool!
>> How much unlike!
> Your hearts are just a standing pool,
>> Your lives, a dyke!   (I, 183)

Certainly Burns is more ambivalent in his response to prudence; partly due to Calvinist shadows, partly due to the harsh consequence of his own impulsiveness, he often suffered agonies over his own lack of caution. Mere respectability and conformity, however, he could never accept as a true virtue. Thus he could write to Mrs. Dunlop in 1788:

> Let Prudence number o'er each sturdy son
> Who Life & Wisdom at one race begun;
> Who feel by Reason, & who give by Rule;
> Instinct's a brute and sentiment a fool!
> Who made poor 'will do' wait upon 'I should'
> We own they're Prudent—but who owns they're Good?
> Ye wise ones, hence! yet hurt the Social Eye;
> God's image rudely etch'd on base alloy.   (I, 241–42)

Consequently the rational rule-bound 'adult' self is anathema to them both. There is a deep desire to return to the spontaneous ground of childhood. Thus in another letter, written on the same day as the above verse, we find Burns employing terms quite compatible with those of Blake's innocence and experience. 'We come into this world with a heart & disposition to do good for it, untill by dashing a large mixture of base Alloy called Prudence alias Selfishness, the too precious Metal of the Soul is brought down to the blackguard Sterling of ordinary currency.'[13] Life's bitter alchemical inversion, where the gold of childhood is transmuted into the sad, grey dross of later life is, of course, an essential, tragic element in the Romantic vision and, indeed, one which the English poets brought to bear on their consideration of Burns. Coleridge, for example, saw in Burns the quintessence of Romantic creativity where one is able 'to carry on the feelings of childhood into the powers of manhood; to combine the child's sense of wonder and novelty with the appearances which every day for perhaps forty years have rendered familiar'.[14] Wordsworth and Keats were also alike in seeing Burns as an archetypal representative of the moral ambiguities and terrible difficulties of sustaining the spontaneity of the child into the calculations and hostilities necessitated by simply surviving in later life.

Though it is by no means always uncloyed by sentimentality, the heart and its spontaneous passion is with Burns, like Blake, the central moral premise. His image of virtue is almost the reverse of Scott's Augustan-inspired model of prudent compromise; life as a series of checks, balances, adjustments and happy dénouements derived from the fictional models of the eighteenth-century comic masters. For Burns life was a more risky and more sad business. He had little or no use for the stereotype of the eighteenth-century moderate gentleman, believing with Blake that:

> He has observ'd the Golden Rule
> Till he's become the Golden Fool.[15]

And Blake's observation that 'everybody naturally hates a perfect character because they are all greater villains than the imperfect' finds precise definition in Burns's remark in a letter of 1790 that:

> In fact, a man who could thoroughly control his vices whenever they interfered with his interests, and who could compleatly put on the appearance of every virtue as often as it suited his purposes is, on the Stanhopian plan, the *perfect man*; a man to lead nations. But are great abilities, compleat without a flaw, and polished without a blemish, the standard of human excellence? This is certainly the staunch opinion of *men of the world*; but I call on honor, virtue and worth, to give the Stygian doctrine a loud negative! (II, 19)

Burns, therefore, is a primary figure in the Romantic psychological insurrection against the attempt of the Enlightenment to define the moral life as a matter of intellection and cool calculation; that kind of moderation which attains to anaemic, sexless absurdity in a poem like Pomfret's 'The Choice'. This abstract superstructure for the flesh, where the moral life assumes the rational clarity of a mathematical equation, is despised by both poets. Remarks such as Burns's 'what a poor, blighted, rickety breed are the virtues & charities when they take their birth from geometrical hypothesis & mathematical demonstration' (I, 343) are precisely correspondent to a multitude of Blake's comments such as 'God forbid that Truth should be Confined to Mathematical Demonstration.'[16]

Behind such formal rectitude in men and institutions we can further perceive in both poets a sense of something not only hypocritical but profoundly sinister so that, as in *The Songs of Experience*, it seems that some terrible and insidious law operates in human affairs whereby everything is actually the opposite of its appearance:

> Cruelty has a Human Heart,
> And Jealousy a Human Face;
> Terror the Human Form Divine,
> And Secrecy the Human Dress.[17]

To both men, therefore, the acceptance of such a world was intolerable. Hence their commitment to revolution, to the French and American Revolutions in particular, as a way of reorientating the social structure into a form suitable for the deepest human wants. Both men, however, wanted simply not a change of political masters but a new integration of flesh and spirit; a democracy to be brought about by a healing, orgiastic release of energy which, damned up and stagnant, had become self-devouring. Hence the consistent use in both poets of images and symbols of fluidity in opposition to those of stasis; released rather than constrained energy which would sweep away the false, corrupt and malign structures of a morbid hierarchy. Or in Blake's marvellous couplet, rescued from the seemingly serpentine confusions of *Jerusalem*:

> Embraces are Cominglings from the Head even to the Feet,
> And not a pompous High Priest entering by a Secret Place

Blake's lines are of the essence of the radical Romantic political aspiration that the rule of love would replace that of power. In Blake and Burns, and indeed in Keats and Shelley too, the erotic content of this love is essential to its nature and successful expression. Consequently there is a desire in Blake and Burns to reintegrate the self and thereby the community by way of a radical revaluation of sexuality. There is little in Burns of Blake's complex metapsychology on this subject; nor did he have Blake's complete faith that the creative spirit could dancingly be completely reincarnated in its fleshly envelope. He is both too guilt-ridden and too sceptical: 'How are your soul and body putting up?', he wrote in 1788, 'a little like man and wife, I suppose' (I, 200). As a creative man born into an extraordinarily repressive culture (repressions seemingly founded on absolute religious principle), Burns sought a reconcilement of faith and eroticism. For example, he wrote to Robert Muir in 1788 that—

> . . . a man, conscious of having acted an honest part among his fellow creatures; even granting he may have been the sport, at times of passions and instincts; he goes to a great unknown Being who could have no other end in giving him existence but to make him happy; who gave him those passions and instincts, and well knows their force. (I, 207)

And this concept achieves poetic form in 'The Vision':

> I saw thy pulse's maddening play,
> Wild-send thee Pleasure's devious way,
> Misled by Fancy's *meteor-ray*,
>   By Passion driven;
> But yet the *light* that led astray,
>   Was light from Heaven.   (I, 112)

Mainly, however, Burns's attempt to translate sexuality into terms of divine, luminous pleasure failed in the face of his own capacity for sentimentalization and of a culture inspired by a Calvinist god; a god, it should be said, whose deeply rooted life he could never quite tear out of his own brain. Also the very excesses of such a god drove Burns into the opposing camp; better, he thought, to live with the devil and his warm, rich energies than freeze in such a grim spiritual climate.

Blake and Burns, then, are both the initiators and outstanding exemplars of the Romantic creative insurrection against established order and authority. In his fine essay, 'The

Times of the Signs', the great Blake scholar, Northrop Frye, described these radical impulses thus:

> Once the starry heavens begin to go as a symbol of divine intelligence, we begin to wonder if the traditional images of divine and demonic do not need reversing. If the symbol of divine order is an empty, dead mechanism, perhaps the idealized cosmological image is merely a front for a political one, a rationalization of conservative authority. Perhaps the erotic and the rebellious are potentially good things, indications of a greater and fuller human freedom. And if the language of poetry seems to be a primitive language, may not that language be the language of human freedom itself, which is now smothered over by the autocracy of civilization and by the rationalizing parasites of that autocracy?[18]

Both poets, then, are to be understood as attempting to renew the missing connections to an earlier, more vital self-hood. This entailed not only the resurrection of buried, repressed individual psychological energies but national ones as well. The eighteenth century had seen the aesthetic triumph of the imperialistic, neo-classic French style. The end of that century saw a break up of this domination and a creative search for national forms. Hence we find Blake consistently identifying with the 'Englishness' of Shakespeare and Milton as opposed to the artificial, imitative and rule-bound cosmopolitanism of eighteenth-century sensibility: 'Shakespeare & Milton were both curb'd by the general malady and infection from the silly Greek & Latin slaves of the sword.'[19] While he himself is not contemporaneous with Blake and Burns, this aspect of their shared Romantic Nationalism is most cogently illustrated in the writings of Professor Daniel Corkery when dealing with the same period in Irish history, the late eighteenth century, as that in which these two Scottish and English poets lived. In his book, *The Hidden Ireland*, Corkery, in attempting to promulgate Irish nationalism in this century, points to the survival of a highly-wrought medieval tradition of Gaelic poetry flowing down through the eighteenth century, despite the terrible deprivations that the Catholic population endured during the Ascendancy. He considered this poetry to be the very core of the authentic Irish spirit and, further, that each nation's moral duty was to return to its own organic roots and escape from

the neo-classic impositions of what he defined as the values of
the Renaissance:

> In this place it is not feasible, even if one were able, to take
> such a wide or penetrating view of modern literature as would
> show whether or not Renaissance moulds are being flung aside
> as no longer of use. One must be satisfied to sketch out roughly
> certain lines of thought which give us to feel a great struggle
> going on in modern literature between the dying spirit of the
> Renaissance and the rediscovered spirit of Nationality. It is not
> to-day nor yesterday that this fight began. What is every
> Romantic movement, every *Sturm und Drang* movement, but a
> skirmish in it? Does not every such movement begin by an
> increased consciousness that the breadth, movement, colour of
> life, the romance of it, cannot be poured into classical moulds?
> . . . Happy England!—so naïvely ignorant of the Renaissance
> at the close of the sixteenth century. Unhappy France! where
> even before Shakespeare was born they had ceased to develop
> their native Christian literary modes, had indeed begun to fling
> them aside for those of Euripides and Seneca. The edifice they
> built up in after years upon these borrowed alien modes is both
> noble and vast, but it is neither a Rheims nor a Rouen: its appeal
> to the spirit has less in it both of magic and depth. The
> Renaissance may have justified itself, but not, we feel, either on
> the plane of genuine Christian art or genuine pagan art. It is
> not as intense or as tender as the one, nor so calm, majestic and
> wise as the other.
> A Romantic movement is not usually thought of as a violent
> effort to re-discover the secret power that lay behind Greek art;
> yet in essence that is what every Romantic movement has been.
> The personal note, the overweening subjectivity, that marks
> such movements is a protest against the externality of Renaissance
> moulds. The local colour, the religious *motif*, the patriotic *motif*,
> these are an adventure in rough life rather than in the pale
> meadows of death. That is, every Romantic movement is right in
> its intention: it seeks to grow out of living feeling, out of the here
> and now, even when it finds its themes in the past, just as Greek
> art, which also looked for themes in its own people's past, grew
> up out of the living feeling of its own time and place.[20]

There is a quite remarkable similarity between this and the
thought of the patriot-artist, William Blake. The vast energies
he wishes to release in order not to create anarchy but to
sweep away the nullities of imposed, false, geometric form are

also locatable for him in the living but largely submerged national consciousness:

> Englishmen, rouze yourselves from the fatal Slumber into which Booksellers & Trading Dealers have thrown you, Under the artfully propagated pretence that a Translation or a Copy of any kind can be as honourable to a Nation as An Original. Be-lying the English Character in that well known Saying 'Englishmen Improve what others Invent'. This even Hogarth's Works prove a detestable Falsehood. No man can improve An Original Invention.[21]

Burns, too, craved that his poetry should also be the vehicle of national revitalization. His national political and literary circumstances, exacerbated by histrionic elements in his personality, made the creation of an authentic Scottish poetic form intensely difficult. Both due to the Knoxian revolution in the sixteenth century and by the Union of 1707, Scotland had suffered severe disconnection from her past. Thus in Burns's lifetime there was no way back to such medieval master-spirits as Dunbar and Henryson. Also with the process of anglicization which commenced with the Union the very language itself was eroded; a fact which Coleridge remarked created 'the possibility of moral degradation in the very vitals of intellectual Life'.[22] Further, if Blake's analysis is true, Scotland was, in imitating the models of English neo-classicism, imitating an imitation since these were actually French inspired; no man can improve what is already an imitation as the sentimental excrescences of so much post-Union Scottish writing have proved. Scotland in the late eighteenth century was, in fact, in literary terms rather like New England and Edinburgh and Boston were, as Eliot has pointed out, similar *provincial* capitals.[23] In part, Burns shared these confusions and deficiencies. As Fairchild has remarked, 'the poetry of Burns, in short, is curiously divided between Mackenzie and Fergusson.'[24] Burns's enthusiasm for Mackenzie is notorious but he could be equally wrong-headed about Home, author of that weird neo-classic melodrama *Douglas* of which he wrote in a prologue:

> Here Douglas forms wild Shakespeare into plan,
> And Harley rouses all the god in man. (I, 331)

At this point we could scarcely be more removed from Blake's vision either in form or content; the god he wished to resurrect was the very reverse of the sentimental man. Burns was, then, deeply implicated in the compensatory politics of national sentimentality which was the false antidote to Scottish guilt over the surrender of the nation in the Union. Like Scott he had rather fervid Jacobite fantasies. Also, as we have seen, he admired Ossian and, initially intoxicated by his Edinburgh reception, perceived himself as a kind of tartan poet laureate. Thus he wrote to Mrs. Dunlop in 1787:

> The appelation of a Scotch Bard, is by far my highest pride; to continue to deserve it is my most exalted ambition.—Scottish scenes, and Scottish story are the themes I could wish to sing.— I have no greater, no dearer aim than to have it in my power, unplagu'd with the routine of business, for which Heaven knows I am unfit enough, to make leisurely pilgrimages through Caledonia; to sit on the fields of her battles; to wander on the romantic banks of her rivers: and to muse by the stately towers or venerable ruins, once the honored abodes of her heroes. (I, 80–1)

Here we can see the appositeness of Muir's line regarding Burns and Scott: 'sham bards of a sham nation'.[25] Burns, however, is a creature of dualisms and central to the ambiguity of his character is the split consciousness that is the political national birthright. The same poet who could be so wrong-headed in his forays into the wretchedly derivative works of Scottish sentimentality could also respond instinctively, as Speirs has shown, to the authentic if etiolated line of vernacular poetry coming down to him from Ramsay and Fergusson. Equally, he had an unerring ear for traditional song and in his conservative and creative response to this medium is characteristically Romantic. Blake himself might have written:

> . . . let our National Music preserve its native features.—They are, I own, frequently wild & unreduceable to the modern rules; but on that very eccentricity, perhaps, depends a great part of their effect. (II, 172)

Burns's letters are threaded with similar pronouncements on the complex linguistic and technical problems presented by the creation of lyrics for traditional Scottish music. Intuitively

207

he responded to the past in the same way as German (especially Herder) and English Romantic writers more theoretically did. Interestingly, he was aware of and enthusiastic about Bishop Percy's ballad collection which was to be such an important source for Wordsworth but he saw a clear distinction between such source material and its Scottish equivalent:

> Your observation as to the aptitude of Dr. Percy's ballad, to the air, Nanie O, is just.—It is, besides, perhaps, the most beautiful Ballad in the English language.—But let me remark to you, in the sentiment & style of our Scotch airs, there is a pastoral simplicity, a something that one may call, the Doric style & dialect of vocal music, to which a dash of our native tongue & manners is particularly, nay peculiarly apposite. (II, 126)

Hence in Burns we can see a congruence with Blake's belief in the organic form of authentic national art. Such recourse to the past tends to involve itself not only with antique texts but also in oral material. This in turn entails a predilection for mythological thought. Romantic thought is replete with such mythological elements. In Blake, in particular, we find a whole pantheon of uneasily stirring or galvanically resurrected giants. We do not, quite correctly, usually associate Burns with the world of myth. He did not have Blake's sometimes questionable facility for engendering mythological worlds. Nor, much as he admired Ossian (another characteristic he shared with Blake) could he claim descent from the Celtic gods. Like many subsequent Lowland Scottish writers, however, Burns felt in the actual Highlanders not simply primitive elements but mythical ones. Hence he wrote to James Dalrymple in 1787:

> I was nearly as much struck as the three friends of Job, of affliction-bearing memory, when 'they sat down with him seven days and seven nights and spoke not a word'; or, to go farther back, as the brave but unfortunate Jacobite Clans who, as John Milton tells us, after their unhappy Culloden in Heaven, lay 'nine times the space that measures day & night', in oblivious astonishment, prone-weltering on the fiery Surge.—I am naturally of a superstitious cast, and so soon as my wonder-scared imagination regained its consciousness, and resumed its functions, I cast about in my pericraneum what this might portend—(I, 75)

Despite the allusion to mythical insurrectionary energy, albeit defeated energy, and to a key-figure in Blake's poetic world, Milton's Satan, this is quite dissimilar in tone to Blake. In his classic account of the archetypal symbols of the Romantic mind, *The Mirror and the Lamp*, M. H. Abrams defines Blake and Burns as the initiators of the reinterpretation of Satan's role in Milton's epic. By describing Burns as a poet who 'light-heartedly gave birth to the attitude of romantic Satanism' Abrams, however, draws our attention to a central distinction between the two men.[26] In his celebrated letter to Dr. Trusler in 1799 Blake wrote that:

> I perceive your Eye is perverted by Caricature Prints, which ought not to abound so much as they do. Fun I love, but too much Fun is of all things the most loathsom. Mirth is better than Fun, & Happiness is better than Mirth.[27]

Burns still retains a great deal of the laughing, mock-heroic caricaturing spirit of the Enlightenment, Blake's deplored 'fun'. He seems to enter the world of the Miltonic sublime either to send it up or to cut the kind of 'demonic', attention-seeking dash which T. S. Eliot condemned in Byron. Hence he could write:

> I never, my friend, thought Mankind very capable of anything generous; but the stateliness of the Patricians in Edinburgh, and the servility of my plebian brethren, who perhaps formerly eyed me askance, since I returned home, have nearly put me out of conceit altogether with my species—I have bought a pocket Milton, which I carry perpetually about with me, in order to study the sentiments—the dauntless magnanimity; the intrepid unyielding independence; the desperate daring, and noble defiance of hardship, in that great personage, Satan.—'Tis true, I have just now a little cash; but I am afraid the damn'd star that hitherto has shed its malignant, purpose blasting rays full in my zenith; that noxious Planet so baneful in its influences to the rhyming tribe, I much dread it is not yet beneath my horizon.— Misfortune dodges [*sic*. dogs?] the path of human life; the poetic mind finds itself miserably deranged in, and unfit for the walks of business; add to all that thoughtless follies and harebrained whims, like so many Ignes fatui, eternally diverging from the right line of sober discretion, sparkle with step-bewitching blaze in the idly-gazing eyes of the poor heedless Bard, till pop, 'he falls like Lucifer, never to hope again.' (I, 96–7)

Here knowing comedy and naïve posturing are both confusingly present. Like his fellow peasant and near contemporary, James Hogg, Burns had a dazzling capacity for astonishingly literate parody and of setting up structures of apparently impassioned rhetoric only to ironically and self-disparagingly reduce them. This kind of caustic undermining is an authentic aspect of the Scottish sensibility. It was also at the beginning of the nineteenth century a healthy antidote to the excesses of 'romantic' feeling so common in middle-class culture. It is, however, an ambiguous virtue. It can also be the evasion of the deeper areas of the spirit by way of the easy or derisory laugh. Hence Carlyle's condemnation of 'Tam o' Shanter'. And also Edwin Muir's disconcerting belief expressed in *Scott and Scotland* that both Burns's final stature and, indeed, the nature of almost all post-sixteenth century Scottish poetry's achievement is radically flawed by an inability to treat with imagination the fundamental areas of creative activity but to retreat into whimsical or comic fantasy.[28] In a later article Muir wrote:

> The movement which made Burns the acknowledged master of Scottish poetry was unlike any other in the history of Scottish literature. Time had prepared everything for it; two centuries of religious terrors had faded under the touch of reason and enlightenment, and the mysterious problems of election and damnation, riddles rather than problems to the new reason, he turned into amusing doggerel:
>
> > O Thou, wha in the Heavens dost dwell,
> > Wha, as it pleases best thysel',
> > Sends ane to heaven and ten to hell,
> >   A' for they glory,
> > And no for any guid or ill
> >   They've done afore thee!
>
> Calvinism, once feared as a power or hated as a superstition, became absurd under the attack of common reason. The growing powers of the Enlightenment encouraged the change in the universities, the churches, in popular debate, and among the people. The ideas of liberty and equality did their part; Scotland became a place where a man was a man for a' that; the new humanistic attitude to religion led people to believe that 'The

hert's aye the pairt aye that maks us richt or wrang.' The story of
the Fall itself became a simple story of human misfortune to two
young people whose intentions had been so good, 'Lang syne, in
Eden's bonnie yard.'

> Then you, ye auld sneck-drawing dog!
> Ye came to Paradise incog.
> And played on man a cursed brogue
>   (Black be your fa!),
> An' gied the infant warld a shog,
>   Maist ruined a'.

Yet the new humanistic theology could not make Satan entirely
to blame either.

> But fare ye weel, Auld Nickie Ben!
> O wad ye take a thought an'men!
> Ye aiblins might—I dinna ken—
>   Still hae a *stake*—
> I'm wae to think upo' yon den,
>   Ev'n for your sake.[29]

Despite the fact that Burns prefaces 'Address to the Deil'
with Milton's 'O Prince, O chief of many throned pow'rs/ That
led th' embattl'd Seraphim to war', this kind of poem is distant
from Milton's demonism and even further from the intensity of
Blake's. Where Blake only wished to heighten the claims of
the spirit and would, had he known of it, been characteristically
denunciatory of Burns's version of inner light (a sentimental
diffused glow quite different from the form-creating illumina-
tion he conceived it to be) Burns mainly wished to undermine
Calvinism with therapeutic laughter. What prevents such a
clear final distinction between Blake and Burns on this issue,
however, is the fact that the devil exists in Burns also as a potent
and insurrectionary energy as well as a figure to be laughed out
of court by being exposed as a mere stratagem of the power-
seeking 'unco guid'. In part this symbol of rebellion had to do,
as we have seen, with Burns's own sense of alienation and
isolation. In part it has to do with the devil's erotic propensities;
the compensatory sexuality that was a covert element of folk-
culture. Perhaps, however, its greatest use is as a political
symbol. Burns, as we have seen, was sympathetic to the

Jacobite cause and his relationship of the Highlanders and Satan, 'their unhappy Culloden in Heaven', leads one in the direction of the devil as a failed political revolutionary. The self-awareness of being part of the failed French-inspired revolution with its subsequent sense of isolation and depression was very strong in Burns, and it may be that this led to his strongest identification with Satan.

Constantly for Blake and quite frequently for Burns, then, the devil was a symbol of revolt. Given their situation, however, the former tended to disguise his insurrectionary tendencies with symbolism and the latter by use of ironic monologue. In the final analysis however, the kind of revolution that Blake and Burns aspired to was radically different. Burns never approaches the transvaluation of values conceived of by Blake whereby he could write:

> The reason Milton wrote in fetters when he wrote of Angels & God, and at liberty when of the Devils & Hell, is because he was a true Poet and of the Devil's party without knowing it.[30]

Blake considered that unless there was a spiritual revolution all merely political ones wrought nothing but a changed form of tyranny—not democracy but only a new master:

> 'The hand of Vengeance found the Bed
> 'To which the Purple Tyrant fled;
> 'The iron hand crush'd the Tyrant's head
> 'And became a Tyrant in his stead.'[31]

Thus while they share impulses of revolt, Blake would have disagreed with Burns's humanism as, though for different reasons, he disagreed with Wordsworth's. For Blake it was the spiritual or nothing. Thus they disagree in their interpretation of Christ as well as Satan. For Burns he is, usually, conceived of in orthodox, rather 'New Light' terms 'that amiablest of characters' while for Blake he is a heterodox, vital force come to earth creatively to destroy the kingdom of legal generalities and moral platitudes which suffocate the human spirit. Such a radical difference is, of course, manifest in the difference in much of their poetry. Burns mainly lacks the symbolical and mythological resonances and cadences of Blake's Bible-inspired imagination. They differ, however, not so much in the authenticity of their revolutionary desires, as Graves suggested, but in the direction they thought such a revolution should take. Which one is the realist depends on the reader's perspective.

NOTES

1. The most significant such misreading is to be found in John Speirs, 'Burns and English Literature', *From Blake to Byron—The Pelican Guide to English Literature*, 4 (London, 1957), pp. 94–103.
2. 'The Caledonian Antisyzygy and the Gaelic Idea', *Selected Essays of Hugh MacDiarmid*, ed. Glen (London, 1968), p. 161.
3. 'Variety in Modernist Poetry', *The Common Asphodel* (London, 1949), pp. 144–45.
4. Robert D. Thornton, *William Maxwell to Robert Burns* (Edinburgh, 1979).
5. *Classic, Romantic and Modern* (New York, 1943).
6. 'Robert Burns', in *From Anne to Victoria*, ed. Bonamy Dobrée (London, 1937), pp. 406–7.
7. *MS. Note-Book 1808–11*, *Blake—Complete Writings*, ed. Keynes (London, 1966), p. 540. All subsequent references are to this edition. This particular notebook is replete with insults aimed at Cromek.
8. Letter 10. 'To George Cumberland', 2 July 1800, p. 798.
9. Letter 28. 16 August 1803, pp. 828–29.
10. 'The Little Vagabond', *Songs of Experience*, p. 216.
11. 'London', *Songs of Experience*, p. 216.
12. *The Marriage of Heaven and Hell*, p. 152.
13. The selfishness of prudence is a recurring feature of Burns's letters. See, for example, II, p. 16.
14. Cited in *Robert Burns—The Critical Heritage*, ed. Low (London, 1974), p. 109.
15. *MS. Note-Book 1808–11*, p. 540.
16. 'Annotations to Reynolds', p. 474.
17. 'A Divine Image', *Songs of Experience*, p. 221.
18. 'The Times of the Signs', *Spiritus Mundi* (London, 1976), p. 84.
19. Preface to *Milton*, p. 480.
20. *The Hidden Ireland* (Dublin, 1929), pp. xiv–xvi.
21. *Public Address*, p. 595.
22. *Notebooks* 3, ed. Coburn (London, 1974).
23. 'Was There a Scottish Literature?', *The Athenaeum*, August 1st, 1919, pp. 680–81.
24. 'Robert Burns', *Religious Trends in English Poetry Vol. III* (New York, 1949), p. 50.
25. 'Scotland 1941', *Collected Poems 1921–1958* (London, 1960), p. 97.
26. *The Mirror and the Lamp* (New York, 1958), p. 251.
27. Letter 5. 23 August 1799, p. 793.

28. *Scott and Scotland* (London, 1936).
29. 'Robert Burns—Master of Scottish Poetry', *Edwin Muir: Uncollected Scottish Criticism* (London, 1982), pp. 199–201.
30. *The Marriage of Heaven and Hell*, p. 150.
31. 'The Grey Monk', *Poems from the Pickering Ms.*, 431.

9

Robert Burns: Superscot

by ALAN BOLD

Since it first materialized in print on 31 July 1786 the Kilmarnock Edition of Burns's *Poems Chiefly in the Scottish Dialect* has remained to haunt Scotland like a ghost that brings out the reassuring best and frightening worst in generations of Scotsmen (though not Scotswomen as Burns, to his admirers, is the apotheosis of the man's man). It is a sheer coincidence that Burns's name alliterates with the Bible but the connection between the great bard and the good book is more than accidental. Scotsmen—and David Hume's essays in empiricism made a philosophy out of this national characteristic—are habitually cautious, immune to the charms of novelty, stolidly prone to shut the mind on a subject once it has been tested then sealed up in a closed book. To Scotsmen the Bible (not the practice of Christ) is religion pure and simple; it is a convenient package that can be kept on the shelves and delved into as the need arises with births, marriages and deaths. In much the same way Burns is poetry pure and simple. He is a revered figure who remains above criticism, God-like in his acts of creation, Christ-like in appearance (by courtesy of Nasmyth, Buego, Skirving and Reid).

Burns and the Bible not only coexist in the Scottish consciousness as the twin pillars supporting a decent life; the twain frequently meet in a memorable way that is admired, if not imitated, in the ideal Scottish household:

The chearfu' Supper done, wi' serious face,
  They, round the ingle, form a circle wide;
The Sire turns o'er, with patriarchal grace,
  The big *ha'-Bible*, ance his *Father's* pride:
His bonnet rev'rently is laid aside,
  His *lyart haffets* wearing thin and bare;
Those strains that once did sweet in ZION glide,
  He wales a portion with judicious care;
'And let us worship God!' he says with solemn air.

                    ('The Cotter's Saturday Night')[1]

The fact that we could substitute the name of Burns for that of
God in the last line of that stanza says much about Scotland's
attitude to the national bard. Burns depicts the Scot as a
rough diamond whose cutting edge may be conversationally
blunt but who ultimately treasures domestic life. The supreme
quality isolated is honesty—which can cover a multitude of
sins. In a letter of February 1794 to Samuel Clarke, Burns
articulates the matter:

> Some of our folks . . . have conceived a prejudice against me as
> being a drunken dissipated character. I might be all this, you
> know, and yet be an honest fellow; but you know that I am an
> honest fellow and am nothing else. (II, 234)[2]

His poetry is full of eulogies to honesty. It is, to Burns, the
virtue of virtues. So the Scot can be objectionable, boorish,
irascible, cruel so long as he brings honesty to bear on his
delivery. It is a credo that has the same visceral appeal as
Burns's poetry. Burns, as the vernacular prophet of honesty, is
transformed into Burns the patron-saint of honesty. In fact he
was martyred by his inability to live with this impossible,
almost solipsistic, notion, for he was also obliged to live with
other people and to be acceptable to them.

Burns certainly suffered for his sanctity. His whole life was
an astonishing exercise in role-playing, and he was so good at
adopting attitudes that he became all things to all men. When
the company demanded it he could turn on whatever charm
would most enchant. He was, by turns, agnostic, religious;
royalist, republican; Jacobite, Jacobin; narrow nationalist,
citizen of the world; 'sexploiter', chaste lover; humble, arrogant; tender, cynical. His perennial capacity to elicit fanatical

216

admiration all over the world is startling proof of his expertise at mass communication. Burns first advertised himself as a rustic bard because he knew this was the image the back-to-nature eighteenth-century public wanted. Although he had a great—and justified—opinion of his own abilities, he managed, by a posture of modesty, to make all his claims seem inconsequential. When we examine the product he was selling—for the sake of fame, not monetary reward—there is much cunning and very little cringing. A letter sent from Edinburgh in January 1787 to the earl of Eglinton testifies to his skills as a salesman:

> There is scarcely anything to which I am so feelingly alive as the honor and welfare of old Scotia; and as a Poet, I have no higher enjoyment than singing her sons and daughters. Fate had cast my station in the veriest shades of Life; but never did a heart pant more ardently than mine to be distinguished, tho' till very lately I looked on every side for a ray of light in vain. (I, 64)

Burns *used* his humble birth to implant a sense of guilt in others who could expiate their sins by bestowing patronage on the unfortunate poet. In this letter there is, superficially, the sound of submission; on a deeper level, though, the authentic voice is authoritative. This is not so much a missive as a piece of advertising copy sent to a brother-mason who could help the poet. The epistolary mastery disguises the appeal in an attractively servile cosmetic wrapping. Burns is ostensibly addressing the aristocrat as his social superior, but in saying that he has 'no higher enjoyment' than to be Scotland's national poet (for that is what the ambition amounts to), he is playing on the credulity of an earl—and we know what he really thought of titled gentlemen:

> A prince can mak a belted knight,
>   A marquis, duke, and a' that;
> But an honest man's aboon his might,
>   Gude faith he mauna fa' that!
>
> ('For a' that and a' that') (II, 763)

To the Scottish people Robert Burns is, and always has been, more than a poet. He is regarded as the rhythmic heart of the nation forever supplying warm sustaining blood to the otherwise cold body of Scotland. He keeps the country alive and the citizens gratefully respond every year by paying tribute to this restorative power among them. Without Burns, Scotland would be a poorer place, a country devoid of a nationally symbolic lifeforce; without the uncritical adulation of Burns, Scotland would be a richer place. Every attack on Burns shakes Scotland like a heart-attack; he is loved, protected, cherished, nursed, jealously guarded. Hugh MacDiarmid, in his magnificent *A Drunk Man Looks at the Thistle*, could say:

> No' wan in fifty kens a wurd Burns wrote
> But misapplied is a'body's property,
> And gin there was his like alive the day
> They'd be the last a kennin' haund to gi' . . .[3]

Yet enough of Burns has been orally absorbed by the Scottish people for them to draw out of the memory-bank an apt phrase or two to give a warm internal glow and a simulation of received wisdom:

> The best laid schemes o'*Mice* an' *Men*,
>   Gang aft agley
>
> ('To a Mouse') (I, 128)

> To make a happy fireside clime
>   To weans and wife,
> That's the true *Pathos* and *Sublime*
>   Of Human life.
>
> ('To Dr. Blacklock') (I, 491)

Burns, with the knack of turning platitudes into poetry, is seen as the Scottish Everyman. This extraordinary status accorded to a poet in a country not especially known for its love of poetry is as much due to perfect timing as to undeniable poetic genius. Dunbar, after all, wrote many quotable lines without making a lasting impression on the Scottish public; so did John Barbour before him and Robert Fergusson after him. Fergusson, indeed, might have filled the role taken up so successfully by Burns, but his death in an Edinburgh madhouse at the age of twenty-four made him, unfairly, an ignominious figure of failure. What Scotland wanted was a man the public could identify with, a man common enough to be an ideal friend, but uncommon enough to command respect outside Scotland. A *Superscot*. If he had the usual human faults, then these could be excused on the grounds of Scottishness, take it or leave it. If his behaviour offended public morality, then his image could be retouched, his icon restored, by a communal exercise in wishful thinking. Scotland was waiting and Burns turned up. So he became The Man, the Superscot. An archetype for every other Scot to aspire to.

Yes, Burns appeared at just the right historical moment to be treated as the saviour of his country. Scotland had a massive spiritual hangover prompted by the toxic taste of successive defeats and retained by a long folk memory of loss. In 1513 the flowers of the forest had fallen at Flodden; in 1603 the crown had gone, with James VI and I, to London; in 1707 the Scottish parliament had been destroyed in the process of English empire-building; in 1715 the Old Pretender staged an unseemly farce in Scotland; in 1746 the clans had their catastrophe at Culloden, and the clan system was subsequently obliterated by viciously punitive legislation that was, at times, positively genocidal. Scotland was at a loss as to its own identity in the contemporary world: it existed in a limbo as North Britain, a mere appendage to the Auld Enemy. All this was hard to swallow and the bitterness shaped the Scottish character into a creature of violent moods whose flag-waving arrogance alternated with a melancholy submission. A modern American scholar, after a visit to Scotland, formulated this quintessential Scottishness:

> There operates . . . in Scotland (as elsewhere), a most important sociological law . . . And that is *the petrifying but protective influence of great military defeats on those nations which have nevertheless managed to survive these defeats.* As the Scots themselves are the first to recognize, the whole cultural and political life of Scotland is still attuned, basically, to no later historical period than the mid- or late eighteenth century . . . Cultured Scotsmen today still brood over their defeat by England—under the flattering pretence of 'Union' of the two kingdoms—in the early and mid-eighteenth century . . .[4]

Into the defeatist cultural atmosphere of eighteenth-century Scotland came a fully fledged national poet, a man who could hold his own in any company—rooted in the Scottish soil but still cerebral enough to sustain impressive flights of fancy. A credit to Scotland. John Wilson of Kilmarnock published only six hundred and twelve copies of *Poems Chiefly in the Scottish Dialect* but the book was greeted by a storm of applause. Not only was the author obviously talented, he was determined to draw attention to his nationality at every opportunity, as witness these lines from 'A Cotter's Saturday Night':

> From Scenes like these, old Scotia's grandeur springs,
>   That makes her lov'd at home, rever'd abroad . . .
>
> O Scotia! my dear, my native soil!
> For whom my warmest wish to Heaven is sent!
>
> O never, never Scotia's realm desert,
>   But still the *Patriot*, and the *Patriot-bard*,
> In bright succession raise, her *Ornament* and *Guard*!
>
> (I, 151–52)

Never mind the rumours that this particular patriot-bard was seriously considering deserting Scotia's realm by emigrating to Jamaica. Here was a poet to be proud of, an independent voice for Scotland. There were folk all over Scotland who had waited for years to hear the sort of thing Burns encapsulated into polished phrases.

The early critics who responded to the Kilmarnock Edition have been vilified for turning the well-educated son of a tenant-farmer into an ignorant ploughman. Yet they were not so much patronizing the poet as gladly celebrating a phenomenon that so decisively demonstrated Scottish greatness. Furthermore, this bard was not contaminated by a foreign education in England. He was the genuine article, a native genius, and—like the earth he ploughed—Scottish through and through. Burns himself cultivated the ignorant-ploughman syndrome and the critics simply acquiesced. His Preface to the Kilmarnock Edition refers to 'the toils and fatigues of a laborious life' and asks readers to make 'every allowance for education and circumstances of life'. If that did not hammer the message home, then the 'Epistle to J. Lapraik' put the matter in a metrical nutshell:

> I am nae *Poet*, in a sense,
> But just a *Rhymer* like by chance,
> An' hae to Learning nae pretence,
>   Yet, what the matter?

> Whene'er my Muse does on me glance,
>> I jingle at her. (I, 86)

Given such autobiographical crumbs of discomfort the critics swallowed the myth whole, then regurgitated it so frequently that it reached legendary proportions.

Far from reducing Burns to the level of a freakish poetic amateur, the first critics praised Burns as the embodiment on earth of the spirit of Scotland. In 1786 *The Edinburgh Magazine* commented:

> The author is indeed a striking example of native genius bursting through the obscurity of poverty and the obstructions of a laborious life.[5]

Henry Mackenzie, The Man of Feeling, felt even more strongly on the subject. In the *Lounger* (97, 9 December 1786), as well as pinning the label of 'Heaven-taught ploughman' to Burns, he made the point that the poet

> has been obliged to form the resolution of leaving his native land, to seek under a West Indian clime that shelter and support which Scotland has denied him. But I trust means may be found to prevent this resolution from taking place; and that I do my country no more than justice, when I suppose her ready to stretch out her hand to cherish and retain this native poet.[6]

In other words, Burns was too precious a Scottish commodity to export to the West Indies. He had to be kept in Scotland, and so the reception of the Kilmarnock Edition continued. The early critics may have raised objections to Burns's use of the vernacular—and throughout his life he was urged to write in English by colleagues as acute as Mackenzie and creatures as crass as the Clarinda on whom Burns so magnanimously bestowed 'Ae Fond Kiss'—but their motive was not unpatriotic. If Burns wrote in English, they reasoned, then his superiority to the indigenous English poets would cut the Auld Enemy down to size.

The Kilmarnock Edition remodelled the face of Scotland in the features so cleverly presented to his readers by Burns. Burns became a Scottish hero whose heroics—like drinking and wenching—were within the imaginative reach of every Scot who thought he had a touch of the poet in him. Burns became,

221

THE ART OF ROBERT BURNS

too, a convenient justification for every Scottish foible. Almost every Scotsman thinks of himself as a reincarnation of Rabbie, so if he is condemned for being typically Scottish—with all that implies—then he can retort that he is simply being like Burns. And Burns was a genius, *ergo* there is a bit of the genius in every Scot. To cite MacDiarmid's garrulous drunk man again:

> As Kirks wi' Christianity ha'e dune,
> Burns' Clubs wi' Burns—wi' a'thing it's the same,
> The core o' ocht is only for the few,
> Scorned by the mony, thrang wi'ts empty name.[7]

The seeds of the Burns cult were carefully planted by his contemporaries. To them Burns was a great Scotsman for whom poetry was a peripheral activity. Mrs. Maria Riddell's *Memoir Concerning Burns* (published in the *Dumfries Journal*, August 1796, and Currie's first edition of 1800) was explicit:

> For the fact is, even allowing his great and original genius its due tribute of admiration, that poetry (I appeal to all who have had the advantage of being personally acquainted with him) was actually not his *forte*. Many others perhaps may have ascended to prouder heights in the region of Parnassus, but none certainly ever outshone Burns in the charms—the sorcery I would almost call it, of fascinating conversation, the spontaneous eloquence of social argument, or the unstudied poignancy of brilliant repartee.[8]

Dr. Robert Anderson, in a letter to Dr. Currie published in the *Burns Chronicle* of 1925, endorsed this opinion:

> No words can do justice to the captivating charms of his conversation. It was even more fascinating than his poetry. He was truly a great orator.[9]

James Currie himself, whose moralistic approach to the poet did so much mischief, wrote in a preface to his 1800 edition of Burns:

> in the summer of 1792, I had [in Dumfries] an opportunity of seeing and of conversing with Burns . . . who in the course of a single interview, communicated to me so strong an impression of the force and versatility of his talents. After this I read the poems then published with greater interest and attention, and with a full conviction that, extraordinary as they are, they

222

afford but an inadequate proof of the powers of their unfortunate author.[10]

All three writers reveal as much about themselves as they do about Burns. First, they are anxious to establish themselves as privileged insiders so that the outside world will take notice of them; second, they are attempting to show that Scotland did not produce only a great poet in Burns but a man—English take note—who could have conquered the world with his eloquence; third, they display a rather low opinion of poetry as something unworthy of such a genius. The man had missed his true vocation, they are suggesting. After all, the saviour of Scotland was expected to do more than write verses for his own and others' amusement. If Burns's contemporaries rather regretted that he had, like Wilde, put his genius into his art (with contradictory results) and only his talent into his life, it has to be said that Burns himself was not conspicuously ambitious as a poet. To him poetry was not an end in himself but a marvellous escape from obscurity so that, however indifferent the performance (and in some of the English poems it was excruciatingly indifferent), the powerful personality of the man shone through between the lines.

In his *Commonplace Book* covering the period 1783–85 Burns described his début as a poet:

> For my own part I never had the least thought or inclination of turning Poet till I got once heartily in Love, and then Rhyme and Song were, in a manner, the spontaneous language of my heart.[11]

So they remained. Burns never attempted a major philosophical poem, totally eschewed the epic, displayed a complete lack of interest in metrical innovations. He was happy enough with the couplet, the quatrain and, of course, Robert Sempill's Standard Habbie measure which he handled with superlative conversational ease. His thematic and stylistic repertoire was extremely limited: to impressions of love and, less commonly, expressions of hate. His poetry was like a small rich vein that he worked with such vigour that he invariably struck gold. Astonishingly, too, almost all his poetry was conceived and executed before he had set a foot outside his native Ayrshire.

That in itself is enough to give the usually pejorative epithet 'parochial' a more flattering connotation.

Once the Kilmarnock Edition had established Burns as a national poet he was not particularly interested in adding to his output, preferring to concentrate on revealing to the world Scotland's rich heritage of folksong. Thus Burns's poetic works—with the important exception of 'Tam o' Shanter'—were pretty well complete by 1786 when the poet was twenty-seven. The First Edinburgh Edition of 21 April 1787 added Ayrshire poems like 'Death and Doctor Hornbook', 'John Barleycorn' and 'The Brigs of Ayr' to the canon; the Second Edinburgh Edition of 18 February 1793 included 'Tam o' Shanter' (written for Francis Grose's *Antiquities of Scotland*, 1791). Other important Ayrshire poems were too provocative to print openly. 'Holy Willie's Prayer' appeared, anonymously, in a pamphlet of 1789, while 'The Jolly Beggars' was not printed *in toto* until 1802 (though an extract was included in a chapbook of 1799). Burns's own contributions to *The Merry Muses of Caledonia* (*c.* 1800) are still not entirely accepted as belonging to the pen of the bard. So Burns began his poetic account with 'My Handsome Nell', written in 1775 when he was sixteen; and closed it with 'Tam o' Shanter', published when he was thirty-two. During the last decade of his life his imaginative powers were almost exclusively concerned with the restoration of Scottish folksong, and he contributed some 160 songs to James Johnson's *Scots Musical Museum* and around 120 to George Thomson's *Select Scottish Airs*.

Although this is an impressive output, it is insignificant in quantity compared to that of a national poet like Pushkin (who was, at thirty-eight, only one year older than Burns when he died). There is no indication that Burns wanted to build up a large body of work. Poetry was an inspirational impulse to him, and when he settled down in Dumfriesshire after the daft days of celebrity in Edinburgh, he was no longer possessed by his visionary muse Coila who, like him, was a product of Ayrshire. He saw himself as someone who had realized his poetic potential and wished only for other Scottish poets to come along and surpass him (something Burns fanatics can never contemplate). When he wrote his 'Prologue for Mrs. Sutherland's Benefit-Night, Dumfries' in 1790 he appealed to poets to come:

Is there nae Poet, burning keen for Fame,
Will bauldly try to gie us Plays at hame? . . .
There's themes enow in Caledonian story,
Wad shew the Tragic Muse in a' her glory.
  Is there no daring Bard will rise and tell
How glorious Wallace stood, how hapless fell?
Where are the Muses fled, that should produce
A *drama* worthy of the name of Bruce.

(II, 543–44)

Where are the muses fled? In Burns's own case they had enlisted in the service of Scottish song.

I can think of no poet with a reputation comparable to Burns who has achieved so much with the one book (plus 'Tam o' Shanter')—the songs, as Burns himself knew, are a separate issue. The Kilmarnock Edition was Burns's passport to territory normally forbidden to an inquisitive farmer's boy. More than most poets he used verse to bring attention to himself, and he has become firmly established as an ordinary bloke who possessed extraordinary gifts. The two most popular portrayals of Burns produced this century treat him as a Scottish Messiah (and if he had blemishes, well then so had Christ). James Barke's five-part novel sequence *Immortal Memory* (1946–54)[12] gives a full-scale portrait of the artist as a splendid young man in pursuit of willing young women, a devil-may-care Superscot. Barke himself acknowledged in his prefatory note to the final part of the cycle the extent of his idolatry:

> Above all, in Dumfries he came to final terms with man in relation to human society: his philosophy ripened to full maturity. He knew all there was to know: saw everything there was to see . . . My portrait of Robert Burns is unashamedly romantic and idealistic . . .

In claiming that Burns 'knew all there was to know' (which is a claim far in excess of Keats's 'all ye need to know'), Barke is telling the public, particularly the Scottish public, a lie to bolster up the myth of Burns's infallibility. It is to make a paragon out of a person.

The second great popular portrayal of Burns is the actor John Cairney's beautifully realized, witty and elegant recon-struction of the poet's life. Cairney has been the poet on stage,

225

television and records. His rich, cultured voice reinforces the icon of Burns the sentimental Superscot. Like Barke before him, Cairney is in the business of hero worship when he speaks of

> the immortal part of Robert Burns—The flame still burning from a brief, bright spark which lit up a grey Scotland so long ago.[13]

What enthusiastic Burnsians do not take sufficient notice of is the poet's hypersensitivity. Every role played resulted in an agony of remorse, every false step was retraced in his Calvinistic conscience. The continuous effort of playing out the roles he had created for himself enervated him and this, as much as his rheumatic heart, darkened his final days. It has long been recognized that Scotland is a country that has built a national culture on contradiction. Burns, as Superscot, demonstrated the internal psychological schism more than most. On the one hand, he was the gentle, lovable, caring Scotsman; on the other, the coarse, earthy, ranting Scotch git—the stage Scotsman. He could woo the members of the Caledonian Hunt with fulsome words of dedication just as persuasively as he could supply members of the Crochallan Fencibles with examples of bawdry. He constantly worried about this split in his personality, but was so caught in the grip of his own publicity that he was reduced to a spectator watching his own public image taking on a life of its own.

Stevenson's division of the Scotsman—and though *Dr. Jekyll and Mr. Hyde* is set in London, it could not have been produced by anyone but a Scotsman—into rational professional and monstrous amateur is perhaps the most profound clinical analysis Scotland has been treated to. The Scotsman's attempts at rationality cost him the suppression of emotions, and the occasional instability that breaks out can resemble insanity. As his letters show, Burns was constantly aware of the appalling effect of his own tendency to break out. His guilt tormented him and he wrote to his cousin James Burness on 12 July 1796 to say that 'my Physician assures me that melancholy and low spirits are half my disease' (II, 328).

According to Currie irresponsibility and high spirits supplied the other half. Currie's infamous judgement on Burns—'He

who suffers the pollution of inebriation, how shall he escape
other pollution?'—so outraged modern Burns scholars that
they have gone to the other extreme and made the often-
plastered saint an almost teetotalitarian figure. The truth is
that Burns, and most Scots have this in common with him, held
a capacity for drink to be a proof of virility; as a virile image was
essential to his poetic *persona*, he appeared to the public, via his
poetry, as a mighty drinker. The second poem in the Kilmarnock
Edition, 'Scotch Drink', not only implies Burns's alcoholic
prowess but explicitly attributes great creative qualities to
Scotland's most precious liquid asset:

> O *Whisky*! soul o' plays an' pranks!
> Accept a *Bardie's* gratefu' thanks!
> When wanting thee, what tuneless cranks
>   Are my poor Verses!
> Thou comes—they rattle i' their ranks
>   At ither's arses!   (I, 176)

Thus began the myth of Burns the dipsomaniac, the careless
genius who could simultaneously knock back a power of drink
and knock out an immortal poem. It was not Currie who
instigated this particular calumny; it was the poet himself.

All the evidence suggests that no writer has been able to
combine the satisfaction of an alcoholic craving with great
creativity. Poe, Fitzgerald, Behan, Dylan Thomas—and hundreds more—found, to their cost, that dedication to the bottle
temporarily obliterated their genius. Alcohol, the blackout
drug, brought release from creative tension by attacking the
creative process. The best creative work is the result of
sobriety; writers *can* drink and write but cannot do either
pursuit full justice at the same time. The public like to think
Burns could, though, and—to this day—Scotsmen think they
are honouring Burns when they become hopelessly drunk.
What was good enough for Rabbie—so the delusion goes—is
good enough for his fellow Scots. The private Burns told a
different story from that put about by the public Burns. In a
letter sent to Robert Ainslie at the end of 1791 he refers to 'the
horrors of penitence, regret, remorse, headache, nausea, and
all the rest of the d————d hounds of hell that beset a poor
wretch who has been guilty of the sin of drunkenness'. In the

notorious Letter from Hell, written to Mrs. Elizabeth Riddell at the close of 1793 as a morning-after apology for drunken behaviour the night before, he is full of guilt-edged insecurity:

> Your husband, who insisted on my drinking more than I chose, has no right to blame me . . . an intoxicated man is the vilest of beasts . . . Regret! Remorse! Shame! ye three hellhounds that ever dog my steps and bay at my heels, spare me! spare me! (II, 227)

I do not believe that Burns could possibly have been the epic drinker he was supposed to be by Currie and Lockhart. Yet, in his role of Superscot, he had to boast about his boozing. He was, in his private capacity, a part-time poet with women and children to care for and jobs to hold down. The quality, if not the quantity, of his work as poet, letter-writer and songwriter, refutes the notion of the habitual drunk. Yet he glamourized drinking and the public have taken him at his word to such an extent that he has become synonymous with boozing. What other poet is celebrated every year in an orgy of alcoholic self-indulgence? What other poet has a type of beer and a brand of whisky named after him? What other poet is freely quoted and discussed in pubs?

As well as being the darling of the drinking classes, Burns is forever associated with sexuality. Here he set, even by his own standards, a new level of ambivalence. In the Kilmarnock Edition the acceptable face of Burns the wholesome womanizer is reflected in a fine song:

> I lock'd her in my fond embrace;
>   Her heart was beating rarely:
> My blessings on that happy place,
>   Amang the rigs o' barley!
> But by the moon and stars so bright,
>   That shone that night so clearly!
> She ay shall bless that happy night,
>   Amang the rigs o' barley. (I, 14)

Note that it is Annie who 'shall bless that happy night'. Already Burns is promoting himself as God's gift to women. This was another of his various disguises. He knew intuitively what the public wanted and served it up to them in an appe-

tizing form. When he collected, from oral tradition, a song
with the chorus

> O gin a body meet a body,
>   Comin' throu the rye:
> Gin a body f––k a body,
>   Need a body cry . . .[14]

he shrewdly appropriated the piece and coyly substituted
'kiss' for 'f––k'. Sometimes Burns's castrated versions of folk-
song were genuine improvements on crude originals; more
often something was lost as, for example, this stanza from the
anonymous version of 'John Anderson, My Jo':

> I'm backit like a salmon,
>   I'm breastit like a swan;
> My wame it is a down-cod,
>   My middle ye may span:
> Frae my tap-knot to my tae, John,
>   I'm like the new-fa'n snow;
> And it's a' for your convenience,
>   John Anderson, my jo.[15]

When he was not expurgating bawdy songs, Burns wrote his
own with relish—'Nine Inch Will Please a Lady' is fairly
representative of his style in this line—yet so pure can he be
made to seem that a modern Scottish clergyman from Ayrshire
can write 'it was Burns's sincere wish to leave behind him a
legacy of those songs only that were pure and good and elevating'.[16]

Burns the poet certainly broke away from the convention of
courtly love (*amour courtois*) that depicted woman as an un-
attainable goddess to whom the pathetic poet poured out his
verses, but he still treated his literary women with respect;
Burns the man was somewhat more basic. Once more he
played two roles to perfection. On 20 December 1787 he could
write to Agnes McLehose (Clarinda) describing her as

> an unfortunate woman, amiable and young, deserted and
> widowed by those who were bound by every tie of Duty, Nature
> and Gratitude to protect, comfort and cherish her . . . perhaps
> one of the first of Lovely Forms and Noble Minds, the Mind too
> that hits one's taste as the joys of Heaven do a Saint . . . (I, 146)

When he came across Jean Armour in a far sorrier state than the 'unfortunate' Mrs. McLehose, he could assume a radically different attitude in a letter, of 3 March 1788, to his pal Bob Ainslie:

> Jean I found banished like a martyr-forlorn, destitute and friendless; all for the good old cause . . . I have given her a guinea; and I have f————d her till she rejoiced with joy unspeakable and full of glory . . . I took the opportunity of some dry horselitter, and gave her such a thundering scalade that electrified the very marrow of her bones. O, what a peacemaker is a guid well-willy p———le! It is the mediator, the guarantee, the umpire, the bond of union, the solemn league and covenant, the plenipotentiary, the Aaron's rod, the Jacob's staff, the prophet Elisha's pot of oil, the Ahasuerus' sceptre, the sword of mercy, the philosopher's stone, the horn of plenty, and Tree of Life between Man and Woman. (I, 199)

No doubt. Burns certainly thought he was doing his red, red rose a good turn, and the letter shows his image-packed prose style at his most engaging; however the fact that Jean was in an advanced state of pregnancy when Burns gave her what he clearly thought was the treat of her life indicates a goodly measure of sexual cynicism in the poet's character.

When Byron, hardly a conventional prude, came across Burns's bawdry, he was amazed at the contrast between the public, poetic Burns and the private, earthy Burns. In his *Journal* of 13 December 1813 Byron wrote:

> Allen [i.e. John Allen, M.D., 1771–1843] . . . has lent me a quantity of Burns's unpublished and never-to-be published Letters. They are full of oaths and obscene songs. What an antithetical mind!—tenderness, roughness—delicacy, coarseness—sentiment, sensuality—soaring and grovelling, dirt and deity—all mixed up in that one compound of inspired clay![17]

Here Byron has summed up the quality that Gregory Smith was to dub 'The Caledonian Antisyzygy'. In Burns it was revealed at its most pronounced; Scotland, in desiring to hold up Burns as a national prototype, has become confused in trying to keep up with his contradictions.

The one thing Burns was constant in was his pride, and Scotsmen have followed him in taking an irrational pleasure in anything and everything they are proud of—including their own worst features. Burns was fired by a conviction that, though social conventions said otherwise, he was as good as— and better than—any other man. In his Autobiographical Letter to Moore he describes the genesis of 'My Handsome Nell' thus:

> Among [Nelly Kilpatrick's] other love-inspiring qualifications, she sung sweetly; and 'twas her favorite reel to which I attempted giving an embodied vehicle in rhyme. I was not so presumptive as to imagine that I could make verses like printed ones, composed by men who had Greek and Latin; but my girl sung a song which was said to be composed by a small country laird's son . . . and I saw no reason why I might not rhyme as well as he . . . Thus with me began Love and Poesy. (I, 108)

He had to prove himself to the world and he went about it in a calculated way. The above allusion to a classical education was a bee that constantly buzzed in his bonnet; eventually, though, he turned his lack of Latin and Greek to his own advantage by painting a picture of cultural deprivation, when he was not ridiculing those who abused their expensive schooling:

> The following trifles are not the production of the poet, who, with all the advantages of learned art, and perhaps amid the elegancies and idleness of upper life, looks down for a rural theme, with an eye to Theocrites or Virgil.
> (Preface to the Kilmarnock Edition)

> A set o' dull, conceited Hashes,
> Confuse their brains in *Colledge-classes*!
> They *gang in* Stirks, and *come out* Asses,
>   Plain truth to speak;
> An' syne they think to climb Parnassus
>   By dint o' Greek!
> ('Epistle to J. Lapraik') (I, 87)

> When I have pressed [Burns] to tell me why he never took pains to acquire the Latin in particular . . . he used only to reply with a smile, that he already knew all the Latin he desired to learn, and that was *omnia vincit amor* . . .
> (Maria Riddell, *Memoir Concerning Burns*)

Burns, with all his shifts of opinion and his necessity to conceal his political beliefs, never evolved a systematic philosophy, nor would we expect it of him. That does not, however, prevent the Scottish public regarding him as the fount of all wisdom. If Burns's cogitations could be paraphrased into a bundle of related ideas—and that would be a difficult task given his circumstances and habits of thought—then we might peel off layers of prejudice before getting to the central insight. This was his conviction that the potential of each individual should be realized without the unfair burden of a hostile environment. Not an original thought in eighteenth-century Europe with the likes of Thomas Paine and Jean Jacques Rousseau about, but one that he expressed in his own particular way. Nor was he a political romantic; he did not advise the poor to accept their poverty while they waited for the promised land. If they had nothing else, they had themselves:

> And why shouldna poor folk mowe, mowe, mowe,
>   And why shouldna poor folk mowe:
> The great folk has siller, and houses and lands,
>   Poor bodies hae naething but mowe.
>
> ('When Princes and Prelates') (II, 668)

Burns left no successors; the Scottish public ensured that he was a one-off phenomenon. They simply were not greatly interested in any poetry that did not have one name Burns on it as a guarantee of excellence. It was a matter of—beware of imitations! Scotland's two finest poets of the twentieth century came to the conclusion that Burns had little to do with the appreciation of poetry. His star shone brightly over all and sundry, but it did not guide the public to other poets. Edwin Muir, a deeply introspective poet opposed to the calculated popularization of poetry, saw Burns clearly as the creation of the public:

> For a Scotsman to see Burns simply as a poet is well-nigh an impossibility. . . . He is more a personage to us than a poet, more a figurehead than a personage, and more a myth than a figurehead. . . . He is a myth evolved by the popular imagination, a communal poetic creation . . . a great man who by some felicitous miracle has been transformed into an ordinary man, and is the greater because of it. . . . He became legendary because

232

he was uniquely ordinary. He was the ordinary man for whom
Scotland had been looking as it might have looked for a king; and
it discovered him with greater surprise and delight than if it had
found a king; for kings are more common.[18]

Hugh MacDiarmid, who wanted to restore a sense of intellectual perspective to Scottish literature, deplored the tendency
of post-Burnsian Scottish writers to sink into a swamp of sentimentality and complacency:

> Burns led directly to this sorry pass through his anti-intellec-
> tualism and his xenophobia. It is nonsense to say that he
> embodies all the great elements of the Scottish tradition when in
> these two main respects he in fact completely betrayed it. . . . All
> that Burns wanted . . . was
>> ae spark o' Nature's fire
>> That's a' the learning I desire.
> Well, it is not enough and less so today than ever. It is a betrayal
> of Dunbar and Gavin Douglas and the other great *makars* to
> whom Burns owed so much.[19]

What Muir and MacDiarmid felt, I believe, was that the
ominous shadow of Burns's reputation hung over the creative
efforts of all subsequent writers. With its penchant for having a
subject settled once and for all, the Scottish public equated
Burns with our entire national literature. Poets since Burns
have hardly been given a hearing by the mass of the public, so
their writing is only accessible to a small minority who already
value poetry. The Scottish poet is literally preaching to the
converted, when it is time he made new converts to the cause
of poetry. If one poet can enrich the lives of the Scottish
people, then it is reasonable to assume that a multiplication of
that one poet will correspondingly increase the quality of
cultural life in Scotland. To ignore all poetry but the verse of
Burns is to deprive Scotsmen of the national tradition at the
expense of the one-and-only. If the public would look at the
situation in its entirety, they would realize that they have an
exceptionally rich literature. For if we see the Scottish tradition
as being carried by Barbour, Henrysoun, Dunbar, Gavin
Douglas, Ramsay, Fergusson, Burns himself, Scott, Mac-
Diarmid and others, then a broader, more realistic picture of
Scotland emerges. It is no longer only the Land o' Burns, but a

national community in which the individual is valued for himself and not for how easily he approximates to a caricature of the Scotsman. After all, Burns's view of Scotland was essentially a superficial one: when he looked for a national hero he went back to 1314 and Bannockburn and a' that; when he evoked his own nation it was as the Latinized abstraction *Scotia*. He looked back in ecstasy and did not take the future of Scotland sufficiently into account.

This is not to criticize Burns, but simply to regard him as a mortal reality, not an immortal memory. We should remember him, but not live on memories. An American scholar has observed:

> His appeal to Scotsmen has served to foster the notion that he is but a local or national poet, and persistent fascination with his personality and his dramatic career, and with his all too human frailties, continues to shift interest from his having been a poet at all.[20]

That is what the Scottish Society for the Prevention of Cruelty to Burns has resulted in. Burns was shaped by Scotland, but his followers have allowed him to remake the nation in his own image. It is a disturbing precedent and undermines the reputation Scots have for commonsense. Burns made such a fuss about his Scottishness that the Scots have come to believe that to be born in the Land o' Burns is to belong to an élite. A female writer on the determinedly masculine Burns commented:

> Scotland, ever since Burns, has become more and more the country of 'The Cottar' and of the political songs and of 'Auld Lang Syne'. The master has stamped himself on the imagination of the people so that they see in each other—and to that extent, reproduce in each other—the qualities he ascribes to them.[21]

That is an egregious example of nature copying art.

In deifying Burns, Scotland does a disservice to itself and to the bard. Herculean labour was required to achieve contemporary fame, but this brought small tangible reward. Hazlitt—in a lecture on Burns at the Surrey Institution in 1818—realized this when he described 'how a poet, not born to wealth or title, was kept in a constant state of feverish anxiety with respect to his fame and the means of a precarious livelihood'.[22] Just how anxious Burns was to maintain his dignity—and what torment he suffered as a result—can be seen in the tone of two letters to George Thomson. On 16 September 1792 Burns wrote his first letter to Thomson promising to provide him with songs. Though at the time he was a fairly impecunious exciseman he said defiantly:

> As to any remuneration, you may think my Songs either *above*, or *below* price; for they shall absolutely be the one or the other. In the honest enthusiasm with which I embark in your under-taking, to talk of money, wages, fee, hire, etc., would be down-right *Sodomy of Soul*! (II, 123)

Three years later, on 12 July 1796, Burns was in a different position and clearly distressed at having to raise the dreaded question of money:

> After all my boasted independence, curst necessity compels me to implore you for five pounds. A cruel scoundrel of a Haber-dasher, to whom I owe an account, taking it into his head that I am dying, has commenced a process, and will infallibly put me into jail. Do, for God's sake, send me that sum, and that by return of post. . . . I do not ask all this gratuitously; for, upon returning health, I hereby promise and engage to furnish you with five pounds' worth of the neatest song-genius you have seen. (II, 328)

There is still the pride, though it has fallen on hard times; still the absurd belief that being paid for artistic work is shameful. Burns suffered endlessly because of his conscience, and his greatest suffering occurred when he imagined he had offended those who were his supposed social superiors. Jean Armour could be toyed with; the tragedy of Highland Mary could be sentimentalized; but he could not live with the knowledge that he had caused offence to the high and mighty. Though born and bred a man of the people, Burns could be obsequious before the spectacle of ostentatious wealth. Though he wore his honesty like a badge of his identity, he could be swayed by a little flattery. Though he genuinely despised pomp and circumstance in theory, in practice he was pleased enough to be a friend to the gentry. These were further contradictions in his character. Walt Whitman, singing his 'Song of Myself', could expansively declare 'Do I contradict myself? Very well then I contradict myself (I am large, I contain multitudes).' Burns, with a theological inheritance from Calvin by courtesy of Knox, could not so easily explain himself.

A distinguished Burnsian has written:

> He saved Scotland; himself he could not save . . . his worshippers are ashamed of the best part of his nature and his work. And nobody else reads him.[23]

That, of course, is an exaggeration, but it is the sort of exaggerated comment Burns invites. Critics find him hard to deal with because of his enormous populist appeal; the populace accept him but do not dare to criticize when criticism is often called for. I do not underestimate the value of Burns's appeal. It shows that poetry can mean something to the mass of the people, and also that it should be properly presented to them. Burns was a superb public relations man who not only produced the poetry but made sure that when it went out into the world it had friends in influential places. If this sounds like a harsh judgement, then consider how Burns paved his way to Edinburgh with useful introductions and masonic contacts. He did not, as he liked to pretend, arrive in the capital as a nameless bard who was miraculously discovered by a startled citizenry. He made sure he would be noticed and dressed and opinionated accordingly.

Nevertheless, Burns did possess enough artistic integrity to stand head and shoulders above his immediate predecessors, Ramsay and Fergusson. He was not always as technically resourceful as they were, but he did have a gift of communication and a big enough personality to supply his work with an heroic quality. If this involved him in romanticizing himself, then that was, and is, a common enough device in poetry. Everything Burns did was grist to his mill; he was one of God's special creatures. If he went astray, then he believed he had divine permission to do so, for as his muse Coila told him in 'The Vision':

> I saw thy pulse's maddening play,
> Wild-send thee Pleasure's devious way,
> Misled by Fancy's *meteor-ray*,
>   By Passion driven;

> But yet the *light* that led astray,
> Was *light from Heaven*.   (I, 112)

Burns was the last man to wish that his light from heaven should settle on his head like a halo. He wanted to be *a* Scottish poet, not *the* Scottish poet. His proselytizing campaign on behalf of Fergusson shows his generosity. If Burns could put up a stone to Fergusson's memory, then the Scottish public should erect an appropriate monument to the memory of the real Robert Burns by considering his poetic colleagues. There is a real point in constructing a Scottish pantheon that would include not only Burns but all the other great inventive geniuses of Scotland. Then—and then only—can Scotland face the future with confidence instead of dwelling on the past and clinging desperately to the coat-tails of the man they suppose to be the only one sublime enough to tell Scotland's story. The story is not over yet, by a long way. There are pages to be filled by Scottish poets who might take a leaf out of Burns's book and push their poetry into public attention. Burns was never indifferent to people; they mattered to him. That is a lesson other Scottish poets could learn.

It is typical of Burns's pride in himself that he became interested in creating armorial bearings for himself to prove— as if it needed proving—that he was as distinguished as the next man. For his motto he took the phrase 'Better a wee bush than nae bield'. Bield, for those who do not know their Scots, is shelter. For more than two hundred years Burns's reputation has sheltered under the umbrella of Scottish public opinion. It is time a little bield was offered to his brother-poets. Up to now they have not even had the wee bush. If the Scots can appreciate one poet, then they can learn to appreciate Scottish poetry in general and, by doing so, facilitate its development. If, after surveying the field, they still hold Burns to be supreme, then that will be a matter of informed opinion and not dogma. With his usual percipience Burns anticipated the problem of his immortality. On 15 February 1787 he wrote to Dr. John Moore:

> That I have some merit I do not deny; but I see with frequent wringings of heart, that the novelty of my character, and the honest national prejudice of my countrymen, have borne me to a height altogether untenable to my abilities. (I, 76)

In deference to these words from the poet's own pen we should honour Burns as a living presence and not as an artificially preserved corpse to whom we owe undying allegiance. We should dip into Burns as the mood dictates, but also remember to immerse ourselves in the Scottish mainstream.

NOTES

1. *The Poems and Songs of Robert Burns*, ed. James Kinsley, 3 vols. (Oxford, 1968), I, p. 149. This text is used throughout.
2. All quotations from the *Letters* follow the De Lancey Ferguson edition, 2 vols. (Oxford, 1931).
3. *Hugh MacDiarmid: Complete Poems 1920–76*, ed. Michael Grieve and W. R. Aitken, 2 vols. (London, 1978), I, p. 84.
4. Gershon Legman, *The Horn Book* (New York, 1964), p. 365.
5. Cited in *Robert Burns: The Critical Heritage*, ed. Donald Low (London, 1974), p. 64.
6. Cited Low, *Critical Heritage*, p. 70.
7. MacDiarmid, op. cit., I, p. 86.
8. Cited Low, *Critical Heritage*, p. 102.
9. *Annual Burns Chronicle*, January 1925, p. 14.
10. *The Works of Robert Burns*, ed. James Currie, 4 vols. (Liverpool, 1800), I, xix.
11. *Robert Burns's Commonplace Book 1783–85)*, ed. J. C. Ewing and Davidson Cook (Glasgow, 1938), p. 3.
12. The five parts are: *The Wind that Shakes the Barley* (1946), *The Song in the Green Thorn Tree* (1947), *The Wonder of all the Gay World* (2 vols., 1949), *The Crest of the Broken Wave* (1953), *The Well of the Silent Harp* (1954).
13. Sleevenote to *John Cairney Tells the Robert Burns Story*, 2 records, Edinburgh, 1976.
14. *The Merry Muses*, ed. E. L. Randall (London, 1966), p. 50.
15. Ibid., p. 48.
16. Rev. John C. Hill, *The Love Songs and Heroines of Robert Burns* (London, 1961), p. 146.
17. Cited Low, *Critical Heritage*, p. 257.
18. 'Burns and Popular Poetry', Edwin Muir: *Uncollected Scottish Criticism* (London, 1981), p. 193.
19. Hugh MacDiarmid, *Burns Today and Tomorrow* (Edinburgh, 1959), p. 23.
20. Robert T. Fitzhugh, *Robert Burns: The Man and the Poet* (Boston, 1970), p. 388.
21. Christina Keith, *The Russet Coat* (London, 1956), p. 218.
22. Cited Low, *Critical Heritage*, p. 300.
23. De Lancey Ferguson, *Pride and Passion: Robert Burns* (New York, 1939), pp. 306–8.

Index

239